GROWING UP IN GARRETT PARK

Oral Histories of Childhood in a Small Town

1940 - 2001

Compiled and edited by Lee Pope

GROWING UP IN GARRETT PARK

Oral Histories of Childhood in a Small Town

Copyright © 2019 by Lee Pope

Lee Pope

17762 Oak Way

Grass Valley, CA 95945

leepo@sbbmail.com

Book Layout © 2017 BookDesignTemplates.com

Growing up in Garrett Park/ Lee Pope. -- 1st ed.

ISBN: 9781700748621

In gratitude to my parents, Barbara and Roger Pope -

who taught me to appreciate good books,

fostered in me a love for nature,

left me free as a child to explore the world around me,

introduced me to the priceless value of community,

and had the wisdom to search for and to find Garrett Park -

a truly ideal setting for a happy, healthy childhood.

Simple old-fashioned values that come from a sense of community are the key to a great society. I believe we all have that sense from childhood memories, when life was simple. It's those memories that should drive us to reflect on our values.

~ Lindsay Fox

MAP OF GARRETT PARK

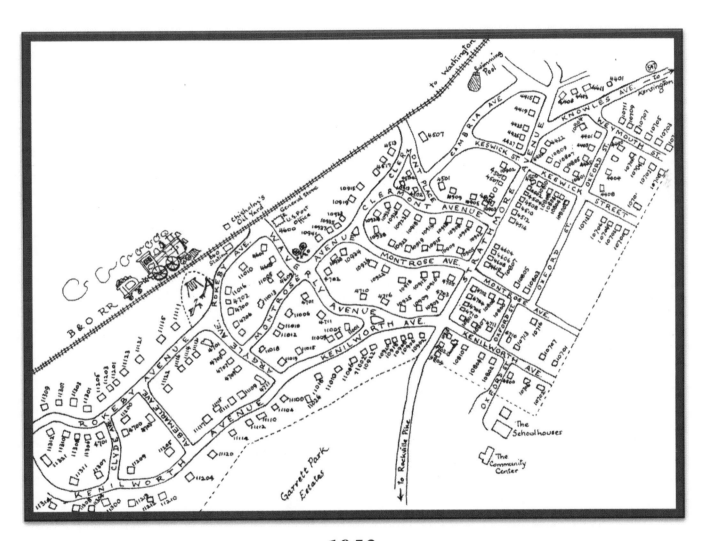

1953

Drawing by Norah Payne

Table of Contents

Introduction

This project began in the fall of 2017, during a time when I was occasionally reading aloud to my disabled next-door neighbor, a retired logger from a rural logging town in northern California called Laytonville. His book of choice was a collection of oral histories gathered from people who had grown up in the Laytonville area in the 1940s and '50s. The book was moderately interesting to me, but no one unfamiliar with the area could possibly match my neighbor's enthusiasm for these narratives, stories of people and places known to him from his childhood and youth. This made me realize how much I would love to read a collection of childhood memories from my own home town of Garrett Park. I wondered if someone had already published a book like this, but I found nothing, so I decided to do it myself. I hope you will enjoy reading these stories as much as I enjoyed collecting them.

Many of the contributors to this project are old friends or acquaintances, but a number of others are people I never knew at all. Re-connecting with people from my past was one of the great pleasures of pursuing this project; getting to know people for the first time by listening to and transcribing their memories was another. The earliest people I spoke with were especially helpful in connecting me to others. Facebook was also a handy tool.

Most of these stories are from phone interviews which I recorded, transcribed, and edited. A few are edited versions of interviews conducted and transcribed in the late '90s during the town's bi-centennial celebration. These, which I obtained from the Garrett Park town archives, were used by permission of the interviewee or family. A few contributors submitted their memories to me in written form. For some of the stories, I combined material from more than one source to create a final narrative. I have indicated the source of the material at the end of those narratives which did not emerge solely from my phone interviews.

I have endeavored to stick with the original words of the story-tellers, only making minor editing changes in the interest of clarity and smoothness of reading. I trust that I have been successful in my efforts to preserve the individual "voice" of each original narrator. For me these stories provide a window into a very special town during a unique time in history – a time quite different from the time we are living in now. When I read the stories, it seems to me that even though the memories reference many of the same places and events, the window is always a slightly different color due to the personality and unique point of view of the narrator. Maybe one big exception can be found in the basically identical memories of sledding on Donnelly's Hill, the most frequently referenced commonality in this collection of memories. For kids in Garrett Park, the Donnelly's Hill experience seems to have been a truly communal one that everyone remembers in the same way. As one person pointed out, it really didn't snow all that often. But when it did, it made a big collective impression on the children of the town. Other big commonalities are found in descriptions of the general store and post office, the swimming pool, and of course, the Fourth of July.

When I started this project, I hadn't been back to Garrett Park since 1979, when, with my husband and baby daughter, I paid a visit to my father's sister, Margaret Leaf, who was living on Rokeby Avenue in the same house that was once inhabited by the owners of Lucy the Goose. My parents had moved out to northern California in the mid-70s, where my brother and I were already living, so there was no longer much occasion to return back east. Even as long ago as 1979, the town, though it looked the same, felt very different to me. The main difference I noticed was that there were not so many people outside, and even though it was summer and school was out, I didn't see any kids on the street. Were there fewer families with children living in Garrett Park at that time, or were all the children playing indoors or perhaps off at camp? I don't know the answer, but I assumed that television, air conditioning and working mothers probably had a role to play in this change.

In May of 2018, I decided that it was time to see Garrett Park again. My husband and I flew out to D.C. and made Garrett Park our first stop in a road trip we took up the east coast. I wanted to visit the archives and hopefully to access more stories that way. We arrived on May 1st during a heat wave. It was 96 degrees in the shade! The leaves on the trees still had their new springtime shine, the azaleas and redbuds were in full spectacular bloom, and the overall beauty of the town was quite breathtaking, surpassing my most nostalgic expectations.

Garrett Park resident Charlie Snyder had kindly offered to meet me in the morning and open up the archives, and that was the first business of the day. Afterwards we walked all over the town, which didn't take long. I had forgotten how close together everything was. It was a weekday, and we saw almost no people on the streets. The only people in the yards were a few hired landscapers.

At noon we joined Steve Sonner, Andy Sonner, and Mike Henley at the Black Market where we enjoyed a very elegant lunch. Even though I hadn't personally known either of them as a kid, both Steve and Mike had responded with helpfulness and enthusiasm to this project. Andy had been my diving teacher at the pool when I was in sixth grade, and later, at WJ, my American History teacher. He was by far the best history teacher I ever had, the one who modeled for me how history taught through story-telling was actually fascinating. I was happy to finally get a chance to tell him in person how much I appreciated having him as a teacher.

When I mentioned to Mike Henley that I didn't remember there being so many Victorian houses in the town, he said, "That's because there weren't." So my sense that the houses were, in general, bigger and fancier was not just a trick of memory. Some of the people I have interviewed said they thought the town was much the same; others have said that it is completely changed and what made it so special is long gone.

For most of my adult life I have had recurring dreams of walking the streets of Garrett Park, usually with the goal of getting "home" to the house I grew up in. Since I began this project the dreams have stopped. In a way I miss them, but I'm pretty sure that the reason I no longer have these dreams is that I no longer need them. The thing I was seeking in the dreams, the sense of community and connection to my past, has been returned to me in the course of undertaking this project. The people who have shared their memories of the town for this book have renewed the sense of community that surrounded me and gave me a sense of place and belonging when I was a child. For that, I am grateful to all of you.

Lee Pope – June, 2019

ANDY SONNER

These were the times that were portrayed on television shows such as "Leave it to Beaver" and "Happy Days." Looking back on my own childhood and youth, it seems that life in the town of Garrett Park was pleasantly simple, unruffled, and relaxed, especially as compared to the times we are living in now. Those days do seem in many ways to have been happy ones. At the least, they were less complicated than they are today.

My parents, Ken and Kathryn Sonner, met after they graduated from Ohio State. My mother was an honors graduate with a major in English, my father graduated from the School of Agriculture. He was a World War I veteran and had been gassed as he fought in France at the Marne River. After getting married in 1924, my father worked the farm with his father until they were struck by the disastrous early days of the Depression. My father and grandfather lost the farm to bankruptcy. My dad, like many farmers back then, was a good shade tree mechanic, and soon thereafter landed a mechanic's job in the rapidly growing aircraft industry.

I was born in 1934, the second of my parent's four sons. My older brother, White, was eight years older than I was, Alan was two years younger, and Steve was ten years younger. About when I was born, Dad was promoted from mechanic with Curtis Wright to a job as an investigator for them to determine if their engines were implicated in various airplane crashes around the country. That promotion moved us to Texas, California, and then back to Ohio in 1942. In 1943, the federal government man who handled the crash investigations for the Civil Aeronautics Board went off to war and Dad landed the government job that took us to the Washington DC area. My folks rented a two bedroom house, a remodeled barn back of an old Victorian home in Garrett Park, our first home in Montgomery County. I was in fourth grade at the time.

Garrett Park then was a small village of maybe one hundred twenty homes, many of them modest three small bedroom bungalows built in the 1920s, called "Chevy homes" because those who purchased the houses for a few dollars more could have a new Chevrolet in the garage. Those houses, many of them wholly modified now, are dispersed among large Victorian homes built around 1900.

Garrett Park was at the end of the old Capitol Transit bus line. The buses ran once an hour from Chevy Chase Circle and headed north on Connecticut Avenue to Kensington and then along what is now Strathmore to Garrett Park and down to a Victorian B&O railroad station that stood at the edge of town. Commuter trains ran down from Brunswick, Maryland, to Union Station in D.C. and stopped in Garrett Park three times in the morning, and then returned in the evening on the run back up to Brunswick. Many of us Garrett Parkers told the time of day from the regular diesels that went back and forth from Washington to Chicago and sounded their horns for the local crossing. We could also tell time by the commuter trains with the steam engines puffing away as they dropped off passengers at 5:22 and 6:30 in the afternoon before departing north for Rockville and beyond.

There was much less automobile traffic. Instead of the roar of the cars and trucks one hears today, back then in Garrett Park, you could clearly hear the clock at Georgetown Prep as it sounded out the quarter hours a mile away and told us elementary and junior high school age kids when to head home for dinner or to listen to *Jack Armstrong* and *Captain Marvel* on the radio. We all regularly listened in those years before television to programs like *Jack Benny, Charlie McCarthy, The FBI in Peace and War, The Lone Ranger.*

The town during those early years was surrounded by woods and farmers' fields, replaced in the fifties and sixties by houses, apartment buildings and Holy Cross High School. Several of the locals hunted in the woods for squirrels and rabbits, and some maintained chicken houses on the backs of their lots. Many of the government workers who commuted to downtown Washington rode in car pools. Gas was inexpensive, but rationed. My father was in a car pool with four others who became close friends and stayed car pool friends long after the end of the war when gas rationing ended.

We youngsters all rode balloon-tired one gear bicycles safely around town. Older boys regularly hitch-hiked to Bethesda and Chevy Chase. We hitched to the movies and some teen agers even hitched on summer Saturdays and Sundays to the popular beaches along the western shore of the Chesapeake Bay in the days before the Bay Bridge.

Garrett Park had no mail delivery. By choice, the residents went to the back of Penn's Store, the one store in town, where there were lines of rented mailboxes, and picked up mail. The postmaster received the bags, unloaded from the local trains or thrown from the fast moving mail cars, as they also unhooked the outgoing bags with a catcher arm from a mail crane beside the tracks. Today the mail comes in by truck, but Garrett Park still has no mail delivery. The post office is now under the Penn Store and the Penn home is an upscale restaurant: Black Market.

Before television, we all spent a great deal of time outdoors. In the winters, we would pack snow and ice it on Donnelly's Hill (Argyle Ave.) for sledding. In summers, we went to the recreation center at the elementary school for supervised games, crafts and sports competition with teams from other towns and neighborhoods around the county. Once a week, a school bus took us to swim at the Chrystal Pool at Glen Echo.

We also went swimming on other days in a swimming hole along Rock Creek. It was a short bike ride across the railroad tracks and down a long hill on an abandoned road to a place where, each spring, for years folks from Garrett Park had rebuilt a damn with rocks across a bend that made the muddy water deep enough to swim and to drop safely from a rope hanging from a Sycamore tree on the bank.

Several of the towns then had county-maintained red clay tennis courts. Garrett Park had a team in an adult county amateur league that competed on weekends. I remember sitting with others on the bank overlooking the courts as the then nationally famous amateur, Barney Welsh, a well-known Montgomery County criminal lawyer on the Rockville team, regularly defeated our town champion, Johnny Darling, six-love, six-love.

Barney, slim with long arms and legs, glided over the court with grace and power as he drove home sizzling winners. We had heard that he often got criminals acquitted, and that made him more interesting to me. Later, I came to know him quite well and remarked to him about his nationally known powerful forehand. A tennis magazine rated it one of the best five in history. He said, "If I had as good a backhand, I never would have become a lawyer!"

Part of the elementary school grounds during the war had been set aside for "victory gardens," where the locals would meet and talk as they cultivated and picked vegetables. Many continued to maintain the gardens for years after the end of the war. We also harvested firewood from the surrounding forests, and at Christmas, we cut pine trees from the nearby fields.

The first four Garrett Park Elementary School grades were in a one-room, one teacher school. After fourth grade, Garrett Parkers had to go to Kensington Elementary School for the fifth and sixth grades. We would catch a public bus early in the morning and then go home by public bus immediately after school.

When I went there for the fifth grade, I experienced constant bullying from a pack of kids who used to go by our bus stop on the way to their homes. They lived in substandard housing in a neighborhood called "Monkey Hollow" just across the railroad tracks from the African American section, Ken-Gar. Those kids were tough, some older because they had failed grades. I suspect now they used to pick on me because I was big for my age, almost as big as they were. The two sixth grade Garrett Park boys were afraid of them and would not come to my aid as the bullies would take turns beating me. A few times while one of them was thrashing me, the bus came by and they did not let me up as the bus went on without me. I had to walk the two miles home or wait for the bus that came an hour later. Some days after school, I waited until I saw all of them pass the bus stop on their way to Monkey Hollow and then ran and caught the bus at the last minute. They made my fifth grade year miserable. By the sixth grade, I had learned from my thrashings how to fight back and many of the older ones had moved on to junior high school. After I fought back a few times, they left me alone. But the earlier thrashing taught me to despise bullies. Over the years since then, I have met several in politics and in court, and I have often enjoyed fighting back.

The experiences at Kensington Elementary School were unhappy enough, but my junior high years were worse. I got into a lot of trouble. I am not sure today why. I got poor grades and skipped school and ran with a similar group of kids. I did manage to play junior high varsity basketball. After three bad years in junior high and after one bad year at Bethesda Chevy-Chase High School, I transferred to Devitt Prep, a boy's school located in Northwest Washington and now no longer in existence.

The following year, the school closed and I went back to Bethesda Chevy Chase High School. When I returned to B-CC, I studied hard while earning good grades as well. I made the football team and was considered by some a hero for some feats on the field that year. I met my first girlfriend, Sandy Shoemaker, and after a few weeks of dating, we "went steady. Sandy encouraged me to get active in student government, so I ran for treasurer and won.

Sandy and I were married the summer of 1958, just before I started teaching at Walter Johnson High School where I had done student teaching. Sandy was the best thing that ever happened to me and made the life I was to lead happy and meaningful. We bought a little one bedroom cottage in Washington Grove, a town much like Garrett Park, where we had six happy years together and started our family.

I was happy as a high school teacher. I loved reading about and teaching United States History. I found that although I was no scholar, I was able to make the subject interesting and even exciting for many. I found that preparing for class was becoming easier each year; I was getting better at it and felt satisfaction because I sensed that the students liked me and I really liked them. I enjoyed the association with the other teachers and I was resigned to a career of low pay for ten months of work. I did like the change that came summers when I managed the Garrett Park swimming pool.

However my observations of some of the older teachers gave me pause about remaining a teacher for life, and after several years of teaching I decided to return to school and study to become a lawyer.

I began as a criminal defense attorney in 1964, next spent thirty years as a prosecutor, and then I served almost eight years as an appellate judge. In 2004, after reaching age seventy, the mandatory retirement age for full time judges, I have presided in the circuit court as a Senior Judge. During more than fifty years, I observed most of what happened around the courthouse and some of Montgomery County politics and elections. I encountered interesting people and had exciting court and political fights.

Sandy and I produced six magnificent children that make me so very proud. Sandy did so very much to help my career from law school through my appointment to the Court of Special Appeals. She had encouraged me to go to law school and was beside me all the way. We had looked ahead to spending what some call "The Golden Years." She left this earth in 2005, and without her, the years have been anything but golden.

As I write this at age eighty-two, I am the "oldest living worker in the Montgomery County courthouse, and now I am on my way to becoming the oldest living Montgomery County lawyer as well. Looking back into the early years of my life, I have memories of the Depression, with Hoovervilles outside of town, the "hoboes" coming to our door and offering to do work for a meal. My mother would give them a glass of milk with a plate of food to eat on the front porch while my younger brother and I watched. Today I see a few people holding up signs at stop lights asking motorists for help, and homeless people live on the street or in shelters, but no one ever knocks at my door and offers to work.

I have memories of World War II. I heard the news about Pearl Harbor on that December 1941 Sunday afternoon while we were living in Glendale, California. My mother came out on the porch and told my five-year-old brother Alan and me the news. I responded that I thought we were already at war with Germany. My mother just shook her head sadly and went back inside. She remembered the First World War and most likely was thinking about my fifteen-year –old-brother and fearing the coming years.

The following day, in elementary school, we all sat on the floor in the hall as a radio broadcast the President Roosevelt's address to the nation asking for a declaration of war against Japan. During the war years that followed, we filled books with saving stamps to accumulate enough to buy war bonds. We sang military songs in school and collected tin cans, scrap iron and papers for the war effort. In 1944, my older brother joined the Navy, and after receiving a commission, served on a destroyer patrolling the Caribbean for German submarines. The whole country seemed to have been involved in that war, far different from the wars in Viet Nam, Iraq and Afghanistan.

The prosperous post war years were interrupted by the Korean War, which took a few of my generation away from the comfort of those prosperous years. Congress restored a draft, but many in college were exempt; there were no demonstrations or protests although the draft deferments were unfair by allowing college students to defer service. And then, after that war, came the war in Vietnam with a draft that produced the protests that helped usher in the counter culture and demonstrations that changed much about America.

Very few of my friends participated in those demonstrations or in the freewheeling lifestyle of the time. By then, most of us were starting careers and taking on family responsibilities. At least at the beginning of the war in Vietnam, most believed those politicians who claimed that fighting there was necessary to stop communism from spreading throughout Asia as had happened in Eastern Europe -- the Domino Theory.

My contemporaries and I lived through the entire length of the Cold War with the threat of a nuclear destruction that led some to build "fallout shelters" in their yards. The fear of the Soviet Union and international communism affected much political thought and discussion. Those who had been or were on the left of the political spectrum were often viewed as socialists or "communist sympathizers," a term from the Fifties.

And then there was the curse of segregation. Most of those I knew growing up accepted the separation of the races as the way of life in Maryland. My folks, coming from Ohio, believed it wrong. Unlike most of the families in town, we referred to African Americans as "Negroes," instead of the pejorative "N" word used by many of my friends in Garrett Park and their parents.

I could not imagine the day when the country would accept civil rights and unsegregated schools. Segregation completely dominated the way we lived in the entire area. Even the ferries that crossed the Chesapeake Bay had segregated rest rooms and water fountains. I don't remember any of my friends or their families working to change it. That is a real stain on my generation and those that came before us in Maryland. Most of us white people throughout the area, if we thought it wrong, just looked the other way. It took the Supreme Court in 1954 to start making the majority do what we had been unwilling to do. Looking back now, I see we were inexcusably insensitive to accept the segregation of restaurants, swimming pools, theaters, sports teams and schools. Most of us did not question those policies and laws that excluded African Americans from opportunity and from participating in what were prosperous years for us. It was a part of life passed on to us by the preceding generation who had it passed on to them as well. I feel shame today for the way we were.

On the other hand, the period following the end of the Second World War was experienced by many Americans as a time of exciting opportunity, of growing prosperity, and of optimism. When the veterans came home from the war, many went to college on the GI Bill. The unions began to experience their greatest strength and helped that generation build the middle class. Many of those during the War had saved and were eager to buy goods – unlike how many suffered during the Depression. The wealthy during the war, and for a while after, had paid as high as 90% income tax, unlike today when the very rich pay less than 40% and often succeed in making it even less. The states and federal governments consequently had revenue streams to support public institutions and build roads and bridges. The debt we owed for the war we owed to ourselves, not as we today owe our debt to the Chinese. College was affordable for all, or almost all.   We had the new antibiotics as well as other medications to cure some of the diseases that had plagued previous times, and we saw the scourge of Polio eliminated. We built the Interstate system for the expanding ownership of automobiles and the arrival of two-car families. Most of my friends' middle class mothers stayed home while we were in school, in part because the professions were largely closed to women.

These were the times that were portrayed on television shows such as "Leave it to Beaver" and "Happy Days." Looking back on my own childhood and youth, it seems that life in the town of Garrett Park was pleasantly simple, unruffled, and relaxed, especially as compared to the times we are living in now. Those days do seem in many ways to have been happy ones. At the least, they were less complicated than they are today.

(Excerpted from: *A Maryland Prosecutor: Fights with Judges, Politicians, Police, and Some Criminals along the Way* by Andrew L. Sonner)

2

BILL MAURY

It was really something that you would never ever be able to recapture - the overall beauty of the place, the huge elm trees that were everywhere arching up and reaching over. Garrett Park was a unique small town, and I recognized it at the time. I know that I thought that it was too idyllic to be real.

On August 30, 1949, my family moved into our house in a little section of Garrett Park called Richterville. I was nine and getting ready to enter the fourth grade. My mother, Priscilla Maury, was a widow with four kids. Richard was the oldest, my sister Ann was the next, and I was the third oldest, born in 1939, followed by my younger sister, Sally. My maternal grandmother, Landon Bunker, also lived with us. We moved just before Labor Day when school was about to start.

My family was a military family. They're all West Pointers, going way back. My grandfather was killed in the war and my father was killed in the war. I didn't know my father at all, though I guess I did meet him because he was around for a year and a half or so after I was born. He left the day after my sister was born in May of '41. He was captured out there in Bataan. So we would get letters and eventually he was on one of those ships that the Japanese put Americans on and stuck out in the middle of Manila Bay and Americans torpedoed it.

Ann, Sally, Priscilla, Richard, and Bill Maury

When we first moved to Garrett Park, we didn't know what to make of it. My mother moved there from Rockcrest because she could afford the house. At that time Al Richter had built maybe ten houses. He had lived originally in the house that was later owned by the Hartmanns (10701 Keswick Street), later moving into a house on Oxford Street. It was then known as the Truitt house. And then the Wagners (10706 Keswick Street), the Goldsteins (10704 Keswick Street) and the Abrams (10702 Keswick Street) had moved in, all in the period of maybe four months prior to that, and the Hartmanns had moved into their house in January of that year. So that whole area sort of came together at that time.

We very quickly became just a part of the place and started checking stuff out, as kids will. Just behind us was Rock Creek and the woods; the area back there was untouched. The Berry Farm, which was down behind us was still a ruins. And we would go there and climb around in that. Down Oxford Street there was sort of a little path leading into the woods where we would wander around. I was very close with George Hartmann, who was my age, and we did everything together for years. We would go investigating with our dogs, and Tommy Richter would come with us occasionally and sometimes David Remley.

Weymouth Street wasn't there, and the Parkside Apartments, nothing like that was there. The nuns had St. Angela's Hall which is now Strathmore Hall. Haile Chisholm was still plowing and working on the huge field back where Garrett Park Estates are. It was called the Flack farm or maybe the Frick farm, two or three hundred acres of mostly corn. He was also farming the area where the Holy Cross School is now.   But

Kensington Estates existed. And down at the bottom of the hill, the Plavnieks had bought out the Mizells' property — Mizell used to own a lumber yard that was down at the bottom of Garrett Park Hill, down by where Rock Creek goes, the bridge over Knowles Avenue. The Mizells had a saw mill back over there, too, back up Howard Avenue.

When we first got here, down across the tracks where Tom Dove and his family lived (where the now-closed track crossing is) there was this sort of shanty house. They had a couple of kids, one of them named Cornsilk. And there was Tom, who worked for Haile Chisholm, and Tom's mother. Chisholm had his place there, I guess it had oil and he also had coal. There were a lot of furnaces in Garrett Park at that time that were coal furnaces, and Chisholm would deliver oil and coal.

Further down that path used to be the way to the old swimming hole. Somebody had been logging down there relatively recently because there were these huge piles of sawdust, two of them. And we used to burrow in them and have BB gun battles, though my mother would never buy me a BB gun because she was afraid we'd put out our own eyes. A couple of people came close to it but nobody did. We could build these foxholes and pop out of them and shoot at people. We used to hang around down in Rock Creek, go to where the old swimming hole was and swim in that, and also swim in Rock Creek. We didn't have a swimming pool. There were no houses. Randolph Hills was a big farm, and there was nothing all the way to Veirs Mill Road.

Then further up the tracks was the old beat-up CCC (Civilian Conservation Corps) Camp. There were a few buildings that were semi-standing, and most of them didn't have floors. They were built on cement slabs and the cement slabs were still there and then there were these pits, latrines or something. Then there was a bridge that went across the tracks, and led to a dump where Garrett Parkers dumped stuff.

My friends and I would take turns standing down on the railroad tracks throwing these ballast rocks at one another, and we'd duck down behind the bridge. One time David Remley threw just as I stuck my head up, and a rock hit me, right in the eye.   It didn't hurt, because it numbed, but it tore the skin, a big flap of skin was hanging down over my face. And I got on my bike and rode home and went to my grandmother and said that we should probably go over to the doctor's to get this sewed up. She was totally unflappable. She just said, "Oh, my God!" We got Virginia Richter and she drove us over to Walter Reed and I got it sewed up.

A guy lived down by the dump named Fred Hendershot — at least that's what he said his name was. And we had always assumed, or pretended to assume, that he was an ancient guy who was a Civil War veteran. Of course, he was probably only about fifty. Now, looking back, I would imagine he was some of the detritus of the Depression that just never came out of it. He had a shack there that was right on the dump, didn't have any running water, and didn't have any heat. It was probably somewhere around twelve by fourteen, something like that, built out of old boards and stuff. He had a little barrel that he'd sit on out in front of his shack, and we'd go over and talk to him, and he would say that he'd been in the Civil War. I remember asking him what side he was on, and he said, "The Blue Bellies." At that point I realized that he was probably lying, because if he had been telling the truth he wouldn't say the Blue Bellies, because that was a term of derogation.

He would tell us stories, and he told us that he would occasionally rent out his cabin to young men from Garrett Park and Kensington who would have trysts up there with their girlfriends. It might be true and might not be true. I would doubt that he would be the most dependable witness. You'd see him picking his way along the side of the tracks and he would take bottles which at that time, you could turn in and get five cents for them – Nehi, Coke and Pepsi bottles. He probably had some sort of pension check or something at the post office.

He hunted for his food with an old twelve-gauge that he used for hunting rabbits. And he would get his water from the spring, which the Doves also used, and which had very clear water. He would hang out with Mr. Johnny, a stumpy little guy that the Penns used for various jobs who lived in an old area down beneath the post office. Occasionally he and Fred Hendershot would just hang around together. I'm sure they would booze it up down there, but they didn't have enough money to do it with any regularity. They were just characters who were around in Garrett Park. Fred was there probably until '52 or 'maybe as late as '55 when they began to bulldoze and build Randolph Hills. They got rid of the dump and the bridge roughly at the same time. I'm sure that all that was put together by the CCC.

Rock Creek was real clear at that time, and all of us would fish in it and swim in it with a great deal of regularity. Sometimes we caught trout. They stocked it in April and there were always pictures in the papers of cars stopped along at various points in Rock Creek. At the opening of every trout season, there always was sort of a standard picture of the opening of the trout season and people fishing there.

We played with the kids from Ken-Gar once or twice. I remember swimming with them in the old swimming hole down there. Then we changed where our swimming hole would be because it was easier for the people from Richterville to go straight down from there where there was another bend in the creek.

My friend George and I built these boats, and we floated all over the place on them, would float on them down Rock Creek, and it was great. I remember a couple of times doing that when it flooded so much that you could float around on a boat in Plavnieks' lumber yard. Rock Creek was really pretty much of a wilderness. There was a big swamp down at the bottom on the southeast side of the Garrett Park bridge, and we used to go down there when it froze and go ice skating. In the spring, Remley and I used to go down there and have frog egg battles, throwing frog eggs at each other. That was a lot of fun.

In the early summer, right shortly after school let out, which has always been right around the second week of June, the wild strawberries would come in the field that is now Holy Cross, but Holy Cross wasn't there. And there was just this big field. And they had all these wild strawberries. They had an incredible smell. It would be baking in the sun and that smell of those wild strawberries was enough to drive you wild. And we'd go and gorge ourselves on them.

The sense of seasons was different. In the fall everybody would burn their leaves. Even at the time everybody thought it was sort of a nostalgic smell of the fall. It was just everywhere, a pervasive smell. I remember the first couple days when people would turn on their heat, and there would be this sulphur-y smell of coal from these awful coal burning furnaces.

Until the early '50s, Mrs. Penn ran both the post office and the store. Her husband was there, too. I think his name was William Penn, and he had a stroke or something and would simply sit on a little table there in front of where the window was. It was sort of a grated old thing like you'd see in a Western, with bars there in front of it, and she would dish out stamps and things. There was ice cream and you could get milk and a few other food items. After school in the fall we would all come down to the post office which was a big hangout area, and was really the only place where kids could hang out. You could go in there and buy candy and ice cream, and just generally cause nuisances.

There were buses that would make the route and would turn around in front of the post office. We used go running over and pull the back door and it would make this hissing sound and the back door would open and the bus driver would get furious. And then we'd go scooting away, laughing uproariously. We called it "pulling the pugle". About twenty percent of people in the town kept chicken coops in the back yard, and on Halloween we could go out and stick cherry bombs under the chicken coops and cause all kinds of grief.

Around '51 or '52, this guy named George rented the store. And he began to make it more like a little convenience store where you could buy steaks and meat. It didn't have vegetables, but then people didn't eat as many vegetables in those days as they eat now. And he had crackers and dog food and milk. People wouldn't do much real shopping but they would pick up extras.

Most of the people had milk delivered. There were four companies that delivered: Sealtest, Thompson's, Green Spring and Embassy, I think were the ones that came around. You could get orange juice and I think you could get bacon delivered to your house and it would always be brought up to the back. The milk was in these old milk bottles. They had the thin top and quite often people would buy Cream Line milk and it would have the cream at the top and in the winter it would freeze very frequently and it would poke out of the top. Of course, refrigerators were smaller, too. I don't remember people having the real big refrigerators.

I remember there was a guy who would deliver bread from Holmes to Homes Bakery. The Hartmanns had a dog named Monty who was an English setter. Monty was a great dog but a very lazy dog. And he would wander off and try to get free stuff from people. There weren't any leash laws. Monty, who lived on the other side of Strathmore, would always go over to the post office. The Holmes to Homes Bakery would deliver bread to the post office, and there would be Monty. Oh, gee! So he'd pick up Monty, stick him in the truck. They were those open-sided trucks, and then he would drive Monty on home to the Hartmanns' house. It was just sort of standard thing.

Nobody locked the doors in Garrett Park at that time, and there was no crime. I remember one time when I was in fifth grade, a couple of kids in my grade went out and broke probably four or five hundred windows where they were building Garrett Park Estates, throwing stones through them. The police showed up at school and began questioning these kids, and they immediately said that they had done it. There was a big brouhaha about that, but that is about the only crime that I remember at all.

One thing I'll never forget is this one time when Bucky Lynch was giving Haile Chisholm hell. Lynch and Chisholm did not like one another, and I don't know what he did, but finally Lynch just irritated Chisholm so much that Chisholm began chasing after him. I remember seeing these two figures running all over the place, all over Garrett Park for what seemed like a long time, until finally, Chisholm caught him. Lynch was fourteen or fifteen at the time, and Chisholm was about fifty, and he was much stronger, and he picked Lynch up. There was a big rain barrel next to the post office, and he took Lynch and stuffed him in the rain barrel. Chisholm was laughing, and we were all laughing fit to kill, and Lynch, you know, he didn't take it as much of a joke. He did not think it was that funny.

There was one kid named Carter Bennett who lived in on the other side of Strathmore, on Waverly. His house had a large carriage house or a barn behind it. It was a neat house, an old farmhouse, and there was sort of tower in the barn. We developed this huge Civil War thing when we were in the sixth or seventh grade, and for maybe three weeks running we had this Civil War battle over there. It would always end up with a siege and kids throwing water. We had developed a way to make these water balloons from folded note paper and we were throwing it at one another. I guess we'd take turns about who was in the tower, and we'd go falling down the stairs and have these huge water battles. We'd all come home beat and bruised and everything and say, "That was great!" And we'd go back and do it the next day until finally Mr. Bennett stopped us.

Whenever there was good weather, we would all meet and play football or baseball or whatever up in the school, and for the boys that would be a daily event. It was odd, though, because the kids who lived in Richterville, tended not to associate that much with the kids who lived on the other side of Strathmore. George Hartmann and I, for some reason, became anti-these people and would occasionally get in fights with John Howard and Bing Reynolds and the Doves. It was some kind of xenophobia or something, and I don't know that there was any particular reason for it, just that they came from another area. But it wasn't really any big deal. We were in the same school together and we'd hang around together. Later, when we went to junior high school, that group feeling sort of broke down for us. But most of the kids got along pretty well. I don't recall more than two or three fights that I got into and I don't recall ever standing around and watching fights, though when we got to Kensington, there were fights all the time. But not in Garrett Park — I guess because everybody knew each other and there was a fairly good idea among the adults of what was going on.

When we first moved here, it was about as idyllic as it could get, even looking at it with the clinical perspective of a historian. Prices were not high. There was very little traffic, and we hitchhiked all over the place. I remember I had a music class that I would take piano lessons down at Chevy Chase Circle. And I would hitchhike down there and hitchhike back and save myself 35, 40 cents, something like that. Then I could buy a big bag of peanuts and a Heath Bar or something, and it was perfectly safe to do it. A kid could go almost anywhere he wanted to go. And every parent who was around knew all the kids, and the kids were generally friends with parents.

Over time, Garrett Park had become considerably more liberal than it had been. In the thirties and forties I think it was really pretty much of a regular small town with a fairly conservative base to it. Montgomery County, which had been very conservative, began to change dramatically, too. The end of the war changed the whole structure of what was going on, and when the war ended there was an explosion of growth. Many people had money to spend, and spending money made more money, and the whole thing began to snowball.

There were very few Jews living in Garrett Park in the twenties and thirties, but when I was a kid, probably half my friends were Jewish. I didn't know that there was such a thing as anti-Semitism. Garrett Park itself was an extremely tolerant place by that time, and of course, as far as blacks, most of Garrett Park was very liberal, at least the ones that I grew up with.

I remember when Bish Thompson moved out to Bethesda. Thompson had been down on E Street in Washington. In '53, they had a test case about the "right to refuse" for segregation in Washington, D.C. Some blacks had gone into Thompson's and tried to get seated and they couldn't. But I guess Thompson saw the writing on the wall and so he moved his place out to Bethesda. Maybe Maryland had different laws from D.C. Of course, there was total segregation in the schools at that time. Brown vs. the School Board was in '54., but we didn't actually desegregate. There were a couple blacks in my high school class but not many.

Very few people had TV's. We didn't have a TV all the way up until the sixties. We would listen to the radio and that was about it. There was a lot that was in sort of the sepia-tone past that you look at and you said, "Gee, wasn't that wonderful!" But there was a lot of stuff that wasn't so wonderful. For instance, I'm sure that there were a lot of kids in the school who had severe learning disabilities, and they were just thought to be dumb - you know, tough darts, they're not very smart, kind of slow. And probably some of them weren't actually slow at all. We didn't know anything about that sort of stuff.

On June 20th of 1950, sometime around June 20, the county had a recreation system where teachers would come around and provide entertainment and recreation for the kids. You would learn how to work with gimp and have some sort of sports. This went on for a number of years. I remember riding my bike up to the school with my friend George Hartmann because it was just the first day of the recreation. And we got up there and were informed that the United States had joined with the movement against the North Koreans in the beginning of the Korean War. I remember that very well, looking at a calendar and the guy was pointing at the date and said, "Remember this day." I guess a lot of people sort of thought it might be the beginning of the Third World War. But we didn't pay too much attention to that.

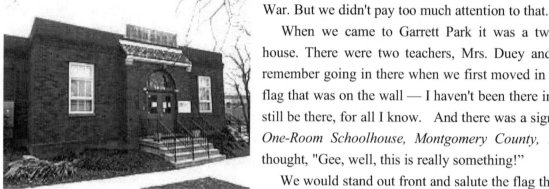

Garrett Park Elementary

When we came to Garrett Park it was a two-room schoolhouse. There were two teachers, Mrs. Duey and Mrs. Reed. I remember going in there when we first moved in and there was a flag that was on the wall — I haven't been there in years, it might still be there, for all I know. And there was a sign that said: *Best One-Room Schoolhouse, Montgomery County, 1934.* And I thought, "Gee, well, this is really something!"

We would stand out front and salute the flag that was raised in the morning. Once a week, I think, a person who was a traveling phys-ed teacher would come around and would give us Phys-ed. There were some bars where we could practice chin-ups, but almost no kid could do a chin-up. There was a little area in the back where the stove was where we would hang up our cloaks. Also a health person would come by every once in a while, and we got weighed by the County Health Examiner. I was a chubby kid, and I think I was the only one in the fourth grade who weighed a hundred pounds. And that, of course, evoked a tremendous amount of laughter and finger-pointing. But that's the way it was.

I was thinking about the way the grammar school operated when we were kids, because that was really when I was most aware of what was going on in Garrett Park. There were two rooms in the schoolhouse, with a large curtain-kind of thing down the middle of it. First, second and third was on one side and the fourth, fifth and sixth was on the other side. The place where the first and second and third school classes were taught had a stage in it. We would have a Christmas pageant and that was always fun.

Mrs. Reed would have one group, the fourth, fifth and sixth grade. And then the first, second and third were behind a curtain on the other side of this one room that had been divided in half. And the first, second and third had a teacher named Mrs. Duey who was the principal of this very small school. I think there were twelve of us who were in the fourth grade. I don't remember all the names. There was George Hartmann and me and Alicia Conklin and Allison Turner and Buddy Sanders— John Howard, of course, Bing Reynolds. The teacher would sort of migrate between these three groups of students, fourth, fifth and sixth graders all in one room. In sixth grade there were six students and I think in the fifth that year - this was 1949 and '50 - in the fifth grade I think there were ten. And in our grade there were twelve. And then there were a lot more in the first, second and third. I mean, there was obvious need for expansion. So that was the way the fourth grade was. Mrs. Reed was very good and she managed to assign each section a project and we'd be working away on it. And then she would move to the next section and teach them. And it was incredible when you think back about it.

School lunches were not served. We usually took our lunches to school. There was no school bus, and we would all just walk to school, and probably half of the kids went home for lunch and would either ride their bikes home or would walk. In the back of the place, there was a little kitchen kind of affair with a small, sort of cast-iron stove. I guess because we were such a rural school, we would get these special gifts from the government. One time, we got these big boxes of pears that were absolutely incredible. Then for some other time — who knows why these things happened — we got potatoes. Mrs. Reed would cut the potatoes in half and we would bake them in the oven and we would all have a potato at lunch. It was terrific. I mean, Garrett Park was hardly a hard-up community.

When I was in the fifth grade, Mrs. Reed decided that what we needed to do was take these nature walks. And so the fifth and the sixth grades on fall days would get to walk through the woods, and behind the school there was all woods. There were some absolutely incredible ant hills down there, ant hills three-feet-high or maybe even more. We would look at them and examine them, and there were two of them that I remember. One of them was very active and Mrs. Reed was very interested in seeing that. And one of the ant hills had fallen into disuse and the ants had all left it, for some reason. We never did figure out why.

We would look for berries and check out what kind was edible. I think it was really a great thing for kids to do because you got a lot more connection with the outside. So we had a very different sort of education. We didn't have bells or anything like that. Because she didn't have any kind of teachers' lounge that she could go to get away from the kids, Mrs. Reed was just surrounded by the kids at all times. She would sit and have her lunch with us since there wasn't any cafeteria.

Then we would have these special projects. I remember one time we got inundated with flies. There must have been millions of these fairly big sized flies, and they were all over the place. Mrs. Reed gave about three of us some rolled-up newspapers and we were allowed to stay after school and create havoc with these flies, killing as many of these flies as we could.

We had recess all at the same time, because that was the only way you could get enough kids to go out and play a game, and generally she would just leave us alone. The girls would do one thing and the guys would do something else. She was a very resourceful teacher and I think all of us really benefitted from having her as the teacher.

In the sixth grade, they started to build the new elementary school. Mrs. Reed thought this was a great opportunity for all of us to have an idea of discussing and describing how things were built. So all of us had to keep a journal of what went on and write a paper. I remember this friend of mine named (Mike) Murtaugh who lived over on Clermont, he came up with the word "superstructure." George Hartmann and I felt that he must have cheated to come up with a word that was so adult. Superstructure? Come on, Murtaugh, where'd you come up with that word?

Garrett Park Estates was ballooning, and in the sixth grade we first began to get Garrett Park Estates kids coming to Garrett Park School. And even though John Howard and Bing Reynolds and George Hartmann and I would fight all the time amongst ourselves, if somebody came from the outside, then it was dog-eat-dog and we were going to fight them tooth and nail. And they weren't insiders, so we gave them a fairly hard time. I remember the first person from Garrett Park Estates to come to our class was a girl named Sharon, a very nice young girl, looked a lot like my sister Sally. But the thing was she just happened to live in the Estates. I wasn't so bad, but a lot of the kids were bad, and it was terrible. She developed a sort of nervous tic, she started pulling her hair, and she actually developed a sort of little bald spot. I began to feel sorry for her, and I got to know her fairly well, and she didn't have any major psychological problems after that. But we weren't real nice to the kids when they first came over from Garrett Park Estates to go to school in Garrett Park.

I remember when they built the pool, there was a big question as to whether to allow the people from Garrett Park Estates to come in. I think that the more open-minded people were saying, "Wait a minute, you know, what are we talking about?" And other people were saying, "Well, you know, they aren't actually from the town." So there was not much relationship. At that time Garrett Park had its own little group called the Garrett Players. And my mom was involved in it and a number of other people in the town. Bing Davis, who lived over on Flanders, was big in the theater, and she began to want to participate. And that was one of the things that began to sort of open it up so there was more participation between Garrett Park and Garrett Park Estates. But most of the people who live in Garrett Park Estates really don't associate themselves much with Garrett Park, but more with Kensington, because that's what their zip code says, their post office says, so it's kind of strange.

When we all went over to Kensington Junior High School, we all thought that that was quite a deal. In the seventh grade I think I took a school bus but after that it became the cool thing to do to hitchhike, because we would generally leave late. Even in the seventh grade, I know that we hitchhiked to school a lot. It was just easier and quicker.

KJH was on Kensington Parkway. The kids from Wheaton came over to KJH, and the kids from Wheaton were a tough lot. Wheaton was tiny and was tough, was very blue-collar. And you would hang around with those Wheaton kids and they'd pop your lights out in a second. Garrett Park had at one time been tough. I remember when we first moved in they didn't have any crime in Garrett Park, but there was this kid who was in jail for murdering a cabdriver and he's probably still in jail. What I heard was that this kid, who lived in one of the Chevy houses, would go down to Washington and rob cabdrivers. He took an iron pipe with him, and he would bop them over the head and steal their money. Well, he ended up killing one accidentally, bopped him over the head and the guy died. And that ended him up in jail.

Both my brother and my sister had been to KJH, and other big kids in Garrett Park had been there - the Doves and Sonny Newhall. And the people in Kensington Junior High School did not like Garrett Parkers. I mean, there was always a period of testing out, and we got into fights, George and I did, probably once a week, when we went over there to Kensington. People would give you a hard time in the locker room or in the bathroom. I remember, there was this one kid, Alwin Merrill, who really didn't like me at all.

I was fairly big but I did not like to fight very much, and I was trying to be as innocuous as possible, but I was getting into fights all the time. And finally I accidentally put my foot on Alwin Merrill's chair, and he said that this was grounds for a major confrontation. I tried to explain to him that this was not grounds for a major confrontation, and he kept insisting it was. And it was finally decided that two days hence we would meet in this fight down at the bottom of the hill where there was this standard place where you met at Kensington Junior High School for the fight. I thought, "Oh, man, this is really terrible," anticipating the thing with great fear.

So I never will forget. It was in the springtime. We ended the school day. Oh, geez. And we walked down the hill, and there was a huge ring of boys standing there, they're all around in a big circle. And I knew I was going to be the star attraction to the thing, which I didn't like at all. I thought, "This is terrible."

This other kid, named Leroy Archer, had a pen his father had given him. And he was going to keep score, and he had a piece of paper. It was terrible. But it was a neat pen. And so I attempted, to the best of my ability, to draw everybody's attention to this pen, a fascinating pen, and tried to make it so that everybody would be interested, and everybody was momentarily interested in it. But they were there for the big event.

Alwin Merrill came running over, fire shooting out of his eyes, and he was determined that he was going to lay waste. I was real slow, but I was real strong. And he threw a punch and I dodged it and grabbed his hand. I grabbed his hand, I squeezed it as hard as I could, and I wrapped his arm back around his neck and just about broke his arm. And the whole thing was over in about ten seconds.

My friend, George, grabbed his wallet, grabbed Alwin Merrill's wallet out of his back pocket and went running over to this little creek that flowed down there and said, "Shall I throw it in?" I thought, "Geez, that's the last thing we need! Then we'll have all these guys jumping on me for despoiling Alwin Merrill's wallet." So I said no, and that was the end of it.

The next day when I went to school, everybody liked me, and I was very popular after that. And that was it. But George had sort of a semi-asthmatic state, and he would get in this fight at noon with this kid named Billy Howard almost every day. And it was terrible. Billy Howard would sometimes beat him and sometimes he would beat Billy Howard. George Hartmann was tremendously strong, and finally he managed to get Billy Howard in this really incredible bear hug and just about squeeze the life out of him. And then after that, nobody bothered either one of us.

When we went to Kensington Junior High School, our nucleus of friends began to split apart. Particularly for me, because I got involved in sports over there at Kensington and I developed a couple of close friends from Kensington that I hung around with. But I still knew much of what was going on in Garrett Park.

Kensington at that time was different, smaller. Where Connecticut Avenue cut through, it was just a dirt road. There was a farm down there. In Kensington there were two places where we would go for ice cream and sodas and things after school. There was Ford's Pharmacy and then a place called Shirley's which had been the old McKeever's ice cream plant. I think both of them had wooden floors. Ford's Pharmacy was an actual pharmacy, the only pharmacy around at that time. There was a soda fountain and a hardware store. Ford's burnt down in the sixties, but by then, the place where the Connecticut-Knowles Pharmacy is now became a pharmacy, and it had a soda fountain.

After school, we would walk up Kensington Parkway and stop either at Shirley's -- and it's funny because Shirley's was where more of the hard guys hung out and Ford's was not as tough as Shirley's. But Shirley's had these fantastic cherry sodas. So quite often people would say, "To heck with the tough guys, we'll go to Shirley's anyhow," and we'd go to Shirley's. For a while it got to be all the rage to smoke these really foul-smelling short cigars, King Edwards I think they were. And Shirley's would sell them to us, but I don't think we could get them from Ford's. This was before McDonald's, before anything. The best hamburgers around were from Markeat, the little shop that was on the northeast side of the bridge across the railroad tracks there. It was just a little shanty owned by this guy named Weiss or Weismann. He made great hamburgers, and they sold milkshakes and hot dogs and stuff like that. There was not much else in Kensington.

Bethesda was not built up at all. Wisconsin Avenue there was lined with cherry trees and it was a very nice scene. The nearest movie theater for us as kids was the Hiser-Bethesda which was the theater that's next to the post office there in Bethesda, or there was also the Bethesda Theater. Either our parents would take us or by the time we were thirteen or fourteen, we would quite often ride our bikes up there. In Bethesda, we'd generally go to the Hot Shoppes to eat when we were teenagers. That was about the only place where we could go that had any kind of hamburger place, and it was jam-packed. But next to the Hiser-Bethesda was a nice little place called the Red Fox and we could go there and get hamburgers.

I don't think many of us went up to Rockville. By that time, the Villa Theater up in Rockville had replaced the Milo, and as late as the fifties, I think the Villa still had a separate balcony area for blacks. At least I know that it did back in the forties. But we always thought Rockville was sort of the "pits," and it was beneath us as far as our station in life was concerned and that normal, decent people went to Bethesda for their entertainment.

The Hiser-Bethesda Theater

There was almost no dating. I remember when Lynch decided that he wanted to ask Cathy Gironda out, but the absolute humiliation of being seen with a girl — that was pretty big stuff. And he decided what he would do is go down to Washington with her. So, of course, he didn't have a car, and he couldn't drive, anyhow, he wasn't sixteen, and the idea of taking the bus wasn't a good idea. So he was going to meet her on the train which stopped down there, and then hop on the train and go down to D.C. with her. He had this huge plan where she was going to get on the train, and then he would suddenly materialize and get on the train, but just by chance. I wasn't there but some kids saw her get on and they weren't stupid, you know. Then maybe a minute or so later, Lynch hopped out of some bushes and came running and hopped on the train. And everybody found out that he was taking Cathy Gironda down to Washington.

For entertainment, we would take the train occasionally on a weekend down to Washington. I think there were only two stops, one in the morning and then it would stop at night as it came back. So if you wanted to get down to Washington by train on the weekend, you had to be pretty careful to catch it at the right time or you were just pretty much stuck. We didn't do anything in particular down in Washington. We would go down to Ninth Street where there were all sorts of these variety stores where you could get all kinds of things.

We were all mail order freaks. We would listen to the radio and order Sky King rings or Jack Armstrong rings. I think it was Lynch who found out that you could order from these pulp magazines little things that looked like BB's that would pop like a firecracker when you threw them or these tiny, little things that we called ladyfingers that were tiny, little firecrackers.

My grandmother smoked, and when we were down there one time, I bought a whole bunch of these things. I hollowed out the end of one of my grandmother's cigarettes and then I put it back in the pack. I put it near the front and I was sitting on the couch in the house. And I said, "Don't you want a cigarette? Don't you want a cigarette?" I think she thought something was sort of strange. Anyway, she lit it and it began to fizzle like a firecracker and exploded. It didn't hurt her, but my mother was absolutely irate that I would do a thing like that, the mark of an absolute scumbag or reprobate or something. But that was the kind of thing that we would do.

Garrett Park at that time had its own fireworks, and they were quite something. I think Clyde Hall was involved with doing them. We had a lot of gatherings that would involve the whole town. There was the Fourth of July, there was a generally a picnic on Labor Day just before the beginning of school, then in the fall the Woman's Club of Garrett Park had a bazaar and that was great fun. I guess they used it to raise funds. That went on for a number of years, probably six or seven years. They had food and candy and cookies and stuff that people had made, and all sorts of games for the kids and bag races. I guess they were doing that to help build the community center and finish it off.

There was a tremendous sense of community. Everybody knew what everybody else was doing, and kids would see each other all around the place, so unlike a lot of schools where you would know people only in your class, you knew people at least in three classes and generally more than that. For two or three years, the big deal was the turkey shoot. And if you shot best, if you hit the bull's eye, you'd win a turkey. I'll never forget that because I had never heard of a turkey shoot before. When George and I first got there in the morning, there was nothing there but a whole bunch of sticks in the ground, spread apart. I think what I thought was that they'd let go all these turkeys that would go running across, and people would shoot. And Hartmann and I were convinced that the place would be littered with turkey guts, and this was almost too much, we were so excited about it, we could barely stand still, and we were really looking forward to the turkey shoot. But what it actually was, they would put targets on these things, and people would shoot at the targets. The idea of shooting guns down in Garrett Park was completely out of the question, but at that one time, that's what they did, and they had tons of people who wanted to do it. It was the first time I ever shot a shotgun, and I was really surprised by the kick of the thing. It was probably a 20-gauge or something. It wasn't a big blunderbuss but it was really something. Of course, I didn't hit anything. That big field was great for all sorts of things, the turkey shoot and the Fourth of July celebration.

The county had some sort of system where they would put us all on the school bus and take us over to Glen Echo about once a week. They had the Crystal Pool over there and we would be able to swim there. A lot of the kids really didn't know that much about swimming, and the idea of swimming teams was completely out of the question. I knew how to swim because I had gone to camp. I don't think most kids went to camp, and most kids were around in the summertime. I remember talking with kids when we got out of school. We'd just say, "Well, for three months we don't have to wear shoes." It was really incredible and just nothing to do, but generally we weren't going to get into problems. Many kids had chores; there were a lot of chicken houses and stuff and the kids had to take care of that usually.

In the summers of '53, '54, and '55, a bunch of us, particularly Howard, and Gieser, and Lamb and I would go down to Washington to watch the Senators get beaten. We would hitchhike to Chevy Chase Circle and then hop a bus and take it down to Calvert Street and then walk across the Calvert Street Bridge and come to the turn-around there and take a streetcar, go down 18th Street. I never will forget where the streetcar would start to turn left on Florida Avenue, there was an old bar. We all knew it because there was a guy who played for the Chicago White Sox named Ferris Fayne who was a real good hitter — he was just a Punch and Judy hitter. But he broke his finger in a bar fight there and we were always looking at that. The four of us would go down there with real regularity, hitchhiking down to the city, and our parents didn't think squat about it. I mean, we'd get down there and the games started at 7:30. We'd get back probably 11, 11:30 at night, having come from the city. I remember one time, it was in August of '53, coming back. And we were coming across the Calvert Street Bridge. The Calvert Street Bridge was famous for people jumping off of it. So Lamb, who was always a daredevil anyhow, decided to hang over the edge of the bridge, and we were holding him as he was hanging. And these cops were coming down the road. Boy, they did a 180 degree turn, you know, one of these power turns and came back, almost made us drop Lamb. And they were really angry at us, saying, "What the hell do you kids think you're doing?" So we pulled Lamb up and said, well, we were just kidding, and got out of there.

I remember in 1953 was the year the seventeen-year locusts came. I was thirteen that year. It was really exciting because this kid named Carter Bennett, who basically could figure out the thing that would most irritate girls and adults, figured out a way to make these paper boxes out of notebook paper. We went through notebook paper like crazy. You would make them and then you'd stick a seventeen year locust down in there and throw it at a girl. It was later that we found out that they would last long enough that you could fill them with water, and we had these humongous water battles with these things.

The area was beginning to lose a sort of rural edge to it. By the time we went to high school, we would still mostly hitchhike to B-CC and that's where we went for the first year, '55-'56. And then in '56, they built Walter Johnson.   And so everybody from here went to Walter Johnson. Before Walter Johnson, the only high schools were B-CC, Blair, Richard Montgomery, and Gaithersburg. That was it. Not many kids had cars then, and we hitchhiked a lot. If somebody had a car, everybody would use the car and you'd all go in it together. It meant five or six kids going in this car to school. But I usually I would be driven by George, who had a car. I don't really remember how I got home.

It's very hard to find photographs of this area from the early fifties. This was the time when all of Montgomery County was just exploding with growth and a lot of the development. When we first started at Walter Johnson, there were cows in the surrounding fields. Some family owned the farm and it was still an operating farm. I remember sitting in class when I was in the twelfth grade at Walter Johnson, sitting in my English class. I remember the date and the time - January 27, 1958 at about 2:15. I remember because I decided that I was going to have this locked in my mind, and I said, "I'm going to remember this time and look at this particular time every day for the rest of my life and just see where I am." We'd had a real heavy snow that winter, and it was a cold winter, too. I looked across the field from my English class, and it had snowed. Now, you can't see squat from Walter Johnson. But I could look all the way directly out to Old Georgetown Road, and it was a crystal clear day, the temperature was about twenty, and the snow was absolutely white. And there was one car traveling on Old Georgetown Road, which was two lanes at that time, one car. And the sun was gleaming off the light of it. It just seemed absolutely perfect out there, so cold and clear and everything.

It really was an interesting time and place to grow up. I think most of us who were around in those years really knew that what we had as a community was very unusual. And I know some other kids would talk about it, and when kids start talking about stuff like that, you've got to realize that it couldn't have gotten any better. It was a totally different kind of environment than you see today. In many ways we as kids were able to benefit from the rural nature of the area, like the way we could go swimming in Rock Creek. I remember that when I was a kid, all over the place we had tree frogs in the summertime. You'd see these things stuck to the sides of trees, ribbiting away as they sat there.

 It was really something that you would never ever be able to recapture - the overall beauty of the place, the huge elm trees that were everywhere arching up and reaching over. Garrett Park was a unique small town, and I recognized it at the time. I know that I thought that it was too idyllic to be real.

(Excerpted from interviews conducted by Rich Kapit on January 9 and February 6, 1994 courtesy of the Garrett Park Town Archives; photos of Bill courtesy of Trammell Maury)

3

BING REYNOLDS

I still think about the generous support the whole town gave me after my car accident, how amazing that was. Growing up, I always felt supported by being surrounded by people who knew me, and I learned that way to be a people person. Today most people don't get to experience that kind of thing.

My parents were Dorothy C. Reynolds and Walter Bingham Reynolds, Sr. I am Walter Bingham Reynolds Jr., but I was called Bing as a child to distinguish me from my father, and I still am. My younger sister, Joyce was four years younger than me, and my brother, Chuck, who passed away several years ago, was three years younger than Joyce.

I lived in Garrett Park from birth until when I joined the Navy when I was twenty years old. My parents moved to Garrett Park in 1939 shortly after their marriage, and I was born in 1940 in Sibley Hospital in Washington, D.C. Our original address in Garrett Park was 63 Kenilworth Avenue, and then they renumbered it, it became 11109. I think when they were developing a fire grid, they gave the houses addresses that referenced somewhere out by Washington, D.C.

My earliest memory was of my mom and dad having a really hard emotional time over something that was happening out in the world. I remember that there was a huge drama over something, and maybe it was Pearl Harbor, though I would have been really young to be remembering it. Dad was in the army, stationed in Ft. Meade, in Maryland. He was too old to be sent overseas, so he was doing postal service, working in D.C. Mom would go to D.C. to meet him and he would sneak off the base. She would leave me across the street with a neighboring girl - I think her name was Libby Ackers, who was only a few years older than I was. I remember being really upset about that and screaming.

Another early memory, from when I was three or four, is of the burial of my first dog, Pete. Pete had become a chicken killer, and in Garrett Park you couldn't really have a chicken killer because a lot of people had chicken coops. The Lambs had a chicken coop right up adjoining our property down the hill from us, and also Pete had gotten into the Acker's chicken coop. So they had to do away with Pete, and we buried him in the back yard. In addition to chickens, there was this goose who lived down on Rokeby Avenue. The family with the goose was on my paper route, and in the big brick house up the hill from them, was a German Shepherd who used to go after me. But when the dog chased me, I would run over to the neighbors and the goose would chase him away.

The Ward's lived on top of Donnelly's Hill across the street from the Donnelly's house. Sandra Ward and I used to play a lot together. One time we were caught by one of Sandra's sisters in the outhouse checking each other out. We were only about six. Grandma at the time was staying with mom, and she would always say "Bing's out playing with that Jezebel!" Of course my grandmother blamed Sandra, not me. There were these corn fields we liked to play in, where Garrett Park Estates was later built. There were these old fashioned corn stalks tied at the top, and we called them "houses" and played in them. They were neat little hiding places.

The Giesers lived originally in a little Chevy house on one of those streets that goes up to Knowles, but then they moved to their big house on the other side of Kenilworth from us. They had three boys – Stevie, Jimmy, and Benny. Mr. Gieser loved to work on cars in that huge shed or garage. When I was really young I played with Jimmy and Stevie Gieser. Jimmy was a year older than I was, and Stevie was a few years younger. Jimmy and I hung out a little, but Stevie and I got in so much trouble that Mrs. Gieser forbade him from playing with me. One time, when I was about ten, we started a fire that started spreading quicker than we thought, right there in the spare lot by their house. Another time, when they had started building the Estates, me and Stevie Gieser went and broke windows in the new houses there. This was like the first eco-terrorism, and it resulted in my only court appearance. The judge asked me if I did it and I said "Yes". He said, well you're honest, so don't do it again. I think we must have been rather nice kids, because most of us did rather well af-

Buddy (a cousin), Joyce, and Bing

ter we got done growing up.

Garrett Park was originally in a very rural part of Maryland, though that was changing quickly. The Doves lived in a tiny little house on a hill across the street from the post office. The boys were Johnny Dove and Abby Dove, who was the oldest, named after his father (Albert). Johnny Dove was a few years older than me, and took me under his wing. I was a fat little kid, and because I wasn't much good at sports, Johnny would pinch bat for me, sort of taking care of me. Grandpa Dove, (Albert Sr.) lived in the house across the railroad tracks by the post office. He was really ancient.

The mail delivery was a big event. The train delivered the mail, and when they threw the bags out, we kids could bring in the bag and get a reward. When I was younger, old Mr. Penn and Mrs. Penn, ran the P.O. and owned the store. Later Mrs. Parsons became the postmistress and Louie Karsh ran, and maybe owned, the store. He was a good butcher and they had a meat case, and I think his wife helped him run it. I ate way too much sugar and was overweight. We would buy cigarettes for our "parents" maybe shoplift little a bit which ended up on our parent's bill. We used to throw rocks and bottles at the railroad warning bell, and we also threw rocks at street lights, and were successful at times. Poor Louie - he'd scream and rant.

Butt's rock was a big rock, maybe eight feet high, just on the edge of the park by the tracks. It was a good hang-out place for us. That probably made Louie happy, when we hung out there instead of in front of the store. I wrote BR loves GP on it. GP was Gina Parsons, the daughter of the postmistress, and she was the prettiest girl in town. At some point, our parents had us go to Sunday school together, and we'd cut class and make out in the car while mom and dad were at church.

My main group of friends was Bucky Lynch, George Hartmann, John Howard, Bill Maury, and the Lamb boys, Michael and Donald. Michael was a little older and Donald was a little younger than me. My friends and I spent a lot of time across the tracks. There was this guy, Freddy Hendershot, who lived in a shack on the CCC grounds. He had a "goldmine" full of fool's gold right near his shack and we liked to go and dig there, which really annoyed him, and sometimes he wasn't so friendly. But he could be sort of nice, sort of ok, and we did talk with him, and sometimes he told us stories. But he could also be sort of scary. It might have been an alcohol thing.

One time I was playing with my gang down by the creek across the tracks when a gang of blacks from Ken-Gar showed up. I believe we had a mud fight but with no rocks (I hope), and It ended with no injuries on either side. They probably thought we were on their turf. I didn't give much thought to it at the time, but there were no black people ever in the town except for workers. I did think about this later, how slavery really hadn't ever really ended.

None of the adults knew where we were when we would be out there playing. My mom had a high, high soprano voice, and she wanted to be a singer, and in fact she did sing in church. Her voice could carry really far, and she would call me way over at the CCC Camp from the back porch, which was not enclosed. She would call, "Biiiing" in her high C or whatever it was voice. I'd get home, and she'd say "Didn't you hear me call?" and I'd say, "Oh, yeah, I was over at the CCC Camp."

Across the railroad tracks there were these huge sawdust piles, at least ten or sixteen feet tall, and we would slide down them and come home full of sawdust and be in trouble for that. My dad took me on hikes down there together sometimes, and when I was about six, he took me down to Rock Creek. We would stand by the creek and pee together – something unheard of today. You would be arrested for indecent exposure. There was a spring down there, just below the post office, where skunk cabbage grew, and we skinny-dipped in the creek.

We boys liked to play in the box cars that were parked on the tracks by the railroad station – all around inside them, on top of them, and we would get covered with soot. We always used to put coins on the tracks and let the train run over them and flatten them. The railroad crews used what we called torpedoes, these little things filled with gunpowder that they'd put on the rail, and they'd go off before the train got there to warn the train that there were workmen on the tracks up ahead. We'd find them discarded along the tracks and put them on the tracks, and wait for the train to run over them, so they would go off and make the train jump a little bit.

The worse trouble I ever got into was when I decided it would be a good idea to put rocks and bottles on the tracks and see what happened when the train came. And when the train came, it caught air, and you could see the gap underneath its wheels. So they sent the railroad inspectors out to find out who'd done it, but Mr. Chamberlain, who had seen us and knew who'd done it, covered for us so we didn't have to go to jail.

One time we got the cops called on us for harassing one of the neighbors who lived in a duplex by the triangle (where Waverly meets Kenilworth). This neighbor was really touchy, and he went off on us one Halloween when we were doing the things kids did on Halloween. So we just picked on him unmercifully. He was scared, and he didn't know the kids at all. He threatened us, and he even had a gun out the window one night, and he finally called Sgt. Brown, the juvenile sergeant for the county police. And Sgt. Brown came and gathered all us boys, and he called our parents, and we were all gathered in my mom's living room. He told us how were really destroying and hurting this family, and I think we felt kind of bad about that. We didn't even get cited or anything. Sgt. Brown was good that way.

So as kids it seems we were always up to something. Mr. Thurston, a next door neighbor, had an old car with a spare tire on the back, and I got in trouble one time for letting the air out of the tire. When the new school was being build we had played chase on the foundation and ruined so they had to rebuild the wall. And once again Sergeant Brown investigated it. There was this construction site where they had sanded the floors and left a pile of fine sawdust. And we, of course, being educated kids had heard about how sawdust was really flammable, so we would build little fires and throw in a handful of sawdust, and watch the flash of the fire. We could walk over to the White Flint Golf Course, and we used to go out there and steal golf balls and sell them back to the golfers. And I have this memory of Haile Chisholm standing out there in the railroad bed near the post office, telling us kids how weak and punky we were, digging stones with his bare feet, and they were big stones, the kind they use for railroad beds. Bucky Lynch was hanging out with us, and he was really trying to annoy Haile and he finally pushed him to the limit. Even though Haile was barefoot, he took after Bucky and chased him all around. I don't remember how that ended. *(To learn how this ended, read Bill Maury's narrative – L.P.)*

Bill and Maureen Gorman lived next door to us in a neat old stone house. They had a son, Mike, who was a friend of mine. Mike had an uncle who had flown the first US mail plane, and we went downtown and looked at it on display at the Smithsonian. I remember that his uncle's name was listed on the airplane. A friend of Mike's dad stored a racing boat powered by a jet engine, a jet-propelled speedboat, in their driveway. It had a real jet engine from a fighter jet plane. Mike's aunt (Bill's sister) had been the first Miss America. I met her once, but by then she seemed old, and she was drinking to excess. I think she was what we would call an alcoholic.

Bill Gorman taught me how to play poker and twenty-one. From him I learned about the odds in a poker game. And one time he took us out to the county's airport, which was on Rockville Pike, near the golf course, and we got to fly in a single engine airplane. Bill loved his beer, and there were cases of empties out in the driveway, waiting for the trash pickup, and cases of beer inside the house. We were still kids, not yet in high school, but Mike and I learned to love beer too, and we never worried about his dad knowing it, because he had so much he couldn't have missed what we drank. Beer got me into trouble plenty of times. Because both of Mike's parents worked, Mike's house was a favored place for kids to hang out, and we liked to play Spin the Bottle. I especially remember playing it with Gina Parsons.

Bill had a Civil War gun collection, revolvers and rifles, and he kept one or two guns and his porn collection in the attic crawl space. So that was a place we liked to hang out. I still have a scar where one of the Civil War cavalry sabers cut me when we were play fighting with them. At some point, when we were somewhere between ten and twelve, Mike Gorman and I learned to shoot some of those guns down by Rock Creek. When I came of age at about fourteen, my dad gave me a .22 for my birthday, and we boys would sometimes go squirrel hunting across the tracks. We never did manage to get any squirrels, until finally Michael Murtaugh did kill one and brought it to school, breaded and fried, for lunch.

There were lots of snakes out in the woods across from the tracks. We never saw a copperhead, but we wanted to. A lot of people didn't like snakes, but Mike Murtaugh and I liked them so much we collected them, and we didn't like people to kill them. We kept our snakes in a sort of a zoo with snake cages. Once we found a dead blacksnake that had been killed by the railroad crew, and we cut it open and found a tiny live turtle inside, just a little bigger than a golf ball. We took the little turtle home and kept it in one of the cages.

There was a lot of history in the area around there, and once I found an arrowhead by the steps of our house. There was an old abandoned cabin across the tracks which could be seen from town. I cannot remember exactly where it was, but we did explore it and maybe added a little more vandalism.

Once Mike Murtaugh and I built a flat bottom boat, like a pole boat, and dragged it over to Rock Creek and floated it down all the way down to Wisconsin Avenue. We could walk over to Viers Mill Road through the woods where there was a housing development, like a little town, with a movie theater. The houses were very small and cheaply made, and I think they were built for the war veterans. We often would hike west along the

B&O Railroad one time past Gaithersburg, and one time some country kids ran us off. The Welles had a garden right near the railroad tracks, so we could easily steal corn from their garden. Mr. Wells wasn't too happy with us. We built a lean-to just off the tracks west of town in the field towards Veirs Mill, over by what became Randolph Hills. We would camp there and cook the corn fresh picked from Wells garden. Mike Murtaugh found a sassafras tree, and we made tea from the bark. It tasted kind of like mud. We found a dead dog and put the scull on a stick so he was looking out over our lean-to. One night we decided to go on a hike. We had a very hard time finding our camp that night.

We had freedom that kids these days don't have. Getting towards the teenage years, we took these long bicycle trips, and once we rode all the way out to Cleaves' Farm out by Gaithersburg. We knocked on the Cleaves' door and Mrs. Cleaves said "Do your parents know where you are?" Of course they didn't. It was getting dark and she called our parents and we ended up sleeping that night in the barn.

Dogs used to be a lot freer too. My dog Paddy, a terrier, ran lose all over town and would return home wounded from dog fights or car encounters. When he was hit by a car and broke his back, we had to put him down. I was about fourteen at the time.

Halloween eve and nights were unreal. One time, Mike Lamb lit bag of poop on fire on the porch of this house on the corner of Rokeby and Argyle. We didn't have anything against the people who lived there, they didn't particularly deserve it, but it just sounded like a good idea. The owner came out chasing Mike, across the park into the railroad culvert. I remember we were watching Michael running, and he ran straight down the hill, across the road, into the park, and into the tunnel. Michael was just the right size, he could fit in there and run through it, but the guy tried to run in after him and bashed his head on the roof of the culvert, so he was quite angry. Sgt. Brown came, and someone found us and told us, "You guys gotta go up to Bing's house", so we all trooped up to Bing's house and there was Sgt. Brown sitting on our couch with my parents. And we had a talk.

Ringing the church bell was another Halloween trick that was started by the older gang and which we carried on. Some of the guys who were more monkey-like would climb up into the belfry somehow. I remember hiding from the police who were searching for us, hiding in somebody's yard while the cops were walking along the bank, looking for us. It was quite exciting. I think that Garrett Park probably had that reputation of causing trouble, and so they had designated patrol cars for Halloween.

Another Halloween, we tricked Stan Woodwell Sr., who was a former track star. We had a good head start, but he was so fast, like a leopard, and he quickly passed up the slower kids and finally caught Bucky, who was the fastest one of us. We stuck around for a firm scolding, and were mightily impressed. I remember both Stan and his son, also named Stanley, who was my younger brother, Chuck's age – good natured people.

We organized our own games and we didn't need a baseball coach. We played baseball and football without any adult to make it happen. Little League started over in Kensington, and I didn't get picked, but I still could play baseball and football with my friends.

I was about thirteen or fourteen when the swimming pool was built. The whole town got together to make that pool happen, and we were really excited about it. To be a member you had to put in $100.00, and my parents weren't at all rich, but they paid that 100 bucks. We really wanted that pool, and one time before the pools was ready, my friends and I snuck under the fence to swim in it, though the water was all murky from the winter.

I attended Garrett Park Elementary when it was still really small. Mrs. Duey taught grades one through three. I sort of held a grudge against her, but now I love her. One time I was sitting in class dutifully copying all the letters from the walls around the room, and I was copying all the cursive ones because I thought they were pretty, and she got mad at me because I was doing that when I didn't yet know my alphabet and how to spell. Mrs. Reed was our fourth through sixth grade teacher. I thought she was old because she was a platinum blonde, but she wasn't really old.   At some point Mrs. Sutherland came and took over the middle grades. I never had Mrs. Sutherland, but I did get in trouble with her. We had discovered auto bombs which are like the bombs that terrorists use, but we could buy them as a kind of fire cracker, and they would whistle and smoke and then go bang. Someone planted one in her car. Though it wasn't me, she blamed me anyway. I think that we also once put an auto bomb in Andy Sonner's car.

Sometimes we would skip school and go into DC on the train. Mrs. Reed was okay with it when she found out we would visit museums or the zoo, and when we came back there was no punishment. It was a good thing for me that my friends all were good students, and I think she hoped some of that would rub off on me. I probably had attention deficit disorder, and Mrs. Reed probably recognized that. Unfortunately, by the time I had her for a teacher, I had been anesthetized to the extent that I thought that in order to be myself I had to be a bad student. That was my identity. Today I more than likely would have been in special ed. and had a set of initials on my school records indicating some disorder, but instead I saw a county child psychologist who said I didn't love my mom.

I was pretty young when my mom read the whole *Kon-Tiki* book to me. And later, when I had the flu or measles or something, I was home in bed, and I read the *Mutiny on the Bounty* trilogy, the whole thing, to myself. I remember that the first book had regular print, but the second two had really tiny print. So even though I wasn't a good student, as I got older I actually became a good reader. I'm planning a trip to Fiji this year, and part of that trip will take me up to the Bly waters. I am really looking forward to that.

Scuba diving in Bali 2018

I think it was Mrs. Duey who at some point showed us the film, *The Lost Weekend*, a movie about alcoholism. I believe she showed it to us because her husband was a fireman, and a lot of firemen are heavy drinkers. That was the first time I learned about recovery and about how alcoholism works.

I attended high school at Walter Johnson, where I hung out with the bad guys. There were only a small gang of them. Some of the kids were beatniks, but I ended up with a few motorcycle type guys, guys who didn't have motorcycles but they had that mentality. When I graduated from twelfth grade I felt I was at last set free from prison.

A year later I ran my car into a tree at the top of Garrett Park hill. John Howard and Johnny Walter were with me. John Howard had a severe broken ulna and radius, and Johnny a busted ankle. My lungs were so badly crushed that they didn't work very well, and when I entered the hospital I was almost dead, and they put me in an oxygen tent. I spent two weeks in the hospital. When I woke up I was in the oxygen tent, and the nurse looked at me when I opened my eyes and said, "I thought we had lost you." I remember looking up when I was in the emergency room, and my dad had tears coming down his face. Before that I had no clue how much he loved me. We had no medical insurance, and when I got out of the hospital, the town took up a collection, and everybody contributed to pay my hospital bill.

Now I had no driver's license, and I wasn't really happy. I looked at my dad and said "What about the Navy?" He said "Good idea son." So I joined the Navy and went to machinist's school, where I learned to operate an engine room. I didn't have any desire to be an officer, so I just went as far as I could go in four years.

I did very well in the Navy, and when I got out of the Navy, Joyce and a friend of hers had come to Garrett Park to visit. I met her friend, who was at the time engaged to be married to a guy who went to the same college (Wilmington) she and Joyce attended, and Joyce's friend and I got enmeshed, and Joyce didn't get to see her hardly at all, and she's been mad at me ever since. "I came with Marty to have fun, and you took her away." I had told the guys in the Navy, well, if I don't meet someone and fall in love and get married, I'll be back in 90 days (the time limit for re-enlisting without losing your benefits). But after I met this young lady, me and her just hit it off, and I spent the summer there in Maryland doing odd jobs, spreading asphalt with an all-black crew except for the foreman. They kept asking me to be a foreman because I was white, but I just hung out with the black guys, and we had good times together.

That was the summer I asked her to marry me. We got married in the fall and came to Boulder, Colorado because she liked Colorado, and I had visited, and I liked it too. I was tired of living at home. I'd seen the world, and I was ready to get away, and so was she. Her former fiancé's father was a pig farmer, and I don't think Marty really pictured herself growing up as the wife of a pig farmer.

I got a job selling insurance. I reflect back to that time, and I cannot put my finger on why I went job hunting but I didn't look where my skills would be appropriate, such as at the public service power plant. But I never thought of it. I was working at a 7-11, and a guy walked in and said "You're pretty good at people relationships. I think you'd be good at selling insurance." So I became an insurance agent. I ended up owning two insurance agencies, the first one which I sold so I could go to college, and the second one I sold after Marty had died, and I was depressed, and I didn't want to be working at insurance any more. I got my geology degree at C.U., and afterwards worked for a time as a miner, which I loved. I was mining for molybdenum, a mineral that strengthens steel, and it's used in bicycle frames. They used to put it in toothpaste, similar to fluoride. I graduated from C.U. at thirty-two, and I did well there for a guy who didn't have much of a scholastic background. I had been asked to be a geologist at the mine, but their pay for a geologist wasn't anywhere near what I was making as a miner, and I excelled at mining and moved to the top. Marty and I were living in southern Arizona, and one day we were listening to the radio, and John Denver came on and we said, "We have to go back to Boulder." We both had tears in our eyes, and we knew we were going home.

The last time I was in Garrett Park was when we were finally selling the house. I think it was in 1994. The town had changed – it felt different and it seemed like there were a lot more cars, and by then I hardly knew anybody in the town. Joyce and Chuck had left me to clean out the house, and I decided to have an estate sale. So I put a sign out on Knowles Avenue saying "Estate Sale", and people would go into the house and grab something and lug it out. I was having fun, joking with everybody. I would say five bucks, and they would say fifty cents maybe. I had a little stew with one parent. His kid had bought something for a quarter. He took off with it, really happy to have it, whatever it was, and his dad went ballistic that I let his kid buy something without his permission. He told me to give back the money, and I said, "All sales are final. And anyway, your kid needs to learn how to deal with his own money." The kid had tears in his eyes when his father dragged him off.

Growing up in Garrett Park was the most wonderful thing. Being in Garrett Park, I knew everybody in the town. I delivered papers – I had the Times Herald route which was about a third of the size of the Post and the Star routes, so I traveled the whole town to deliver those papers. It was the kind of town where I knew every-body, and I'd knock on the door and the husband would come to the door and say, "Oh, it's Bing Crosby!" and they'd pay the bill. Even though Louie, who owned the store, would scream at us, I think he loved us. We used to shoplift, and if he knew we had stolen something he'd tell our parents, and our parents would pay it. For some reason we didn't get into much trouble for doing that, and eventually I graduated out of it. I still think about the generous support the whole town gave me after my car accident, how amazing that was. Growing up, I always felt supported by being surrounded by people who knew me, and I learned that way to be a people person. Today most people don't get to experience that kind of thing.

4

FELICITY PAYNE CALLAHAN

That pool was so seductive. When it first opened, I remember having this, "I live in paradise" kind of feeling when I would ride off to come down to the pool to swim. Not in those exact words, but I thought, "What more could anybody want?" I knew this was a wonderful town, and I was very happy with my childhood.

I was born on July 30, 1942 in Washington, D.C., and I lived in Garrett Park from the age of practically zero through 1960, when I graduated from high school and went away to college. My parents, George and Norah Payne, had three daughters. My full name was Felicity Anne Payne, and my two younger sisters were Pamela Nancy, born on December 8, 1944 and Jenifer Anita, born on August 14, 1948.

Our first house in Garrett Park was on the corner of Montrose and Argyle at 11018 Montrose. Then in 1948, the first day of school when I went into first grade, my parents moved to 26 Pembroke Street, now 10707 Kenilworth Avenue. My recollection is that I left home from the old house and then, during when I was in school, they got me out from under foot for the first time in their lives and quickly moved house, so I came home to a new house on Pembroke Street, which was right in sight of the school.

When we were living at the Montrose house, my parents had a fenced-in area that my sister, Pam, and I would play in, with a swing set and a sandbox. I figured out a way to get out of the fence, and when I did, I would usually go down to the playground at what is now known as Wells Park, though it wasn't called Wells Park at the time. Another place I went was the well that was next to what I called the Turner's house (4701 Argyle) on the corner there. It was an enticing and spooky little place, with a stone grotto with two seats on either side. There was this attraction of the water down in that well. I was told not to go there, so of course that's exactly where I wanted to go. We could drop things in and listen for how long it took till you heard a sound or the splash or whatever. When it would rain, I would play in the granite gutters, and we would build series of dams on the slope of Montrose, right in front of my parents' house. I would float sticks and little home-made boats.

At the T-shaped intersection with Argyle, which is Donnelly's Hill and Montrose, there were some Chevy houses, and one of those had a family called the Foxes. My very, very earliest memory was actually of Mr. Fox hammering a dent out of the fender of his car and hitting his thumb. I was very little, and I remember knowing I shouldn't laugh, but I wanted to explode with laughter. I went behind the car and I remember crouching down and laughing into my hands because he was swearing a blue streak. I just thought it was hilarious.

They had a boy, Buddy, and a girl, Lois, who was Pam's and my favorite babysitter. She told these incredibly good stories that she seemed to make up on the spot, stories about a green monkey with purple polka dots, a mischievous, tricky monkey, with powers and capabilities. We knew that we would get these stories when we went to bed and we were always very good about it because we wanted the stories. If Lois was busy and couldn't babysit, it was crushing. We were always kind to Lois because she told such great stories, but we were pretty horrible to other babysitters.

I thought her brother, Buddy, was very cool. He would ride over Montrose on a bicycle and down into his driveway with his hands stretched out while I watched from the higher level of our front lawn. He would ride down and up his parents' driveway, and he would jump off the bike onto this little bank to the left of the driveway, and let the bike of its own volition go right on careening up the driveway, until it crashed against the bank. It looked very neat, so one day I decided to be cool myself. I don't know if I had a tricycle or a bike with training wheels, but it was not quite as effective as when Buddy Fox did it. I came tooling down Montrose Avenue and I made my left turn into the driveway and I did my best to jump off, and I kind of leaned against the bank, and dumped this little bike over, and went in feeling very cool. Then the next morning my father came in very abashed looking like he had terrible news. "I just ran over your bike. It was behind the car." He didn't expect it to be there and then he backed out, crunch, crunch.

When it was snowing, I loved it that we were right there at Donnelly's Hill because we would sled and sled and sled and sled. And then we would come in, have a hot chocolate, warm up very fast, and maybe even go out and sled some more. I was very good friends with Michelle Berrigan, who lived at the top of Donnelly's Hill, and it was through her that I met Jim, the man I'm married to. My parents were good friends with the Reynolds' family, so I spent a lot of time with the Reynolds family. Living at the Howard house I think I had a feeling that we were living in the center of things, as opposed to when we moved down on Kenilworth, or Pembroke, as it was then, where I felt a little bit that we were on the fringe.

I have a vague recollection from when we were in the Montrose house of a man coming around collecting things, and he had a horse drawn cart. I'm not sure if it was somebody who came from Kensington or whether it was somebody local. He was collecting stuff like pans to help the war effort, so that's pretty early because I was born in '42. I remember my parents discussing about whether it was practical doing without the pans, which we maybe needed, questioning whether they really were going to be making a difference. And I remember my mother mending pans that had holes in them using circular discs of metal and little brads that held them in place. She would fix them into the hole and then she would hammer hard into the bottom of the pot. Imagine that, mending a pot!

I also remember stirring the yellow into margarine and we'd be stirring and stirring, whipping it hard to make it look like butter. It was white, like lard. I also remember lighting the broom on fire. I was sweeping embers vigorously back into the fireplace, all the way in to the point at which I noticed the broom was on fire,

and then I got scared. I started to leave the scene of the crime carrying the broom, which was on fire, with me. Then I thought I was bringing the evidence with me; so I quickly dropped it right on the rug, which was woven grass and rattan, and it went up in flames. Then I shrieked and my mother came in and poured water on it. Then we had to stare at that hole in the rug. That's a pretty early memory.

My father was co-director of a Sunday school, which was in what is now the Town Hall. If you memorized the Bible verses you could earn a card that would have more Bible verses on it. I don't know where they came from, and I don't even know why I wanted them, but I was just so darn competitive and I would spend Sunday morning plowing through the Bible looking for the shortest possible verse I could find that I could memorize.

I think one of the really charming aspects of Garrett Park is that people pick up their mail at the post office. My earliest memory of the post office is of the boxes behind where Mrs. Lina Penn sold stuff. There were open boxes and I would say my name, and she would give me the mail for my parents and I would carry it home. My mother remembers that I actually earned a dime doing a special delivery letter. It was to Mrs. Lucille Stevens, and it was on my way home. My mother explained to Mrs. Penn that it was excessive, and Mrs. Penn said that she was required to pay a dime for a delivery, so she had asked me to deliver it and knew I would be responsible.

The general store was almost like a community center before the community center. There were always people in there, men standing around talking, and mothers who would wheel their children down in some sort of carriage from any part of the town. There was sort of a chaotic feeling to the store. It was semi-hardware store-ish, and it had things like rakes and buckets and nails and other kinds of implements, some school supplies and batteries, and I think maybe there was some clothing and maybe even bolts of cloth. There were barrels and boxes of things that were sold in bulk and grains and cereals. Kids would come in for bubble gum, and later the baseball cards and stuff. It was just a real country store with candy in round or square jars that stick together that were behind glass and you would point and she'd pull them back and pull out the candy that you wanted. I definitely remember the big red Coca Cola metal container that was not in any way, of course,

electric but had ice floating in it and all the bottles. And I would sometimes be allowed to load the bottles in and they'd clink — of course they were glass — and clink, clink, clink I would be squeezing all these bottles of pop in tight, little bottles of orange or root beer. It was important to mix them up so that there was a sense of total selection.

Later there was this incredible modern innovation - an electric rotating hot dog cooker. That must have been when I was maybe eight, maybe in the early '50s. For 25 cents you could get a hot dog and a soda, and I was just so enamored of that. I just thought there was noth-

Garrett Park Post Office and general store

ing more gourmet than going down to the post office and getting one of those hot dogs — it smelled so good, that rotating cooker, and she would put a whole bunch of relish and chopped onions and mustard and stuff on it.

Both the railway station and the town store had these pot belly stoves that were nice and radiant and warm. In the railway station there was actually a person behind the grates in a little office where we bought tickets, and there were benches all the way around the outside that you could sit on. It was an exciting place to be because this was the place that you actually left Garrett Park from. I am very sorry the town ended up pulling down that railway station. It was a beautiful building.

There was no television, so you had to make everything up. We had these incredibly inventive games involving so much imagination and lots of very vigorous activities, teams and lots of running and chasing. White flag was a big favorite. The game might have been centered around a house, but in our mind's eye the boundaries that would divide those two teams would essentially go from South Carolina to Canada. It extended like the Mason-Dixon Line and if you were caught across that line you would be nailed and brought in as a captive for that flag on that side.

At night, we'd play flashlight tag. It was particularly fun in the Chisholms' pasture (where Holy Cross now is), but it was a little nerve wracking because there was a low area with a creek in it and the cows would sometimes come down. It was fairly brushy and built up, with trees around it, so the cows couldn't get in too easily. But if you could get across, you really had to keep your eye out for those cows, because sometimes they'd decide to come thundering down the hill toward you, and then you ran like crazy either out of the pasture or into the creek area where they were not too easily able to get in. We played a lot in that creek. There were little insects there with little pod feet on the water, and little squiggly things and tadpoles that we caught.

When the Garrett Park Estates was being built, one of the things I remember was a new revelation: cement sidewalks with cracks in them. And I can remember spending ages roller skating and that smooth sound, clunk, smooth sound, per clunk, just roller skating and roller skating with your legs getting that swish-gunk-swish-gunk.

The Garrett Players present "Affairs of State" L to R: Bing Davis, George Fills, George Payne, William Frost, Priscilla Maury, and Charles Ofenstein

I regret it but there was always the feeling that the old Park was a little bit better than the Garrett Park Estates. But there were things like the Garrett Park Players, where there were some really talented and wonderful people who lived in Garrett Park Estates who were big, particularly talented participants in the Garrett Park Players. Since my parents were involved, particularly my father, who acted, I was always very excited by the annual play.

Mr. George Kirby, who was the director, had a heart attack at one of the productions, and I was there in the audience. They called out, "Is there a doctor in the house?" Unfortunately he died immediately after, in the hospital. I remember my father coming home, and we said, "How's Mr. Kirby?" and he said that he had died. I remember crying and crying and feeling very shocked that anybody could die. It was the first time that I actually knew about death.

My very best friend for many years was Tim Honey. (His mother, Mary Honey would later be godmother to our adopted daughter, Marijke, whom she had helped us to find when we were looking to adopt.) The neighborhood children had the Little Garrett Players, modeled after the adult Garrett Players, in the Honey's basement. They had a furnace at the end of the room, and they built some archways to the left and right of the furnace so we could have a dressing room off to one side. We had a curtain that we could pull forward, and a space for a stage. The Honeys actually constructed this. We made the scenery, had costumes, wrote scripts, rehearsed and had props, and we made programs, just like the Garrett Players. We thought it was great. One play I remember involved soldiers and guards. In addition to my sisters and me, the neighborhood kids were

Martha and Timmy Honey, Wendy and Jeffie Johnston possibly, Tam and Jimmy Wilson across the way, Johnny Lamb, Steve Sonner, maybe the Thompson girls occasionally, and Karen Modine.

The backyard of the Honeys was also made into a baseball/kickball field, so we always had a diamond there to do things with. It just seemed to me that there were always quickly available games. We also would make forts in the woods or there might be events that would be happening in the town that everybody would be excited by.

They also organized teams, and we had the Garrett Park Summer Team of girls' softball. I was always very chunky but very strong. I remember that especially if we were playing a new team, that I would deliberately kind of waddle up to the plate in this very shluppy, chubby kind of way, and the outfielders would come in, and then I would hit it over their head. I didn't develop physically or emotionally to become a teenager quickly, and even into junior high I wanted to be an athlete. My goal, one of my earliest goals was to be the first woman professional baseball player.

They had Mayday celebrations at the elementary school. In the sixth grade, one girl would be the Queen of May, and then there would be her court, and they would all be dressed up, and there was a clown…A Mayday version of the Nutcracker Suite, because then there would be all these acts for the court and the different grades would put on different performances. One of them was bouncing big rubber balls to music. You would bounce and then you'd twirl around and pick the ball up or throw it, and everybody would throw it up and catch it at the same time. Some of the little children would miss the ball and while the choreograph stuff were going on, there were kids running this way and that way trying to catch their red rubber balls which were going astray. It did infuse the Park with a lot of red rubber balls, which meant that we could get a game of kickball.

There was something called summer school, which I loved. It was held at the community center and it was through the Recreation Department with programs every day. They had really nice young people, probably college students, who came in from outside the town. This was part of the allure in a way. And I would rush over there to see what all they were going to do that day because I might work with Sara on gimp lanyards which she was going to do from 10:30 to 11:15, and then there was going to be a story time. And I'd say to myself, well I'll go over and I'll catch the story, and then there was lunchtime and I'd zoom home for lunch.

There used to be a Garrett Park bazaar. Talented people from the town made things and you would go to these various card tables where there were all sorts of things there to buy. I can remember how exciting this bazaar was. It must have been held in the fall, a pre-Christmas kind of thing as a good time to put craft things out.

That pool was so seductive. When it first opened, I remember having this, "I live in paradise!" kind of feeling when I would ride off to come down to the pool to swim. Not in those exact words, but I thought, "What more could anybody want?" I knew this was a wonderful town, and I was very happy with my childhood.

Because I was strong, one of the sports I was good at was swimming. I swam with my face out of the water and I swam competitively with my head up, but I could actually win with that. So when I took the lifeguard course with Andy Sonner, most of the people taking the Red Cross course were men. I swam faster and stronger than anybody there because you have to swim with your head up when you are a lifeguard. You keep your eye on the person splashing and in trouble, and I was all set. But then for some reason, I think because I was beginning to notice the male lifeguards, I didn't want to be noticed as a female athlete.

All of us would ride our bikes like maniacs all over the town, and we had tremendous freedom, with no sense of any restrictions. The thing that was so striking is that there was no fear. Down where the pool now is, there were men who lived there across the tracks, and I remember going over the tracks. While there was something forbidden about the fact that it was actually over the tracks, I never, ever felt afraid of them. I felt that there was something remarkably exciting about their life, and I liked the idea of the adventurousness. They were hobos. They had very poor huts of sheet tin or maybe even cardboard, and inside they had a bed, a place where they could lie down. It was very cramped, but for a kid, it was like a neat little fort. They cooked a lot of food in cans on a fire and I thought that was neat.

After all, *The Boxcar Children* by Gertrude Warner was one of my favorite books. *The Boxcar Children* are four children that for some reason are without parents. They make their way into a forest and they find a boxcar, and that's their shelter. And then they find a place where people have discarded broken china, and they find some cups that have just a little chip in them, and they put together some utensils and stuff. They find berries, and they find places where they can get water and they make their own way. So there were these guys living across the tracks and cooking their food in cans, and it was all very innocent and nice to me. I didn't see the social implications of poverty.

A friend of my parents came from out of town, it might have been during the McCarthy era, and he was very exercised about Communists and talking with my parents, and I remember him saying passionately, "I'd rather be dead than Red!" And I really thought about that. I thought, wait a minute, dead is better than being Red... what are you saying here... and I thought if being dead is so terrible, if that's better than being Red, being Red must be really terrible. I thought, "Well who are these people that are so frightening to us in this country?" These Communists? I mean it must be that they are really, really awful, but how can they be really,

The Community Center Building Committee: W.D. Quigley, Ilah Gieser, Al Richter, George Payne, Alice Thurston, Sam Powell

really awful? I mean, what does it mean to be really, really awful so that we should be better off dead and would it come true when I say, yes I will die? You know, this is going on and on in my mind. I think adults should be very aware that a kid can have those strong feelings in reaction to an adult conversation.

The whole of Garrett Park was just an enormous playground. So if anybody deigned to build a house, it was invitation to climb on it while it was being built. As soon as the construction people would leave, the kids would swarm all over the construction. I remember being at the building of the community center and when they were putting up those flats and the excitement of each flat being framed, and it would kind of teeter in, and everybody would shove and push it back and trying to nail it together and getting the frame up and getting them, you know, rafters up for the roofing and stuff like that. I remember running all over the place. I'm sure I was just under foot.

The community center really was a center for many things.

Garrett Park Community Center

There were square dances and we had Girl Scouts there. I was first a Brownie and then a Scout, even in junior high. I liked the uniforms and particularly the badges. We had craft activities, learning activities, field trips, camping trips, things on buses. I was very big on leading the songs like "Hundred bottles of beer on the wall". I thought that was great, and particularly because when you started up, the leaders would go Uuuugghh. They didn't want to hear that again. I don't recall any downside to the Girl Scouts, and it was considered to be a pretty nifty thing.

In my memory Kathryn Sonner was the person who got the notion of getting the town together to have a George Payne Day. My father was trying to put an addition on the back of the house where the dining room now is, and George Payne Day was a way to help him out and get that darned thing built and closed in. So they brought bowls of food and even beer and stuff, and a huge number of people came to the house and worked and they put up that whole room in one day.

My mother was always somewhat self-effacing, but from my child's point of view, my father didn't do more for this town than my mother did. There was so many things that she was here in the town doing - she ran off the Garrett Park Bugle, and she was also the librarian. I think she was very much the starter of the Garrett Park Library. My mother had the degree in library science and she also believed in public libraries and books and she was an incredible reader. She collected books from people, and she was very pleased with it, but my mother was not a person to require acknowledgment of her own contributions. At some point Mrs. Bunker came kind of zooming in and pronounced herself head of the library. She could be very bossy toward my mother, but my mother just kind of hung in there because she liked the whole idea of being around the books. Also I think it was important for her to continue in her own field.

Mrs. Stevens' house is where the library started. It was very informal. You'd check the book out by writing on a slip of paper and putting it in a wooden box or a cardboard box. But they eventually got more and more books and they connected to the county system and got money to buy books and built it up. I would go down to the library a lot, as that's where my mother was. I wasn't a very good reader but I was competitive. So, at one point I'd just go (to the Garrett Park Library) and I'd keep picking books randomly. I would start at the A's and just read across. So I started really vigorously reading so that I would read every single book. When I got to about 'F' or 'G', I noticed they were buying more books and now there were new books behind me, so I gave up the endeavor.

My mother had a good friend and partner in Marguerite Murray, and they were very simpatico. Mrs. Bunker wasn't very patient with children, but Mrs. Murray told and read us wonderful stories. She had a particular flair for telling stories. She not only told stories of her own creation, she also told us stories from books. We didn't have television and we were used to hearing things on the radio and imagining, and it was much more vivid if someone told a story while we would use our imagination for the pictures. I always had a story of some sort, either told or read, before going to bed, and having stories told to you was especially satisfying.

At that time my mother didn't have a car as such to drive around independently. The groceries were delivered by the grocery man, and the milk came in a truck. So you would wait until the milkman, clink-clink-clink went up to the door with the things and you would be hiding in the bushes and you would streak through the milk truck, scooping your hand in and grabbing up the ice, and out the other door and the milk man went away. The ice was circular and had little indentations on the top and the bottom; that was the way it was made, and you could hold it like this with your thumb in the bottom indentation and your forefinger on the top and lick it. We had to make our fun where we could.

The Jewel Tea man would come and almost looked like a UPS truck but a little bit smaller. And he would have a stock of things that if my mother had an impulse that she needed suddenly some margarine (never butter), flour, whatever, eggs, he would have those kinds of things. But he also gave her a list and she would order things, then he would bring cans of stuff or whatever.

I remember going with both my parents and the whole family grocery shopping to Kensington, to the Safeway. Also I loved going to Mr. Victor's, which was a five and dime store. So we would go shopping and get a whole slew of stuff that was supposed to last a week or maybe two weeks. Then in-between we'd be supplemented by this person going around, the Jewel Tea man.

I also have a little recollection of my father bringing things home through the British Embassy where he worked. I was brought up conscious that my parents were English, and we were connected through the embassy. Sometimes we would be taken out of school to go down and wave the Union Jack for certain special events, such as visiting royals. And every Christmas all the children were presented to the ambassador and you had to be dressed up and it was a big deal.

I guess my mother sometimes must've had the car sometimes because I do remember her driving down to the embassy to pick up my father and I would go with her and she would send me in and I would scamper up, and it was a very much protected, you had to be acknowledged by the guard and they were very proper but of course I was only six, and I was hardly going to be a terrorist. My parents took us children down to Washington quite a bit. My parents, my father in particular, oddly had a notion that there was something improper about going to movies, but he did take us to a lot of concerts. My parents were very interested in music, and we went to a lot of things as children to Constitution Hall.

We had movies in the one-room schoolhouse every Friday morning. The movies were a particular problem for me because I was frequently very frightened by them, and could not handle them at all but I was too humiliated to admit it. Mrs. Duey finally talked to my parents and said "Why don't we just take this poor girl out of her misery and not send her to school on Friday morning? Let's not make her see these movies." But I insisted I wanted to be there. It was just movies like Swiss Family Robinson, but they were terrifying to me. In fact, I've recently seen that same Swiss Family Robinson movie on television, and there's one part where they are going down a path, and they look up, and there's a big spider. I ended up being very afraid of spiders for years and years.

My way of coping was to whisper, "I have to go to the bathroom", and I would go out, and I would get into the girls' bathroom and I would feel so safe. I would sit there for a while, and then I would have to come back out into the hallway, and I would peak in to see if I could stand it, but of course I let this big shaft of light in. The teacher had her hands full because I was wrecking it for the other kids by opening that door. I wanted to be in there, but I was too afraid to be in there. How many times can a kid go to a bathroom in fifty or seventy-five minutes? Even today, I do not have the disposition to see frightening movies. But this was part of what I was expected to do as a child. I wanted to be considered the most daring, and yet I just couldn't handle these movies, so it was a big dilemma for me.

When I got to elementary school the teachers had a bit of a handful. I probably would have been considered hyperactive today. We girls wore these dresses to school with sashes that tied in the back, and they used my sashes to tie me in my chair. I think it was very effective, about the most practical way of keeping you in one place. The thing that was nice about Garrett Park is that for all that, there was such a good feeling, so much affirmation, that I had a great childhood and I did feel good about myself, and I always liked going to school.

I felt that the new school building was not as nice the old one, that the old building was what school was supposed to be like. The new building had that long, narrow hall, where we had those bomb drills out in the hallway. You crouched down and put your hands over your head to protect yourself from the atom bomb that was going to be dropping in Washington. But, oddly enough, I wasn't frightened by those, since I didn't have any idea of real danger. Nobody went out of their way to say, "Look, if we drop this bomb on another country and vaporized tens of thousands of people..." It was a break in the routine of the school day and I didn't take it in as anything serious.

At school there weren't organized games or teams or anything like that. There might be a game but it wasn't organized. Sometimes we would play games like Red Rover. But much of what we did was just playing, using exactly what was there, the trees, the fields, whatever. When I went to first grade I don't recall that I particularly knew anything like letters and numbers, and there was no kindergarten. I think we were just allowed to play and have fun, and a lot of that play was in many ways very important.

I remember the fear of reading, not knowing how to read and being at the point of just learning to read. Mrs. Duey had us take turns sitting in a circle, and as it came closer and closer to my turn, I'd begin to panic and wonder, "How am I going to get through this? I'm going to stare at these groups of letters, and I've got to say something." Then there was such relief when she would pass by me for someone else.

In third grade, Mrs. Sutherland came. She was really one of the nicest teachers that I remember, though I can also remember her getting angry with me, and she would certainly want to tie me to my chair. But she did lots of things that really taught us about crafts and how things were done. We got lots of old, used clothing and ripped them into long strands and made rugs that we wove or braided. It was fun going to school with her, and she was a wonderful teacher.

She had a heavy poster board that was very glossy pink, fluorescent pink on one side, and white on the other side, which she cut into little rectangles, making them an inch by three inches or something like that, and folded them over so that the pink glossy was on the outside. When you read a book, you would tell her about the book you read, and she would write the title on the white side folded over. Every time you read a book it was stapled to this long strip of dark colored felt with your name above it. I would keep my eye out to see if anybody was coming close to the number, and I would read like crazy. I needed to have the most books stapled to my stupid felt.

Mr. Horan was our sixth grade teacher. I remember him with some chagrin, poor fellow, recalling that we were something of a challenge for him. He was a nice young man, and our class may have been his first teaching experience; I sure hope we weren't his last. He was never mean or angry that I recall, and indeed he seemed to like us and liked teaching. I hope we didn't make him too miserable. Unfortunately many of my memories are of me finding things very funny and laughing a lot, probably making "classroom management" more difficult for him. Our sixth grade class graduated and I don't know if Mr. Horan came back to Garrett Park Elementary the next year.

In sixth grade I was a safety patrol. My post was right on the corner of Kenilworth and Oxford, which was the closest post to my home. Of course I was always late. I would come out of the house and grab my books, and I had to wear that patrol belt buckled around me, and I would look up to see if there was an adult guard up there, and there was a captain who would check to see if people were late. You would get in trouble if you were late because, theoretically, you needed to be there to help the children safely across the road. I was on an inside curve, and they just had to walk by me, but I had to look very official and stand at attention and make sure that they were in some way proper. When I was late I would have to creep up from tree to tree and make a dash for it, and then appear very leisurely as if I had been there all along, just out of sight slightly or around the corner or whatever. But I loved being a patrol. It was a big honor and you got to go to Glen Echo as a reward at the end of the year, which was a big deal.

That sixth grade year was one of the years of the seventeen year cicada. Boys would string the cicadas through their eyes, and then would swing them around and around on sticks and sling them at me on patrol. Of course at that point they were dead. It was horrible. All around me were these buzzing cicadas, and you couldn't walk because they would crunch under your feet. Now, if anybody needs to know when the cicadas are, I count seventeen year increments from my sixth grade year because I'll never forget having to be at my post with these cicadas all around me.

That same year, somebody brought in an egg case from a praying mantis, and over the weekend, it hatched. That little egg case produced more praying mantises that you could possibly imagine. When we came to school, all these little teeny things were hopping like crazy all over the room. One of the things I liked doing at the end of the school year was going back to school and helping them pack up the school for the summer, you know, banging all the erasers, putting everything away, cleaning the desks. So I went that year, and even at that point, there were still these little praying mantis carcasses.   We had to shake all the books and get all the praying mantises out before we put them away, and we had to brush them out of the cupboards. Mr. Horan had hurt his back, and he had strapped a heating pad on it, so he only could move from outlet to outlet, where he would plug himself in, and then he would only be able to deal with the radius of around six feet.

In seventh grade we started at Kensington Junior High, a very big junior high where all the Garrett Park kids went.   I remember being panic-stricken when I was going to have to get on a bus and go beyond Garrett Park because it was impossible to imagine. KJH was a long, flat two-story building in three sections on top of a big hill. It gives me the strangest feeling to go along Beach Drive there and look up that same topography, where I spent three years of my life. I look there now and there is a flat ground, and it feels like there should be like dotted lines in the air or something. There was a school there. There were kids that were walking up and down this space, kids that learned Latin here and played in an orchestra and behind the school did these sports, and now there's nothing... it's gone, it's like a dream, it's like it was never there. It's weird to me.

I went to Walter Johnson its first full year. When we started in 10th grade, it was the first time they had the whole school start out in September. In 1957 the Walter Johnson football team won against BCC. I remember that so well, because the big thing was that Bethesda-Chevy Chase was the high school, it was number one in everything, the premier top-notch academic high school, and always won for every sport. We were out there with the smell of the cows and named after a baseball player, and they just scorned us. When we won, I remember it was just ecstatic, it couldn't have been sweeter. We were amazed and thrilled to have won, and then the BCC team was so humble. Some of the football players were crying as they left the field, they were just dragging off the field. That football game more or less said this is a high school that has arrived.

After graduating from Walter Johnson in 1960, I went on to Oberlin College and got a degree in mathematics. I graduated from Oberlin in 1965. I've worked in computers mostly, and I've done a little bit of teaching math. I'm interested in civic things, I'm a town meeting member and have worked in Wetlands Preservations, and in protection of children with special needs.

(Excerpted from an interview conducted by Henrietta Keller on December 29, 1994, courtesy of the Garrett Park Town Archives)

Comments added by Felicity Callahan in 2019:

My father died in 1998, and my mother in 2007. In 2009, the house I grew up was torn down and replaced by a newer, Mission-style house. There was an empty lot next to our house that my parents had planted with thousands of bulbs, special bushes, and flowering trees. In the spring people walking up Kenilworth Avenue to and from Parkside would stop and stare. It was such a "park" of spring beauty. Well, that was all plowed up and cut down, and a second house was built on that lot by the same person who tore down the Payne house and built a new house for himself.

Growing up in Garrett Park gave me a really solid beginning, and I think that the way the town insulated itself, along with my parents own desire to protect us, is why I actually did experience a fantastic childhood without worry. I have always had a deep fondness for Garrett Park, and especially the wonderful childhood there in the 1940s and 1950s, and the amazing sense of community.

5

BARBARA HORN WAGNER

When I applied to the PhD program in Pharmacology at GW's Graduate School, I wrote in my essay that they should admit me because of the town I grew up in. I wrote that "it was a place where I learned that I can do, so admit me to your program." From living in Garrett Park I have learned to be able to say "I need this and how am I going to be able to accomplish it."

My parents, Harold and Louise Horn, were both teachers. They were living in a rooming house in Cumberland, Maryland when they first met. My mother was an itinerant music teacher who went from school to school. I think that my father was teaching either general science or physics. They met before the war, and they were married in a Presbyterian church in Takoma Park, on December 27, 1941, right after the war had started. My father wore an army uniform for the wedding, and my mother wore a suit.

My mother was born in West Virginia, and later her family moved to Cecil County, Maryland. She grew up in Cecil County in a little town called Rising Sun. My father was originally from a little town in Kansas called Glasgow. He somehow ended up working as a teacher in Cumberland, Maryland. I thought it was sad that my father always blamed his lack of success on his poor schooling, because he had grown up in this little town.

I was born in 1943. My mother, who moved around a lot while my father was in the army, was living in Fort Jackson, South Carolina at the time. My father was on maneuvers, so she was alone. It was not an easy birth, and they were thinking about a Caesarian, but they finally got me out without one. It must have been really frightening for her to give birth all alone in this army hospital. I have to admire my mother for what she went through, giving birth to me.

After I was born, my mother returned with me back to her family farm in Cecil County. After the war was over, we lived with my father's sister in an area of Washington D.C. called Mount Pleasant. My aunt, who worked as a clerk for the government, supplemented her income by renting out rooms. Later, Ron and I were able to get a lot of entertainment out of spying on her roomers.

My mother didn't like her sister-in-law, and I'm sure it was a frantic search on her part to find us a house. We moved to Garrett Park in 1946, when I was almost three. The first memory I have from that time is of trying to stand on a box of kitchen utensils on the floor in front of the dining room window. I wanted to see the train as it went by. We lived on the part of Rokeby that was across the street from the train tracks, so the trains were right there. I'm not sure I could actually see them, because of all the trees on the property across the street and in front of the tracks, but I sure could hear them, and that's my first memory of Garrett Park. I also remember that I was amazed by the grass and the fact that there were no sidewalks. At my aunt's house in Mt.

Pleasant it had been all concrete. She had only this tiny little patch of grass that was her driveway, two concrete strips over the grass leading into the garage.

My younger brother, Ron, the first Garrett Park native in the family, was born in May of 1947, when I was almost four. I remember when he was born, and that we had a baby nurse who lived with us for about two weeks. She lived on a farm with these little lambs, and we went out to get her and bring her back so she could take care of this baby who cried all the time. She made peanut butter and banana sandwiches.

The Horns' house in center between the Lambs' and the Kizers'

The neighborhood I remember from my elementary school days was very small, consisting of the lower part of Rokeby Avenue. I remember playing in the park across the street, Wells Park. There was a big slide in the part of the park that was directly across the street from our house, and there were these big swings in the part of the park that was across from the Crichtons.

Next door on one side of us lived the Kizers, Mabel and Al, with their five children. Richard Kizer was either a year older than I was or the same age, and Susie Kizer was a year behind. It was really fun going to the Kizers' house. Mrs. Kizer was the manager of her house, and she sat at her table with the telephone at her side, the commander of her ship. In the spring, when there would be a carpet of pink and white flowers in the park, Mrs. Kizer had us make May baskets out of construction paper. On May Day (May 1st) we would gather the wildflowers from the park to fill the baskets, hanging the baskets on the neighbors' doorknobs. Gathering the flowers was an especially important part of this ritual. Another thing I remember about Mrs. Kizer was that she made cream puffs. When I was young, Mrs. Kizer was really the social director

Barbara (on right) with a friend

of our part of Garrett Park. Later she became a Jehovah's Witness, and I think she was too busy with her church to continue in that role. Mr. Kizer was a very successful barber in Bethesda. My father, who didn't drink and didn't approve of people who did, thought it was just terrible that Al Kizer would come home from work and walk around the yard with his beer.

On the other side of us lived the Lambs with their five boys. Later the Lambs moved over to the other side of that house. The Bolton's were very interesting. They were well-known people in their field, which was diplomacy or politics. Mrs. Bolton hired me as a baby sitter the first summer that I was out of high school, and she had very high expectations, giving m e a lot of responsibility. She would make up her mind in advance who she wanted as a baby sitter, and if I said "No, I have other plans" she didn't like that. She had a lot confidence in me, and she would get angry if I let her down. We were both very strong willed, so we butted heads. But I really admired her and respected her very much. Sadly, Mrs. Bolton died of Myasthenia Gravis, an autoimmune neuromuscular disease, when her kids were still quite young. She was the first person I knew who died.

I have a vivid memory of one neighbor I didn't know at all, Mrs. Butts. She lived on the other side of the street from us. As far as I know she lived alone. She was pretty old and rarely came out of her house, and she was very mysterious to us, though I don't know exactly why. We kids were afraid of her.

Next door to her little house was the house where the Dubinskis and the Punga families lived. They had come over to the U.S. from Latvia. I was in elementary school when Solveiga and her sister first moved into the Dubinskis house, and Solveiga hadn't yet married Harry Dubinskis. They were married after they arrived. Solveiga's wedding to Harry Dubinskis was the best neighborhood celebration that ever took place in our part of Rokeby Avenue. They invited all of the people on our street. I have vivid memories of tables being set up in their living room and just piles of food. It was so exciting. I thought Solveiga and Harry were wonderful and so exotic. As far as I know they were the only family in Garrett Park who came from a foreign country. I remember that my father wasn't very welcoming towards them, and that he made fun of them because they were from Latvia. I don't know what my mother felt – she was pretty silent most of the time.

It's amazing what I don't know about my parents. I don't think they participated a lot in the town events, though I do know that the Garrett Park Community Center was one of the few Garrett Park projects that my dad worked on. The town got the buildings for the community center from an abandoned army base, and townspeople got together to fix them up. My dad also served one term on the Garrett Park Town Council. I noticed that there were these recurring names on the town council, and I always wondered why my father was on the town council only once. My parents seemed a little separate from other folks, but maybe that was just my perception.

Only once I do remember that my mother was in a Garrett Park Players play called "The Gypsy and Me", but she got so put down by my father for that, and she was never in another play. When I saw the fabulous 1998 movie "Pleasantville" I could see my family in it. William Macy comes home from work and hangs up his hat and says "Honey, I'm home! Here I am!" That was my dad.

I have recently come to understand that my parents didn't have the same politics, but my mother never expressed a political opinion. I was aware that my mother didn't like my father's sister, the one who lived in the district, and who was so conservative that she got all her newspapers from Kansas. I now know that Mrs. Woodwell was the chair of some Democratic faction, either for the county or within the town, and they had meetings in the Woodwells' basement, and I have since wondered if my mother would have liked to be involved with that, and my father had nixed it.

However, we were charter members of the swimming pool. It was unusual for our family to be on the forefront like that. I was on the swim team at first, but I didn't stay on for long. It was too challenging and I didn't like it. One summer I worked in the booth at the swimming pool, selling and eating ice cream.

Our family was poor – there was no extra money. We got our first television set in 1952, for Eisenhower's inauguration. My father was really into Eisenhower, and I remember watching the Eisenhower inauguration on TV. I was so happy when we got that TV, because everyone else had TV before us. Before we had our own television, I remember gathering at the Wagner's house, just up the street from us, to watch Howdy Doody.

When I started school, the town didn't yet have its own kindergarten. We rode the Capital Transit Bus, which picked us up at the post office, to Kensington Elementary School. The bus stop in Kensington was at the corner of Strathmore and Summit. My mother couldn't drive me to school because we only had one car.

For first grade I attended school in Garrett Park, in the two-room school house. Mrs. Duey was my teacher. One of my first memories of school was when Mrs. Duey introduced the word "and" and I popped up my hand and said "that's my middle name!" She lost no time in correcting me. She told me that my middle name was

Ann, not "and". I felt really humiliated. Another thing I remember was that I forgot to do a page in a work book and I got a big, red, "E". I was only six, and it was a terrible experience, especially since my father was a teacher, and very authoritarian, and of course I was expected to do well.

One of my friends was Bessann Abrams, who was a year younger than me. I remember one time in the two-room schoolhouse when I was in second grade, Bessann got a little spot on her skirt, and I took her into the bathroom to help her clean it off. By the time we were done and ready to go back to class, she had this really big wet spot on her skirt, which was very embarrassing for her.

Ron and Barbara - 1948

Louise holding Ron, Barbara right front
with an aunt and cousin, 1950

Barbara as a Brownie — 1951

My best experience was with Mrs. Sutherland in third grade. We did pottery with her, and I made a little angel that I still have. She is very clunky, short and mainly skirt with wings. Once we were having a yard sale because we were moving and someone saw my little angel and said, "You made this in elementary school!" I remember Mrs. Sutherland taking us to visit G.W. (George Washington University), and that we did some sort of group reading there. I think maybe she was taking a class and was using us for some kind of demonstration. She also taught me to brush my teeth when I first got up in the morning. To this day I always start my day with brushing my teeth.

I remember my fifth grade teacher, Mr. Horan, as kind of a doof. As a class we set the clock an hour ahead, so he dismissed us early for lunch. I was almost kicked off the patrols for participating in that.

In sixth grade I had Mrs. Ruckle. At this point there really was a clique made up of new girls from the Estates. Mrs. Ruckle tried to make the girls like a girl that they were excluding, but it didn't work at all. I think that she was the first person who demonstrated to me that you can't manage groups of people, you can't just make them do what you want them to do.

The building of Garrett Park Estates brought a lot of changes to the town. I remember we used to walk to the woods at the end of Clyde Avenue, where Garrett Park Estates was later to be built, and we would cut our own Christmas tree. It was a huge change and a loss when that wooded area was replaced by Garrett Park Estates. In order to make room for the new students from Garrett Park Estates, the new Elementary School was built. The Estates introduced a whole new group of people into our school, and when all these new girls came into my class, I didn't at the time see anything good about it. They displaced me at the top of the pile, and now there were cliques forming, where we hadn't had them before. And just the fact that they had a Kensington mailing address made them seem different to me. In many ways it felt like an intrusion, because before we had been an extremely small class.

I went to Kensington Junior High, and then I attended Walter Johnson for high school. It was the beginning of the '60s and everything was changing. With the election of JFK when I was in high school, the country was right on the cusp of a huge change. I still have this visual image of Kennedy delivering his inaugural speech. I thought Kennedy was a miracle, and I sat transfixed listening to him. And then just three years later he was killed. I have had so many of these moments in my life where I've thought "Life is going to be better because of this elected official", and when Kennedy was assassinated it was just the most horrible thing imaginable. I was watching television at my parent's when Lee Harvey Oswald was shot on TV. It felt like life was going to all fall apart. I think that in many ways this country has never really recovered. There has never been any transparency about what really happened. They just said, "That's all been taken care of, there was the commission". It was such a terrible thing for our country.

Of course it's been disappointing, the way things have turned out. But I tell my son, "If there's peace in your heart, there's peace in the world". In the movie Pleasantville, the people who had passion were the ones who had true colors. The rest of the movie was a black and white movie. And starting with Kennedy and ending with Bernie Sanders, I thought that they were the people that could make the change that needed to happen in the world. Of course there have been others as well who came after Kennedy and before Sanders.

After I graduated from Walter Johnson, I married my high school sweetheart. I had three children before the age of thirty. When my youngest was a baby I enrolled in classes part time, eventually graduating from George Washington University with a BS in Chemistry. I dreamed of going to medical school at G.W. but had not taken the MCATs so I applied to the GW Graduate School's Department of Pharmacology PhD program as an interim step. Life intervened and I left the program with a MS with Distinction in Pharmacology.

I ended up going back to school when I was fifty-one and doing a second degree in nursing. I became a hospice nurse, and for all the troubles I had, I felt they had prepared me for this work. I felt very successful at hospice nursing. It had taken me all that time to find what I loved. I was a hospice nurse for almost 20 years and I loved it. Now I have taken two training classes in becoming an end of life doula, which is a new category. In my retirement I have been volunteering as a doula at Gilchrist Hospice in Baltimore. I may start doing Death Cafés here in Delaware. Right now there are none here. I'm very comfortable with the dying and with death, and I can help other people be comfortable.

I live part-time in Delaware and Chevy Chase, Maryland. Delaware is my official residence and I'm on the Milton Historic Preservation Commission. Most important, Delaware is where I studied yoga and learned the Ashtanga yoga primary series which I practice daily.

Chevy Chase is where our vacation home is, in the village of Friendship Heights and we are in Chevy Chase every weekend. I drive on Strathmore Ave. pretty regularly, and I am familiar with the changes in Garrett Park. It's lost its socio-economic heterogeneity, but I think the changes are in the whole area in general. The world has changed so much since I was a child, and it continues to change.

When I look back on my childhood in Garrett Park, one thing that I think was special about it was the socio-economic diversity. There were all kinds of people in the town, and yet it was a real community. Because Garrett Park was such a melting pot of different kinds of people, I was able to know and learn about people who were very different from my own parents. For instance, Mr. Abrams, Bessann's father was the first person I had ever heard of who was an atheist.

Garrett Park gave me my "Can Do" spirit. The town has done so many interesting things, the celebration of their longevity, their house tours, and the way they had themselves put on the National Register of Historic Places. Most towns just have their historic districts, but because Garrett Park had all different types of architecture in each neighborhood from different period, they had the whole town listed as historic.

When I applied to the PhD program in Pharmacology at GW's Graduate School, I wrote in my essay that they should admit me because of the town I grew up in. I wrote that "it was a place where I learned that I can do, so admit me to your program." From living in Garrett Park I have learned to be able to say "I need this and how am I going to be able to accomplish it."

I subscribe to the gratefulness word for the day, and recently the word was "wanderer". The wanderer has no path. So that's going to be my mantra, because I keep wandering off the path and then I have to get back on it. It may look like you have left the path, but you really just need to keep going forward. If you want anything it's up to you to figure out what you need to do to get it. I ended up being one of the founders of the Kensington Historical Society because I believed Kensington should be on the National Register of Historic Places. When the Town of Kensington wouldn't support an application to the National Register of Historic Places, the newly-incorporated Kensington Historical Society developed and submitted the application to the National Register. I have done lots of things because I saw a personal need and I went out and worked towards achieving something that would help me to meet that personal need. I think growing up in Garrett Park has made a significant impact on how I see the world. For me it really taught me that anything is possible.

Jim and Barbara Wagner

6

JOYCE REYNOLDS KURTH

When my own children were born, I knew that I could never recreate for them the magical childhood that I had experienced. I could never create the deep, deep sense of a community that shared the tears and laughter, the fears and the hope, the happy hour on my parents' porch, the sound of the freight trains rumbling through in the middle of the night. It, of course, saddens me greatly that I could not give this gift to my own children. And I don't even try to explain what Garrett Park was to my Wisconsin people. Explain the unexplainable? We were there; we were blessed.

In June of 1940, my parents, Dorothy and Walter Reynolds, moved to the little village of Garrett Park. At the time, my mother was pregnant with my older brother, Walter Bingham Reynolds Jr., known by everybody as Bing. The house they had built was at 11109 Kenilworth Avenue, and Bing was born soon after they moved into it. I was born on October 26, 1944, and my younger brother, Chuck, was born in 1947. My parents lived in that house for fifty years, until my mother died in 1990. When we loaded my dad up and said goodbye to Garrett Park after her death, it was probably one of the saddest days of my life. Bing was living in Colorado, and I was living in Wisconsin, as was Chuck. We moved Dad out to Wisconsin, and he died three years later, in 1993.

My dad was a lifelong resident of the D.C. area, born on Capitol Hill in 1908. My mother was born in Iowa, lived for quite a while in Kansas, and then lived on the west coast of Florida. In the 1920s, when the hurricanes came ripping through Florida and the depression hit, she took herself to New York City, where she worked in Bloomingdales' basement at the bottom of the escalator, demonstrating a kitchen tool used for grating called "The Wonder Shredder". I still have some of those Wonder Shredders.

After New York, My mother moved to Washington. Her sister and the rest of her family were already living there, and her father worked there as a civil servant. He was a guard at the National Gallery, and at one point he was part of the detail for Franklin Roosevelt. One summer they went up to Hyde Park, N. Y., where FDR had his family home. My grandmother liked to tell of how she would be hanging the laundry out early in the morning, and Mrs. Roosevelt would ride by on her bike and wave to her.

My parents were introduced on a blind date arranged by the people who would become my aunt and uncle, their brother and sister respectively. Right after they married, my parents lived in Tacoma Park, eventually buying the lot in Garrett Park where they were to build our house. In Garrett Park the land was a little cheaper, because it was farther out into the countryside.

At first Dad and his brother worked for the B.S. Reynolds Co. in downtown Washington, near Chinatown, which was the family business. It was a souvenir business, which meant they sold any kind of junk that people would buy. For a while souvenirs were a big deal, but after the 1940s, after the war, the bottom just kind of fell out of the whole thing. My dad, as the younger brother, was the one who was let go, and so he eventually got a job working for the Montgomery County Liquor Dispensary. During the time when he worked in D.C. he would ride the train into work every day and come home on the 5:15. When I was a kid, you had to head for home at 5:15 when you heard the whistle blow because we always sat down to eat at 6:00. As for my mother, she took over the school cafeteria once the addition to Garrett Park Elementary was built. My mother was largely self-educated, and she did a damn good job of self-educating too. Because she had grown up during the depression, I don't think college was something that she could have done, but she should have.

Such a different time; such a different place. Family lore has it that my D.C. grandfather wanted to know what in the world they were going to do way out there—raise chickens? Yes they did, for a while anyway. I still remember the smell of scalded chicken feathers. It's a smell you never forget. And at some point they had a duck of some sort who liked to clean his bill on the wet laundry hanging on the line, but that didn't last long

Walt and Dorothy with Joyce

either. My parents gave up their "farming" attempts much sooner than the Lambs, who at first lived down the hill from us before later moving across Strathmore Avenue. And then there was Lucy—the goose who terrorized the small children down on Rokeby Avenue. We could hear her honks from our house. Poor perpetually angry bird!

And dogs… So many dogs. Most of them un-neutered and all of them free to roam when they were not on duty protecting their strip of road in front of their houses. On my stretch of Kenilworth, Spike would start in front of Donnelly's house; Brownie would pick it up at Giesers'; Paddy had the stretch in front of my home and Fritz took the last leg in front of Mahaneys'. All of this within a one block obstacle course.

Our house was on Kenilworth between Argyle and Albemarle. The Giesers lived near us on the other side of Kenilworth. They had three boys, and there was always something going on there, some kind of game going on in the vacant lot on one side of the house. They had an old barn, which was kind of a neat place too, and it had a basketball hoop next to it.

When I was very small I think I was just surrounded by boys. Ilah Gieser was very kind to me, perhaps because I was the only girl in the midst of so many boys, and years later, after my mother died, she wrote to me on a regular basis. There were the Gieser boys, and my brother Bing, so I'm not sure I knew what my gender role was supposed to be or exactly where I fit in. This influenced me a lot, because there were things they could do that little girls weren't supposed to do. But they didn't exclude me, and Bing would ride me on the crossbar of his bike and take me places. But Bing grew up very quickly and started moving with a faster crowd, and then he kind of ditched his little sister.

There was a family right across the street whose last name was Love, and they had moved into that house when I was two years old. (Later the Melvilles lived there.) My mother always talked about how I just walked across the street and introduced myself to these people. I played a lot with their son, Bobby. He was kind of a daring, foolish little boy. One time he wanted to ride his wagon down Donnelly's Hill on Argyle, and I knew that it was crazy, it wasn't something you were supposed to do, but that's what he tried to do. A particular rite of passage was getting up the courage to ride our bikes down that hill, let alone go down in a wagon! Right where Montrose joined Argyle, there was a big hump, and when he hit the hump he went flying off and got all scraped up. The Modines were living nearby, as this was before they built their house on the other side of Strathmore, and Barbara Modine picked him up and cleaned him off.

I remember playing with Sally Lou Zanelli. She lived in that little gray house on the other side of Kenilworth from our house, which was a Sears and Roebuck house, as was the Guernsey's

Joyce's birthday party, clockwise L to R:: John Collins, Joyce Reynolds, Susie (a cousin), Ann Thurston, Steve Sonner, Pam Payne, Jeannie (a cousin), John Lamb

house. They owned the big lot on the other side of the house also, and we loved to play there, as it was nice and

The Zanelli house

level and perfect for playing games. Ann Ross, who lived in the house right next door to us when I was a teenager, got me in touch with a young woman who is the daughter of Sally Lou Zanelli, and she told me that Sally Lou lives there still.

We were forbidden to play on the railroad tracks, but we did anyway. We liked to play on the part of the tracks where the cut went through, with those steep banks. Chuck was just a few years behind me in age and he liked to follow me, to try to play with both me and my friends, driving me crazy because he followed me everywhere, and a lot of the time I tried to ditch him, but I wasn't always success-

ful. One time when maybe he was six and I was nine, we were playing over there, and he got into a place he couldn't get out of – it was on that steep embankment, and he couldn't go up and he couldn't go down. He was begging and pleading with me to go get daddy with a ladder. And I wasn't telling Daddy we were playing on the tracks! I knew there was no way I could have told my dad, and Chuck did get out on his own eventually.

It was probably the best childhood anybody could have had. We played outside all of the time, and I came home so many times with bloody knees. My parents would just shake their heads. A good friend of mine was Winnie Keene, who lived down Kenilworth on the other side of the street, over by Albemarle. I remember that Winnie and I were afraid to walk home alone in the dark, so we would walk together to the street light there at Albemarle, and then run like hell towards our respective homes. She and I loved to head out into the woods together, and there was plenty of woods to play in.

I also played a lot with Susan Kizer. Susan and I loved to play in the field behind the Giesers' house, which is now Garrett Park Estates. One of my finest memories is of playing horses there with Susan, running and having so much fun. There were these depressions in the ground, and I remember hunkering down in them to shelter from the cold March winds, and just listening to the wind, and it was so wonderful. We grew up outside, and usually there was always a dog with us, and we did that kind of stuff all the way through grade school. We talked a lot, and told each other stories. We loved the woods at the very end of Rokeby, down near Well's house. I remember that there was a spring down there with a cup. We thought that was so cool, that you could drink that water right out of the ground. My parents knew Mr. and Mrs. Wells very well, because they were so much into gardening, and my mother was really into plants.

I remember that it would take forever just to get home from school, especially in the fall when you spent all that time kicking the leaves. We spent a lot of time raking the leaves in the fall, jumping in them, and burning them - that was so much fun. Maybe we would even have some marshmallows in the house and we could toast them.

My birthday was right before Halloween, and Mike Henley's birthday was a few days after mine, and we had a shared birthday one year at my home, a Halloween birthday party. My parents took us blindfolded into the basement and had us feel peeled grapes that were supposed to be a dead person's eyeballs, and spaghetti that was their brains. Everybody was either horrified or they thought it was hilarious. It really scared my friend Chris Woodwell, who hasn't forgiven my parents for that yet!

Winnie Keene and I just loved Halloween. One Halloween my brother Bing, who was big for his age, took Steve Gieser in our old wooden wheelbarrow, and Steve was dressed up as a baby and Bing was dressed up as an adult. I think they might have even won a prize for that. The Chisholms had the scariest house on Halloween. Haile Chisholm would dress up as some kind of monster, and he would lurk outside the house. You knew he was going to get you, that he was going to scare the daylights out of you, but you didn't know how or when. But it was worth getting through the test, because they would serve cider and doughnuts once you got into the house. As far as costumes went, we were usually tramps or something like that, and we would stay out late. And then of course the boys would break into the chapel and ring the bell – we had to stay up to hear that. No-

Dorothy in front of Reynolds house

body ever worried about you back then. Talk about Free Range Kids – we were the real thing.

It was so fun when it snowed, and Donnelly's Hill was right there near our house. We only had one sled, so we argued a lot about using it. We had to take turns – we didn't have a lot of stuff. But we frequently could double up with our friends, so it worked out. The challenge was always to see if you could get across Rokeby and over to Wells Park. My brother and his friends would open the fire hydrant, but it usually ruined the hill for sledding, because too much water would come out and wash all the snow away.

The town was so beautiful in the spring, and our yard was pretty special. My mother had the most stunning azaleas, and the whole yard was just full of them. She got them when they first moved out there and they grew to be just enormous. My father did a lot of yard work, with my mother directing him. I remember him saying, as he got older, "I want my ashes in this yard where all my sweat is."

We took our shoes off in the spring and we would never put them back on again until fall. But in the spring this fear of "polio weather" came up. It was before the Salk vaccine and nobody really knew what it was that caused polio. People thought it might have to do with not wearing a jacket or getting too cold or something like that. I knew at least two kids in my class who had polio, and maybe it happened in the spring. There was even a girl in my class who spent time in an iron lung. It was very scary.

Easter 1948 - Chuck, Joyce, and Dorothy Reynolds

There was the May Day celebration at Garrett Park Elementary, with a May Queen and a flower girl, and one year I was a flower girl. I think Sandra Ward was the May Queen that year. We even had a Maypole Dance, which eventually went by the wayside, but we did have some kind of May celebration in the years to come.

I remember how hot it could be in the summer, but we loved summer, and we loved that we didn't have to go to school. Before the pool was built, we just sweated a lot in the summer. After the pool was built, I especially remember the evening swim.

Garrett Park is famous to this day because people pick up their mail at the P.O. The post office and general store, which we called "Louie's", was a hub of activity, and it was the place to go. They had a pot-bellied stove there when I was real little, and people just hung out there and talked. I knew Mrs. Penn, the post mistress, and later Olive Parsons. She was always so happy to see me.

I was a Girl Scout. Annavieve Abrams, whose roots were in New York City, took her little group of Girl Scouts just about anywhere and everywhere. We walked down to visit Freddy the Hobo who lived along the train tracks. We went on marvelous but usually rainy, overnights, cooking our suppers on top of buddy burners (cooktops fashioned out of #10 cans with paraffin-filled tuna cans for heat) and sleeping on shower curtains converted to ground covers and sleeping bags repurposed from our dads' army days. Cold and wet, I loved every minute of it. Once when we were returning from a weekend away to a camp on the Chesapeake, traffic was pulled over on Rock Creek Parkway for no reason that we knew of. After what seemed like a forever wait, along came a motorcade with Queen Elizabeth II and Prince Phillip!!!! And under Mrs. Abrams guidance and sense of adventure, some of us continued in Scouts through our junior high years into the first year of high school. We were Mariner Scouts then and after paddling lessons in Georgetown, we canoed along the C & O canal up to Seneca Falls and an overnight. We canoed the upper Potomac on a wonderful three day trip. And we even spent time learning to sail on the Chesapeake.

When we were in kindergarten, we took the Capital Transit Bus to Kensington, and that was always quite an adventure. We would all bring our coins wrapped in a cloth handkerchief, and this poor bus driver had to untie all these handkerchiefs. After kindergarten, we attended Garrett Park Elementary. The grades were combined when I first started there – there was a combined first and second, and a combined third and fourth, as well as fifth and sixth grade class taught by Mrs. Reed, who was the bane of my older brother's existence.   I had Mrs. Duey for first and second grade, and then for third grade I had Mrs. Sutherland. I loved Mrs. Sutherland especially. She had spent time in Latin America, I think it was Guatemala, and she was just fascinating to us. She was a very good teacher, who imposed a lot of discipline, and she did crafts with us – pottery and weaving, which was something I think she had brought back from Guatemala. She certainly showed us a bigger world. That year, the year we had a split between third and fourth grade I always was assigned to sit next to the naughty boys, to keep them in line, and it never worked.

In fourth grade we had a new teacher, Olivia Sims. Her one method of discipline was to have us write seventy-five times (I am almost seventy-five years old and I can still recite this), "I will be quiet, polite, business-like and self-controlled in the classroom". She was just awful, a tyrant. There were some very obstinate kids in the class, but anyone would have rebelled against that. She took a normal class where you had your hell raisers and you had your good kids, and she turned us all into hell raisers. I want to say we fired her, because we made her life so miserable that she left mid-year. It was quite an experience. Then someone had to step in and tame us. Our first teacher after that was a substitute, Elsa Keene, who was my best friend Winnie Keene's mom. She was smart enough to read to us, and it really took the sting out of the whole experience. We were enthralled with the stories she would read us and we would just sit and listen, which was wonderful. I think she was replaced by Mrs. Ruckle. I believe that the lesson we learned as fourth graders was the Margaret Meade lesson – "Never doubt the power of a group of committed individuals to change things." We needed to get rid of that teacher and we succeeded. So for good or for bad, and I want to say for good, we realized then that if you work at something hard enough and long enough you can get where you want to be.

After sixth grade I went to Kensington Junior High, and I just hated it. There was Mr. Cross, with his corporal punishment, with his wall full of paddles, and how proud he was of that, and how he got away with that, and I look back at that and I wonder, "How did they ever let that happen?" I remember some of the teachers at KJH. I had Mrs. Nachman for math, and to this day Chris Woodwell and I like to talk about how she would rock in her shoes. For some reason I thought I had to take Latin, and the Latin teacher, who was named Mrs. Davis was a real witch. There was a wonderful English teacher, also named Mrs. Davis. Her class was the one class that I really liked and remember.

KJH was a huge change from what I had known before. For the first time we were in school with African American kids. We lived in an all-white area, and the only black people we had known were the "colored girls" who came in by bus and cleaned out houses. Later, when I attended Walter Johnson for high school, I don't remember a single black face there. I suppose that any of the kids from Ken-Gar who went on to high school perhaps went on to Wheaton, if they went at all. Looking back on how it was, I think about how destructive de-facto segregation was, that if you were poor and black, you could just disappear and stop going to school and as far as the people in charge were concerned the problem was solved. No one was going to Ken-Gar to make sure you were attending school, and those kids lost out on their one ticket out of poverty - education.

Walter Johnson was certainly a lot better than junior high, but it still wasn't that great. I was very shy and I kind of got lost in the shuffle, though I did have some good learning experiences. In tenth grade I had Miss Robinson for a history class. She required a research paper of some sort, and my topic was something to do with the Civil Rights movement. I actually drove by myself down to the Library of Congress to do research, which was quite an experience for me. But overall, I don't think my intelligence was appreciated by any of my teachers, except for my senior English teacher, Miss Kauffman. She realized that I could write and that I read a lot, and she brought that out in me. She was so good for me.

After graduating from high school in 1962, I attended Wilmington College in southwestern Ohio. It was quite a culture shock going to this little tiny Quaker college after Walter Johnson. All of a sudden I was at the top of the heap, where I had already done a research paper at the Library of Congress. I found Wilmington College for myself, choosing it because it had a good work study program. I majored in English Literature and later became a high school teacher. Back then girls had three choices – you could be a secretary, a nurse, or a teacher. But marriage and children was the ultimate goal.

I followed my eventual husband to Wisconsin and a teaching job in the Milwaukee Public schools. My first year of teaching was sheer hell and culture shock. That summer I made a decision to learn how to do this well, and I came back and was a much better teacher. For two years I was in a classroom with a cap of only fifteen kids on the class size. Because of the Space Race, the government was investing in at-risk kids, putting more money into education than they do now, and it was wonderful. We read a lot, and it was like a family, and it kept me in teaching.

Jim was younger than I, and the draft was breathing down his neck, and so we decided to go into the Peace Corps. Everything back then was determined by the Vietnam War. You didn't make choices, and instead circumstances made choices for you. First we were selected for a program in Malaysia, and then we got a letter that they wanted us to be in a program in Korea "because we were so brilliant and gifted in languages," they wanted us to teach at the university level in Korea. But what we were too naïve to understand at the time was that with the Peace Corps, being in Korea and teaching at the college level was in direct exchange for Korean troops serving in Vietnam. It was part of the package. We went to Hawaii for a very intensive training though, and it was the most wonderful three months of my life. Then they instituted the lottery, and Jim got a really low number, so we decided we didn't really want to go to Korea, and we went to Europe for two months instead. After we came back Jim started law school, I got pregnant, and we had four kids. I taught for twenty years in the state of Wisconsin system, mostly high school and some junior high. Those last years of teaching were an especially wonderful experience.

My parents have been gone twenty some years now. I remember from the time when my parents were still alive, when I was visiting them in Garrett Park, I would go for walks in the evening, and it was just quiet. Nobody was outside playing. Air conditioning has really changed things. I was last in Garrett Park four years ago, the year I turned seventy. I went with Chris Woodwell, we went to a big birthday party for Mike Henley, and we saw people I knew from the town. But the town I remember isn't there anymore, it's gone.

I remember when I was in high school and people were so envious of the Garrett Park kids. Everyone wanted to live in Garrett Park, because it was even then considered to be a very special and unusual town. If you were a child in Garrett Park, the adults always looked after you, and you were raised by a community. You knew that if the woman across the street didn't approve of it, your mother wouldn't approve of it. Because people were home a lot, you knew you were safe, and that if you needed help, some adult would help you out. Looking back, I am really grateful for the freedom and the safety of growing up in Garrett Park, the sense of being held by a real community, of being surrounded by good people. From that influence, I like to think that I try to be a good person.

Joyce, Chuck, and Bing Reynolds

Even though Garrett Park was a small town, because there was such a diversity of interesting people living in the community, I had that knowledge growing up that there was a greater world out there. I was fascinated by the people who surrounded me, how they had traveled all over the world. There were people who were involved at the State Department, and who were always going off to exotic places. The Turners lived for a time in Iran, and the Howes went to Vietnam. I remember babysitting for the Howe's kids after they got back, and they were calling water "l'eau" because they had been living in Vietnam and were bi-lingual. When I was in high school there was the civil rights movement going on, and though I wasn't to become directly involved with those issues until college, I certainly knew where my family stood. I knew and admired people like Silvia Lichtenstein, who would participate in sit-ins in DC. Then there were other families who weren't so liberal, some who were prejudiced, and I was aware of that too. It was such an interesting mix of haves and have-nots. There were people who had attended Ivy League colleges, and people like my dad who worked for the county, selling liquor, and all were part of the same community.

I think somewhere I have an old telephone directory that has a picture of the men and women who worked to convert the community center from old army barracks into the central gathering place for the town. There were the women, dressed in seldom-worn slacks, with their hair tied in bandanas, sawing and hammering and sweating to provide this little community with a place to gather and connect and eat and laugh and sing.

The women, the strong, intelligent, determined women - what powerful role models for all of us! They pulled together during the war years. Victory Gardens were numerous in the field that was to become Garrett Park Estates. They looked out for the less-fortunate with clothing drives and donations. Some of them worked outside of the home and others were involved in politics and important social action movements. Their homes were always open and their dining table was always big enough for one more.

L to R - Mary Borror, Leone Lamb, Janet Howard,
Ilah Gieser Elsa Guernsey, Dorothy Reynolds

I have remained in touch with many of these people who have made me what I am today – the good and kind and generous people who knew what I knew. On sleepless nights, in my imagination, I walk the winding streets of Garrett Park.

When my own children were born, I knew that I could never recreate for them the magical childhood that I had experienced. I could never create the deep, deep sense of a community that shared the tears and laughter, the fears and the hope, the happy hour on my parents' porch, the sound of the freight trains rumbling through in the middle of the night. It, of course, saddens me greatly that I could not give this gift to my own children. And I don't even try to explain what Garrett Park was to my Wisconsin people. Explain the unexplainable? We were there; we were blessed.

(This narrative was taken from a transcribed phone interview, with parts written by Joyce Kurth)

Joyce with her grandson, Anders

7

MIKE HENLEY

Having a group of friends who have all seen each other at our best and our worst, we have no secrets. We don't have to portray ourselves in any way, because all of our secrets are out on the table. You're different with people you've known all your life, people who have seen you at your worst and love you anyway, versus people you are just meeting.

My parents, Alfred and Lillian Henley were both from New York, and I was born in Brooklyn in 1944. I have an older brother, David, and a sister, Elizabeth, who is six years younger. My family moved to the Washington D.C. area in 1946, when I was two. I think there were several reasons for the move. My father was a labor organizer who would get himself hired by engineering firms with the unexpressed purpose of organizing a labor union. Then he would get fired as soon as he was discovered. Sometimes he was successful creating the union and at other times not, but after a number of years he was well known enough that he couldn't get a job in New York. That was one of the factors behind our move. The other factor was that he had cerebral palsy, which affected his gait. A place in D.C. called the Kabot-Kaiser Institute had a reputation for being a top place to rehab people with various neurological disorders, so we went down there and stayed there for a couple of years while he was getting rehabilitation services. It was a residential place, and at some point I'm told he felt like it was more important for him to get on with his work than to continue to spend most of his time and energy at the institute. We moved to a few different places over the years. We lived in Takoma Park, and then we moved for a sustained period of time to Kensington, where we stayed until my mom was pregnant with my younger sister, Elizabeth. At that point the house wasn't going to be big enough for all of us, and as they scouted around they found Garrett Park.

We moved to our house on Kenilworth in 1952, when I was in the middle of third grade. Changing schools was hard. In my Kensington school we had been still printing, but when I moved to Garrett Park Elementary they were writing in cursive. It was bad enough being left-handed in a right-handed world, and my handwriting still reflects that trauma. When I first moved here I was terrified, having lost all my friends at sort of a crucial age. I was so heartbroken by it that for my first birthday in Garrett Park, my parents had all my Kensington friends come to the party in Wells Park. But then I began to make friends.

John Lamb was the first Garrett Parker I met. I think the reason for that was that my older brother and his older brother knew each other from high school, and they were already good friends before we moved to Garrett Park. John's brother made sure that John came down and introduced himself, since John was in the same grade as me. Another friend was Tom Guernsey, who lived just a couple of doors away on the other side of Kenilworth. We were the same age, in the same class, and we both had fathers who were disabled. John Hall, who was a grade below me in school, was another early friend.

We had lots of space to play. The Guernsey's barn was a hangout for us when we were little, though over time it fell into disrepair and was eventually torn down. The closest house across the street was the Chisholm's, and right next to it was an empty field we could play in, and we also played in the woods over near Holy Cross, across the highway. Another playground we had, which was unending, was the Estates that were being built. When we first moved to Garrett Park, the Estates themselves were just a couple of streets of recently built houses, and the whole rest of the development was in various stages, starting with pits that were just excavated. There were houses that were up but not yet with doors and these were our clubhouses. It was a great playground for kids.

We were cowboys and Indians in the trenches, and the frontier moved along block by block as the years progressed. In 6th grade, after the movie "Helen of Troy" came out, we divided up into Trojans and Greeks, and we built forts and had maneuvers and battles and stuff.

When it snowed, Donnelly's Hill was just steps away from our house. We thought it was pretty cool that they would block off the street and let us build a bonfire at the top of the street. At some point we were either allowed, or we allowed ourselves, to open the fire hydrant so the water would run down Donnelly's Hill, and turn to ice. Your sled could really get going on that. The goal was that if you could get down to the creek at Wells Park you would have had a good ride. And as a seventy-three year old geezer now, the thought that we could sled to the bottom of the hill and then walk up that hill over and over and over again just amazes me.

Summers were great. They lasted forever, and we got to play and play and play. When you're nine years old, two or three months of no school during the summer was a good percentage of your lifetime. We took advantage of it and just played. There was no such thing as worrying about kids being out on their own. Summer nights we played white flag, a kind of footballish game in Tam Wilson's yard. (Tam was another member of our gang of friends).

There were girls I spent time with too - Bessann Abrams, Karen Hartmann, Susan Kizer, and Debbie Chisholm, who lived across the street. I had a horrendous crush on Karen Hartmann starting in third grade. Karen lived on the end of Keswick Street in this big house that used to be a farmhouse. Originally that house had all the land that eventually became Richterville.

An interesting anecdote about that house was told to me by my high school friend, Joe Triplett. At one point Walter Johnson stayed there. Joe's father was hired to transport Walter Johnson from that house to some other place, which is how Joe knew about the house and its legendary status.

I had a little crush on Debbie Chisholm too. Recently, when Fats Domino died, his death brought up this memory: When I was about fourteen, I bought Debbie Chisholm a Fats Domino record for Christmas. I had started playing piano by then, and before giving the album to her I had opened it and played along with the song, and I had written on the album what key every song was in. It was kind of cheesy of me, but she forgave me.

Debbie's father, Haile Chisholm was a wonderful neighbor. Though he was also a very politically con-servative guy, an American Legion guy, somehow his sense of community overrode his hatred of commies. He was a fountain of stories. You had to be careful if Haile was outside and you were in a hurry - you had to duck him, because he always had a story and you might not always have time for a story. One of his stories was about how he had a farm in Poolesville, and he used a horse and carriage to get there. He said the horse knew the way, so he could just get in the carriage in Poolesville and nod off, and he would wake up in Garrett Park.

That's how much things have changed. When I was a kid, a trip to Silver Spring or Bethesda was a trip through the countryside. The roads were one lane and there was parking on the side. Now Rockville Pike is filled with high rises. When my mom had dementia and I took her there to the doctor, she saw all those tall buildings and said, "Is this New York?" Today I'm struck as I drive down the streets of Garrett Park Estates. As kids we ridiculed these houses with these little twigs growing in the front yards, and now these twigs have grown into giant venerable trees.

Here is the true story behind the founding of the town newspaper, *The Garrett Bugle*. When I was ten or eleven, Tom Guernsey had a little one page paper called *The Garrett Park Gazette*. His parents had gotten him something called a Hectograph, which he used for a printing press. It was some kind of gelatinous pad, and you would write with a special ink and press it on the pad, and then you could put subsequent pieces of paper on it and press them down to make copies. I think it sold his paper for a penny. Before the fire that destroyed my house in 2008, I actually had a copy or two of *The Gazette*. Tom recruited me and John Hall to go around the neighborhood to hawk the paper. Characteristically, Hall shirked off on his duty, didn't sell any papers, and so Tom fired him, and in revenge, Hall wanted to start his own newspaper. Since his dad was a writer with the National Science Foundation, John utilized his father's abilities, and I think John put out the first Bugle. John, again characteristically, lost interest after the first *Bugle*, but his dad, Clyde, thought it was a pretty nifty idea to have a town newspaper like that. So Clyde just took it over, and for many years after that he was the editor of *The Garrett Bugle*. It contained all the news around town. With the Gazette it had been "Jeff Miller fell off his bike and skinned his knee. He's ok." It was kids' news, and I think probably the first Bugle, the one John did, was the same. But when Clyde took over it really became a town newsletter. This is the real story behind "The Garrett Bugle", though John says it's bullshit.

Garrett Park was a sort of a haven for Jewish commies from around the area. I believe that because of this Jewish commie network, the first families who found the place told others about how nice and accommodating a community it was, and a number of them ended up congregating there. However, I did take some shit while living there for being a Jew. For the most part, I would say it wasn't so much outright hostility as it was teasing, at least when it came from friends and older siblings of friends. We all teased each other about everything. But it wasn't always just teasing. For instance, my friend, Tom Guernsey had a paper route, and one of the customers, a neighbor, wasn't paying his bill for the newspaper, which Tom was required to collect. Tom asked me to go and ask for the payment and give him the bill, and later Tom reported that the man had said to him, "I don't like the way you sent your Jewish lawyer to collect for you." And this was when we were little kids.

Having grown up in the McCarthy period with commie parents I was terrified growing up. Once when James Lamb had applied for a position (in Navy intelligence as I recall) I was alone at home and there was a knock on the door. When I opened it there was this big intimidating guy in uniform standing there, and I thought they were coming to get me. James Lamb (inscrutably, considering the political circumstances of the time) had listed our family as a character reference for his job application with the Navy. The scary guy in uniform was there to speak to my parents about James. This happened when I was about ten or eleven. Another time, my mom was approached by the F.B.I. at the Garrett Park Post Office. They made it plain that they knew who their kids were. Those were rough times.

I'm a musician, and I play old rock and roll with a band. The first time I ever performed in front of people was for my sixth grade graduation. They had just built the new auditorium, and it was on a stage, and I played a duet with the aforementioned Karen Hartmann. She played the piano, and I played the accordion. We played Kay Starr's "Rock and Roll Waltz".

Later, when I was in high school we would have little sock hops in the gym. The buses would arrive way earlier than homeroom, and wisely, the administrators allowed some of the musicians to put on hops between 7:30 and 9:00. It was a good idea, and it kept us out of trouble. A bunch of us played together at those before-school events. Because Tom Guernsey was also into music, we started played music together. I played the piano, and Tom was a guitarist. We formed a little band, "The Reekers", and hooked up with a very good singer, Joe Triplett. When the Garrett Park gang had first hit high school we were just sort of the odd balls, the clannish ones, and only as the years passed did we become "cool".

During the early music experience with Tom and Joe, we made a record. Tom wrote the song and we went to a recording studio to record it. At that time this was very rare, and it cost a relative fortune, unlike today where every musician has his own basement studio. It was a big deal, it was very exciting, and it kept being exciting because we got the thing sold onto a label and it went on the air. We were playing in a club in Rehoboth, and we knew at a certain time this song was going to be played on WWDC. We couldn't quite get the station so we all went on the roof of the club, and there we heard our song, D*on't Call Me Flyface* on

The Henley family - David, Elizabeth, Mike, Lillian, and Alfred

the radio. It was the thrill of a lifetime. Later we went into the studio and recorded *What a Girl Can't Do* and it was a hit. Again, this was back in the days before people could make their own records.

It was a gigantic influence on my life. This came out during my junior or senior year in college, and Triplett and I had to decide whether we were going to finish out our year in college or take to the road with the record. We both did the conservative thing and finished college, and I can't speak for Joe, but I just ate my heart out all through graduate school. Meanwhile we had given the record to Tom's other group called The Hangmen, and they were making tours, and putting on concerts, signing on to a record contract, and getting mobbed by girls, and I was just eating my heart out.

I was primed for a life in academia. I was in graduate school for a year, studying Political Science at Tufts University on a full scholarship. After that one year I said "Fuck it, I can get a doctorate any time I want, but I can only be a musician when I'm young." So I dropped out of graduate school. I wanted to be a rock and roll star. My parents must have been very disappointed, but they accepted it.

The story has a happy ending. But first I spent a year suffering mightily. Tom and I would try to put a band together and somebody would get drafted, and we would have to start over. It was just like Sisyphus, and I didn't have a penny to my name. I was dependent on my parents and got involved with drugs, and I was depressed because of the events and the weird decisions I had made.

Then one day I was hitchhiking home from a dentist's appointment, and a VW bus passed me by with three hippies in it, and someone in the car said "That looks like an interesting guy" so they

John Guernsey, Mike Henley, Frank Sprague

doubled back and picked me up. I saw that they had a speaker in the back of the car, and I said "I bet you guys are going to Howard's Speaker Repair" and they said, "Yeah! How did you know?"

My music equipment was set up in Benny Gieser's living room, where there was a continual party going on because his parents were out of town. They drove me there to pick up my equipment and we went back to their house on Military Road and jammed all day long. So we formed a band, and as they were hurting for a good singer, I told them that I knew Triplett. They recruited him to be the lead singer, and that band catapulted to the top of Washington's charts. This was around 1968. The band was called Claude Jones. We had a glorious history, and for three years we were at the top of the heap. We put out a lot of good music.

Claude Jones and friends

John Guernsey arranged for the band to play at a Halloween party for the inmates at the Maryland State Mental Institution in Sykesville. What with the patients having free reign for their fantasies with their Halloween costumes, and everybody in the band smoking pot, it was a pretty profound experience. Profound for us and I'm sure for the patients as well.

I've lived in Garrett Park pretty much my whole adult life. After spending four years away at college and

the one year at graduate school, and of course the obligatory time with the band commune in Warrington, Va., I came back to Garrett Park and lived in the house I grew up in. That house burned down in 2008, and I had to rebuild it, but my address is the same. Geographically I'm the last man standing here (living in Garrett Park) of my gang. Though we are geographically scattered now, when we get together it's just like old times. John Lamb hosts reunions for us on his farm in Iowa.

My childhood experiences have affected my adult life in ways both positive and negative. I've noted that people who've moved around a lot and learned how to integrate in different communities with different kinds of people have developed social skills that I could envy, but only dream of. I believe that this is because I grew up with the same group of people, and they are still my friends. While my friend universe has expanded enormously with the musician part of my life, if I walk into a party where I know only one person, I don't know what to do with myself. I see that other people, who have grown up differently, have a set of skills that allow them to be more comfortable and interactive. I guess the flipside of that coin is having a group of friends who have all seen each other at our best and our worst, we have no secrets. We don't have to portray ourselves in any way, because all of our secrets are out on the table. You're different with people you've known all your life, people who have seen you at your worst and love you anyway, versus people you are just meeting.

I've been a musician my whole life. It's not the only thing I do, but it's something I've done consistently. In addition to playing in a band, the other half of my life is that I have a small "interior landscaping" business. I take care of plants in offices and restaurants and residences. That was my other hobby, so I've been blessed my whole working life doing what I enjoy.

8

TOM PINKSON

To this day I value the gifts of community. I have worked to build community where I have lived, and for this I owe a "thank you" to the people and spirit of Garrett Park, the place where I grew up during the formative years of eight to seventeen. If it existed on the west coast with its better weather I would live there again today.

My family moved first to Garrett Park Estates from California in 1953, and then a few years later to the Park, living at a house we built at 10709 Keswick St. I lived there with my parents, Ray and Ruth Pinkson, and my two younger sisters, Ilsa and Briane.

When we moved to the area Steve Sonner was the first kid I met. It was a few days before school started and my mother brought me to the school to register for the year. Steve was playing out in front of his house and I joined him. Garrett Park School had just expanded beyond the one-room, red brick school house, so I was among the first group of kids to go to the new school.

My first day of school as a new kid in second grade, I got into a fight with Benny Gieser right in front of the principal's office. Benny started it. The principal brought us into a back room and fed us some line of crap, which Benny and I rolled our eyes at and then we became friends. Benny, Steve and a whole gang of us grew up together - Tom and John Guernsey, John Hall, Timmy Honey, John Lamb, Tam Wilson, Mike Ofenstein, Dave Simpson, Mike Henley, a few years later Eric Harris, and a few years after that, Jim Frid.

Before the Estates were expanded, and all the shopping malls were built, we used to go out exploring and playing in the woods and open spaces that abounded at the time. Way out there was an old rickety broken-down house that we believed was haunted. A test of bravery was running up to the door, touching it and then running back to the woods where the rest of the guys were waiting. We'd spy on it from the woods, and one day we freaked out when we saw what looked to be a ghost in a window.

One memory that comes back strong is how we used to frequently cut through a yard that separated Garrett Park from the Estates. Once the owner got pissed at Jim Frid and me, and began to chase us through the neighborhood. He chased us for a long time, and eventually he called the cops to cruise the neighborhood looking for us, but we managed to evade them all and make it back to Jim's house without getting caught.

Another adventurous time was when Mike Henley and I, with a few other guys, almost got run over by the train. We got stuck in a narrow place not too far from the post office, and had to jump up on a steep hill and hold on to bushes to keep from falling back on the track as the train zoomed by.

Tom Guernsey organized us into playing a war game based on the Iliad, and we each got to choose which character we wanted to be. We got our stick swords and garbage can lids and did battle in the Guernsey back yard. We had many adventures at that house. Later, Tom turned me on to Elvis as we waited for the bus on the first day of seventh grade in front of his house. After that, I remember coming home to listen to his record of "Hound Dog" and "Don't Be Cruel".

During the winter after a snow storm, the older guys would turn on the fire hydrant on top of Donnelly's Hill to ice it up and we would sled down the iced street in trains, crashing into each other and having a great time. We played sports non-stop: hide and seek in the Guernsey back yard, basketball at Benny's, little league and tackle football up at the schoolyard, and basketball next to the tennis courts by the post office. Later we played football games against guys from Kensington and Ken-Gar, kids we knew from junior high, and the neighborhood rivalries were intense. It was always a thrill when we tried out for little league, and Mr. Williams would tell us who made it, and then we were to run across the field to the parking lot to get our new uniforms.

What I didn't like about the area had nothing to do with Garrett Park but instead with the humid weather, the gnats and the lack of consistent sunshine in the summer. But good times at the Garrett Park pool made the humid summers somewhat bearable.

Us kids at Garrett Park Elementary School grew up during the height of the cold war, and we frequently had atomic bomb drills where we had to get down under our desks and close our eyes. Talk about a bad joke!

In fourth grade we had a really grouchy teacher. We eventually caused her to quit because of the spitball wars we would have in class with pee-shooters. I remember that Mrs. Mueller was a favorite teacher and Mrs. Deaderling was good too.

One very stressful event took place in sixth grade. For some reason I was selected from the music program at the school to play a solo on my clarinet. This was at a big school assembly, and I was a nervous wreck. I didn't like the clarinet to begin with and I hated that music teacher! Today I play the saxophone, piano, guitar and harmonica but no clarinet.

I started mentally dropping out of school when a teacher told me that I wouldn't be able to communicate if I didn't learn the grammar we were supposed to be studying which I was totally not interested in. I already knew how to communicate, so what line of bull was she giving me? That caused me to begin looking more closely at what other teachers were saying. As the years went on into junior and senior high school, I noticed more and more b.s., so I started skipping school and acting-out in other ways that got me into trouble with the law. I barely graduated from high school at Walter Johnson and was happy to be done with it.

I left Garrett Park in 1962, after working that summer to raise money for an old Chevy. I came out to Southern California to attend junior college and after several years there transferred up to San Francisco State for my undergraduate work, living in the Haight-Ashbury during the height of the hippy scene. After graduation I moved across the Bay to the University of California at Berkeley for graduate work from which I went on to earn a Ph.D. in psychology. I married Andrea, a Hungarian woman, when we were twenty-two, and she became a pediatric nurse helping to put me through school. We had two daughters, who in turn had three sons. Currently we live Northern California, about fifteen miles north of the Golden Gate Bridge in Marin County close to our girls and grandkids.

It's been some years since I was last in Garrett Park to attend my 50th high school reunion, the only one I ever went to. Sadly I was back again shortly thereafter for a memorial service for dear friend Tom Guernsey with whom I had stayed in touch through our later years.

Garrett Park was a small town with a sense of community, a place where people cared about each other and looked out for each other. When you went down to the post office everyone knew you. As we walked around the neighborhood, the houses were known for the people who lived in them; "Oh, that's the Sonner house, that's the Hall house, that's the Gieser house." Growing up there gave me a great appreciation for living in such a place. I loved and still love the houses with their distinctive architecture, the big yards. On the infrequent times I visit the east coast I love walking through the neighborhood reliving memories, friendships and adventures.

To this day I value the gifts of community. I have worked to build community where I have lived, and for this I owe a "thank you" to the people and spirit of Garrett Park, the place where I grew up during the formative years of eight to seventeen. If it existed on the west coast with its better weather I would live there again today.

(Written by Tom Pinkson)

9

STEVE SONNER

Team sports were played as a team. That meant no one bragged or claimed individual credit, whether earned or not, over the collective contributions of the team as a whole. During my working career, I found that experience and legacy particularly useful, even though some of my colleagues, and perhaps too many, never seemed to have learned that lesson. It was in that environment that I really grew to appreciate and value my experience in Garrett Park playing team sports like baseball.

My parents, Ken and Kathryn Sonner, moved to Garrett Park from Columbus, Ohio, in 1943. My father started a new job that summer in Washington, D.C., as an air safety investigator with the Civil Aeronautics Board (now the National Transportation Safety Board). He had grown up on a dairy farm near Delaware, Ohio, and, after graduating from high school, served in the army during World War I. After leaving the army, he attended Ohio State University, where he met my mother, who was born in Marion, Ohio, and later lived in Bucyrus, Ohio. In 1924, following their marriage, they settled on the Sonner family farm and lived there for four years until the agricultural difficulties that preceded the Great Depression and some unfortunate business decisions caused them to lose the farm.

Not long afterwards, my father went to work for Wright Aeronautical Corporation, a company founded by the Wright Brothers, also Ohio natives, that would soon become the leading manufacturer of airplane engines. It proved to be a fortunate career choice, giving him a reasonably secure job in a reasonably stable industry at a time of high unemployment and economic hardship nationwide. Over the next decade and a half, before moving to Garrett Park, they lived in Buffalo, N.Y., Elizabeth and Clifton, N.J., Atlanta, Ga., San Antonio and Brownsville, Texas, and Glendale, Calif., in addition to Columbus.

For the next 21 years, Garrett Park would remain their home. They first lived in a converted carriage house they rented at 11005 Montrose Avenue. It was situated in the rear of 4609 Waverly Avenue, one of Garrett Park's original Victorian homes. At the time, a man we knew as "Major Hudgins" owned the property, and he and his family lived in the main house. Temple Bailey, a prolific and popular novelist and short story writer in her day, had once lived in the same converted carriage house during the 1920s. As noted in "The History & Architecture of Garrett Park, Maryland—A Walking Tour," one of her novels, The Dim Lantern, published in 1923, "is set in a fictionalized version of Garrett Park."

In our family, we always referred to the former carriage house, affectionately, as "the Barn." That term, however, was a source of some embarrassment to two of my brothers, Andy and Alan, who at the time were nine and seven years old, respectively. My third and oldest brother, White, 17, had just finished his first year of college and would soon join the Navy.

I was born on December 31, 1944, in Suburban Hospital in Bethesda, which at the time had a maternity ward. Back then, Suburban Hospital consisted of a connected maze of flat-roofed single-story white buildings strung along the same location it now occupies on Old Georgetown Road. The arrival of a new baby to a mother and father who were both in their mid-40s may have been one of the factors that prompted them to settle in Garrett Park, after what had been something of a nomadic life. More important, however, was their love of the town and its people, many of whom became fast and lasting friends.

Joyce Reynolds' birthday party, top to bottom: Steve Sonner, Pam Payne, John Lamb - 1949

Clockwise from top: John Hall, Benny Gieser, Steve Sonner, and Ned Conklin Indian Rock in Kensington, MD - 1951

Donald Lamb, Steve Sonner, Timmy Honey John Lamb, and Martha Honey – with pet rabbits in Lamb's side yard, 1955

Steve with his pet squirrel, Whiskers - 1954

A year or so after I was born, my parents decided to leave the Barn and, in its place, have a new house built in Garrett Park on land that had served as a victory garden during World War II. Located on the corner of what is now Kenilworth Avenue and Oxford Street, next to Garrett Park School, it was one of the first 10,000-square-foot lots in town. The house itself was a three-bedroom, one bath, prefabricated Gunnison home. Next door lived the Woodwell family. Stan Woodwell, the family patriarch, saw that construction of the house was getting started one morning early in 1947. He decided he'd like to have a look when he got home from work that afternoon. When he arrived to take his tour, the frame and sides were up, the roof on, the windows installed, and the doors locked. The entire exterior of the house had gone up in a day.

I have vague memories of living in the Barn (and its knotty pine walls), and I remember once walking into our new house while it was under construction and seeing carpenters and sawhorses in what became our living room. I also remember the trauma of moving day and being upset at leaving behind what had been our home for my first two years on earth. My mother told me, many years later, that she took me back to the Barn that day to show me it was empty of furniture and uninhabited. Apparently, that return visit was enough to get me to accept my new home, where we'd remain for the next 17 years.

While living in Garrett Park, I attended Garrett Park Elementary School (Class of '57), Kensington Junior High School (Class of '60), and Walter Johnson High School (Class of '63). During my school years, I had various jobs, starting with cutting grass while in elementary school and, one year, delivering the weekly Maryland News to various houses in Garrett Park before dawn every Thursday morning. During my senior year in high school, I worked for an hour each morning, from Monday through Saturday, at the Garrett Park Post Office. My chores consisted of raising the flag, sweeping the floors, and helping to sort some of the mail, under the supervision of Postmistress Olive Parsons and her three assistants, Billye Ofenstein, Ruth Newhall, and Ruby Freer.

After graduating from high school, I attended what was then Montgomery Junior College in Takoma Park. In 1964, following my freshman year, my father retired, and my parents sold our home in Garrett Park and moved to a house they had bought a few years earlier in Irvington, Va., along the Rappahannock River. They also bought a one-bedroom co-op apartment in the Woodley Gardens area of Rockville as a place for me to live while I attended college and as a place for them to stay when they visited the area. I lived in that apartment for the next four years. Having my own place, in a manner of speaking, helped to overcome the sadness I felt about leaving behind forever our home and our life in Garrett Park.

After three semesters at MJC, I transferred to the University of Maryland. While at Maryland, I was fortunate to have some outstanding teachers, including John Snow (economic history), who later became the Secretary of the Treasury; Gordon Prange (WWI and WWII history), who wrote the book that became the movie "Tora, Tora, Tora"; and Larry Hogan (law of the press), who went on to serve in the House of Representatives and whose son and namesake became governor of Maryland.

In 1968, I graduated from the University of Maryland with a bachelor's degree in journalism. Before graduating, I had decided that I wasn't suited for a career in the news business. Instead, I spent the ensuing 45 years working as an editor and writer, primarily for government contractors based in the D.C. area. For the majority of this time, more than 30 years, I worked as a health information and communication specialist and project manager for private companies that provided professional services for the National Institutes of Health and other government health agencies. My work included preparing print and multimedia materials for health providers, patients, news organizations, and the general public about the results of health-related biomedical, clinical, and behavioral research. Over the years, I also provided similar information and communication services for other government agencies. I retired from full-time work in 2014.

Shortly before I graduated from college, my father died of a heart attack. He was 68 years old. My mother died nine years later of congestive heart failure, two months after suffering a stroke. She had just turned 75. As for the rest of the Sonner family, my oldest brother, White, held management positions in advertising and marketing and, later, started his own consulting business before retiring. He lives in Lometa, Texas, in the hill country west of Austin. Alan lives in Norfolk, Va., and had a successful career in sales and management for a variety of businesses. After retiring, he went to work part-time for the Norfolk Public Library. Andy taught at Walter Johnson while attending law school. He subsequently served as the State's Attorney for Montgomery County for more than 25 years and then served as a judge with the Maryland Court of Special Appeals. He lives in Rockville.

As for me, I got married in 1968. I met my wife, Kathy, while I was a student at Maryland and she was a student at Marjorie Webster Junior College in D.C. She subsequently took a year of Montessori training and had a long and successful career as a preschool teacher. We have one child, a son named Michael, who was born in 1970, and two grandchildren, one a girl born in 2008 and one a boy born in 2013.

After getting married, Kathy and I moved to a rented house in Falls Church, Va., and then, in 1970, bought a house inside the Beltway in Annandale, Va., where we have lived ever since, in a neighborhood of winding tree-lined streets that reminds me a lot of Garrett Park.

TV Comes to Town

Late one afternoon in the fall of 1950, I sat with a group of kids on the floor of the Walker's living room, all of us transfixed by what we were seeing on the small black and white screen before us. It was "The Howdy Doody Show," featuring Howdy Doody, Dilly Dally, and Phineas T. Bluster, all marionettes, along with their human companions Buffalo Bob, Clarabelle the Clown, Chief Thunderthud, and the beautiful Princess Summerfall Winterspring.

In 1950, some 10 million households across the United States, or about one out of four, had a television set. One of those television sets belonged to the Walkers, the first family in our Garrett Park neighborhood to get a TV.

The Walkers lived in a white Cape Cod house on the northeast corner of Oxford Street and Kenilworth Avenue. Mr. Walker (James, Sr.) owned a gasoline station in Bethesda. Mrs. Walker (Victoria) belonged to the Dove family, longtime residents of Garrett Park. They had two children—Dianne and Jimmy. At the time, Dianne was about six years old and in the first grade, and Jimmy was one or two.

Late one afternoon in the fall of 1950, I sat with a group of kids on the floor of the Walker's living room, all of us transfixed by what we were seeing on the small black and white screen before us. It was "The Howdy Doody Show," featuring Howdy Doody, Dilly Dally, and Phineas T. Bluster, all marionettes, along with their human companions Buffalo Bob, Clarabelle the Clown, Chief Thunderthud, and the beautiful Princess Summerfall Winterspring. With them in the studio, watching the live broadcast, were a group of kids collectively known as the Peanut Gallery.

It was my first exposure to this new and rapidly growing form of home entertainment. I can't remember for sure who was there that afternoon, besides Dianne Walker and me and maybe her brother, Jimmy. But the audience probably included some combination of kids from our neighborhood: Donald and John Lamb, Anita and Christine Woodwell (and Stanley?), Felicity and Pamela Payne (and Jenifer?), Ned Conklin, and perhaps Martha and Timmy Honey and Wendy and Jennifer Johnston, whose families would have recently arrived in Garrett Park.

We all lived along Kenilworth Avenue, south of Strathmore, and our ages ranged from about three or four to about ten. I was five, going on six, and had started kindergarten in September at Kensington Elementary School. Garrett Park Elementary School, still just two rooms at the time, didn't offer kindergarten. So I and my classmates had to ride a Capital Transit bus to Kensington Elementary and back on school days, at a cost of seven cents each way.

Those of us who didn't yet have a TV set relied on radio and movies as our entertainment media. Radio in those days offered a mix of drama, comedy, quiz shows, variety shows, and music. My favorite radio shows were westerns such as "The Lone Ranger." We had a console combination AM radio and 78 rpm record player in our living room. I would lie on the floor and listen as the Lone Ranger and Tonto took on the bad guys and rescued the good guys, all the while imagining the two of them on horseback, riding across the plains and mountains and valleys of the Old West.

Movies, of course, didn't require that kind of mental imaging. We had a variety of movie theaters to choose from back then—the Bethesda and Hiser-Bethesda in Bethesda, the Avalon in Chevy Chase, the Viers Mill in Wheaton, the Milo in Rockville, the Silver in Silver Spring, and the Apex and MacArthur in Northwest D.C. In those days, first-run movies first appeared only in posh theaters in downtown Washington such as the Warner, R.K.O. Keith's, Loew's Capitol and Loew's Palace. After several weeks on the downtown screens, the movies would finally make their way out to the suburban theaters.

In addition to the commercial theaters, Garrett Park Elementary occasionally offered 16mm movies on Saturdays. The cost of admission was ten cents, or less than half the price of a ticket at one of the neighborhood theaters. The Guernsey home at 11002 Kenilworth Avenue also served as an occasional movie venue. Mr. Guernsey, an official with the CIO labor union (later the AFL-CIO), would show a variety of 16mm movies in the family's living room. Those free movies introduced us to characters such as W.C. Fields and Abbott and Costello.

Then, almost like magic, television brought a combination of motion pictures and radio into the home. My first real exposure to TV that afternoon in the Walker's living room ended when my brother Alan showed up at the front door and told me I had to come home for dinner. My parents surely knew where I was and had sent him to fetch me. If Alan hadn't come, I probably would have stayed indefinitely, until the Walkers finally told me to leave.

I don't remember ever going back to watch TV at the Walkers. My guess is that we neighborhood kids quickly wore out our welcome. And it wouldn't be long before we got our own TV.

Our first television set arrived a few months later, in February 1951. It was a boxy RCA Victor 10" table model, with a rabbit-ear antenna that sat on top of the set. The TV took its place on a combination cabinet and bookshelf at one end of the living room of our house at 4800 Oxford Street, a dog-leg across Kenilworth from the Walkers. I don't know what my parents paid for it, and I'm not even sure if it was new or second-hand—I suspect the latter. But either way, my guess is that it would have cost somewhere approaching $200.

At a time when the average annual income in the United States was a little more than $4,200 and a house in Garrett Park cost anywhere from $5,000 to $20,000, a new RCA Victor table model TV cost at least $200 at local department stores. Hecht's, for example, advertised 16" Crosley table models for $290 and consoles for as much as $480, or equal to $2,875 and $4,759, respectively, in 2018. In the early 1950s, at those prices, a TV purchase represented a sizable financial hit. Nonetheless, many families in Garrett Park soon were bringing TV sets into their homes and living rooms. The growing popularity of television prompted families like the Walkers and the Sonners and, soon, many others in Garrett Park to spend a sizable portion of their income on this exciting new entertainment medium.

The first thing I remember seeing on our TV was a professional basketball game. We watched the Washington Capitals, the name of D.C.'s hometown basketball team at the time, running up and down the court. It seemed like magic to me, as if we were actually there, watching a miniature version of the game.

Soon after that first home viewing, my parents must have decided to use the TV as a babysitter, leaving me alone one afternoon with my friend and kindergarten classmate John Hall. I can't remember from this distance what we were watching, but out of nowhere some jagged diagonal lines appeared on the screen that obliterated the picture. I'm sure we both thought it was a serious problem that could destroy our "new" TV and perhaps even threaten our safety by exploding.

I must have already learned some simple operational procedures, such as how to turn the set on and off and how to change channels. But at that moment I was probably afraid to turn it off or change to another channel, fearing that it would only make things worse. All we could do was wait for my parents to return and hope that they could fix whatever was causing the problem.

As we waited, I stood at the living room window that afternoon and looked out toward the street, watching for my parents' car, anxious for them to return from wherever they had gone. I became more and more frantic and desperate while the TV picture continued to malfunction. As the time crawled by, with the picture still acting up, I started banging the palm of my hand against one of the panes in our casement window until it finally broke. At last my parents returned to find that broken living room window, the TV picture full of squiggly lines, and two hysterical kids, one bleeding from some minor scratches on his right hand and wrist.

I don't remember my mother and father being angry about the broken window. I suppose they were just glad that my cuts weren't any worse than they were. And, with a simple twist of a knob labeled "horizontal hold," they were able to correct the problem with the picture.

With the picture working properly, we would often sit together, as a family, watching the popular shows of the time. Back then, the Washington, D.C., area had four channels, all VHF. Those four channel numbers remain today, but three of the four call letters have changed: Channel 4, WNBW, is now WRC; Channel 7, WMAL, is now WJLA; and Channel 9, WTOP, is now WUSA. The fourth local station, Channel 5, then owned by a company called DuMont, is still called WTTG some 70 years later.

Television programs on those four local channels largely reflected the programming on the radio, consisting of variety shows, quiz shows, crime dramas, music, and sports, with the addition of cartoons, cowboy movies, and other B movies out of the 1930s and 1940s, along with kids' shows like "Howdy Doody." National news broadcasts such as the "Camel News Caravan" on NBC, featuring John Cameron Swayze, were mostly limited to 15 minutes around dinner time. It would take more than a decade before network TV news would expand to 30 minutes and include both national news and more than five minutes of local news.

I would often watch the news, along with the other members of our family. But like most boys my age, I was partial to westerns, such as "Frontier Theater," which showed cowboy movies that featured such stars as Bob Steele, Hopalong Cassidy, Lash LaRue, and Gene Autry. And at last I could see exactly what the Lone Ranger and Tonto looked like in real life, along with their horses, Silver and Scout.

Steve and Tex - 1951

"Howdy Doody," "Frontier Theater," "The Lone Ranger," and other popular kids' shows back then, such as "Kukla, Fran and Ollie," "The Sealtest Big Top," and "Captain Video," were broadcast nationally while others originated locally. One of those local originations was "The Pick Temple Show." In the 1950-51 season, it was broadcast live on Channel 9 from 5:00 to 5:30 p.m. every weekday. The show featured cartoons and short westerns, along with Pick's collie named Lady. Pick Temple, the host, wore a cowboy hat and cowboy outfits and played the guitar and sang cowboy songs coupled with jingles to promote the show's sponsors.

In the spring of 1951, not long after we got our TV, I somehow managed to join a group of kids on the "Pick Temple Show," taking my place one day among other boys and girls about my age from the D.C. area. We all sat in Pick Temple's version of Howdy Doody's Peanut Gallery.

One of the show's props was a small western saddle perched on top of a hitching post (later replaced by a pony named Piccolo). I was selected to sit on the saddle and fire my toy pistol toward the camera to introduce the next feature. I'd ridden a horse before and, more important, had seen cowboys mounting horses in western movies and on TV. I walked up, confidently grabbed the saddle horn, and attempted to pull myself onto the saddle. Unfortunately, however, the saddle wasn't securely fastened to the cross member on the hitching post and started to come off. Pick Temple quickly grabbed the saddle, returned it to its place, and carefully lifted me onto it.

When the show ended, Pick Temple invited kids in attendance that day to his office, where he autographed 8 x 10 glossy photos of himself as a memento of our appearance. When I walked in, I was more than a little shocked at what I saw. He was seated at a desk. He wasn't wearing his cowboy hat. Not only was he hatless and seated at a desk (rather than on a horse?), but he was wearing glasses. In all the westerns I'd watched, I'd never seen a cowboy wearing glasses.

The next day in school, several fellow kindergartners from Kensington told me, excitedly, that they'd seen me on TV. They seemed almost in awe of it—and of me. My classmates from Garrett Park were much more blasé and failed to see it as big deal. I guess we regarded my status as an ephemeral TV celebrity in 1951 as somewhere below the ability to ride a two-wheeler or to ride a sled fast enough down Donnelly's Hill to reach Wells Park.

About a year later, I also appeared on a local kids' TV show on Channel 4 called "Dick Mansfield's Safety Circus," sponsored by Mason's Root Beer, a local soft-drink company. Dick Mansfield, the show's host and namesake, was a D.C. police officer who used various types of kid-friendly entertainment to encourage safety while walking and biking, such as looking both ways before crossing the street and holding on to the handle-bars while riding a bike.

My appearance on the show resulted from winning a contest where the prize was a brand-new 26" Schwinn bicycle. I needed that new bicycle. A car had run over and destroyed my first bicycle. The contest consisted of asking kids to submit a reply, in 25 words or less, to the following: I like Mason's Root Beer because . . . Actually, I wasn't particularly fond of Mason's Root Beer or any root beer for that matter. My mother was responsible for crafting the response, which claimed, falsely, I like Mason's Root Beer because it is foamy, sparkly, and it tastes so good. I printed the words on a sheet of blue construction paper, folded in half to form a card shape, and decorated the card with my first-grade class photo and a drawing of a bicycle.

Not long after submitting my response, we learned that it was selected as one of the winning entries, result-ing in a new Schwinn bicycle and my second appearance on local TV. While on the show, I read aloud the words of praise for Mason's Root Beer that I had submitted with my entry. Then Dick Mansfield said, "Wow, Steve, that was really good! How would you like a great big Mason's Root Beer float right now?" Whereupon I replied, "Oh, no thank you." I can only imagine what Dick Mansfield's response must have been, but my friends who were watching were at once shocked and amused.

One by one, more and more families in Garrett Park brought TV sets into their homes. One day Benny Gieser and I and a few others kids were playing outside Benny's house at 11104 Kenilworth Avenue when his parents drove in. As his mother, Ilah, got out of the car, we could see that she was holding something in her hand and, with a big smile on her face, put a rabbit ear antenna on top of her head. It was her way of telling us that the Giesers, too, now had a TV. Other families all across town, with and without kids, soon added TV sets to their homes.

I'd guess that by 1952 or 1953, the majority of families in Garrett Park had a television. The Paynes were one of the last families in our neighborhood to get one. Sometimes when I was playing outside near their house, I'd see Mr. Payne standing in their living room, seemingly frozen in place in mid-stride, with his eyes glued to the TV screen.

As for us, we tended to watch the popular shows of the day while seated in our living room. Those shows included "The Toast of the Town" (later to be named "The Ed Sullivan Show," after its host), "Twenty Questions," "Omnibus," and "You Bet Your Life," with Groucho Marx, as well as live broadcasts of basketball, college and pro football, and baseball games.

The effects of this new and growing form of entertainment quickly reached both movies and sports. To compete with TV, movie studios began introducing—and promoting—innovations such as Cinemascope and 3-D as a way to give the "big screen" a competitive advantage over television. Movie studios also restricted the TV release of box-office favorites as a way to limit the threat. Old low-budget B-movies tended to make their way to the small screen, but not popular films regardless of their age.

As for sports, an article in the Washington Post on January 2, 1951, noted how attendance at Washington Senators' home games had fallen significantly during the 1950 season, despite the team's rise from the cellar the preceding year to fifth place in the American League. (For a team that hadn't made it to a World Series since 1933, I guess that three-place rise in the standings represented a significant accomplishment.) In an attempt to boost attendance for the upcoming season, the Senators' ownership announced that it would televise only twenty home games in 1951, down from seventy-seven in 1950.

As the 1950s progressed, new and popular programs such as "Dragnet," "The Adventures of Ozzie and Harriet," "Medic," "Alfred Hitchcock Presents," and "I Love Lucy" would add to TV's appeal. New shows aimed specifically at kids like me, such as "Disneyland," "The Mickey Mouse Club," "The Adventures of Superman," and "Lassie," joined and eventually supplanted shows like "Howdy Doody" and "Pick Temple" as we grew older.

One new show stands out in particular. On January 14, 1952, when I was in the first grade, our family watched the inaugural broadcast of "The Today Show," with Dave Garroway serving as the host, a position he would hold for the next nine years.

"The Today Show" would prove to be the exception to our family's rule about not watching television during meals. After that first Monday morning broadcast, we would turn on our TV set promptly at the show's 7:00 a.m. starting time every weekday, and it would remain on while we ate breakfast at the dining room table. This routine would remain nearly uninterrupted over the next 12 years, until we left Garrett Park.

We enjoyed not only the news and features on "Today," but also seeing the people who gathered on the sidewalk along West 49th Street in New York City to watch the show through large windows that gave them a view into the studio. One morning, a year or so after that first broadcast, the camera panning the people assembled outside came to a sudden stop and zoomed in on one member of the audience. There among the crowd on the sidewalk, wearing a fedora, was former President Harry Truman, who smiled and waved to the camera and viewers.

In the mid-1950s, "The Today Show" network, NBC, started broadcasting shows in "living color." Most TV programs, however, would remain black and white for many years, and color TV sets, which first sold for $1,000 or more, would remain a rarity in Garrett Park. One exception, however, was Garrett Park Television, a retail TV sales and service enterprise owned by Charlie Chamberlin and located where the Garrett Park Post Office is now.

One warm Sunday evening, a few friends and I stood outside his shop and, through the window, watched what was probably "The Steve Allen Show" on NBC. It was the first time we'd seen a TV program in color. The store was closed and locked at the time, and the lights inside the store weren't turned on. The only light came from the glow of the color TV as Mr. Chamberlain and members of his family sat watching the show.

Color TV was one of the ways the television business competed with movies for audiences. Another major breakthrough, also in the mid-1950s, was a show called "Million Dollar Movie." It promised for the first time to bring first-rate big-screen movies to the small screen. The first one I remember seeing was "Casablanca." Beforehand, there was a lot of excited talk in our household about "Casablanca" and what a good movie it was, unlike the normal B-rated film fare on TV. As we watched it, however, I wondered to myself what all the fuss was about. Where was the action? Was that the same Peter Lorre I'd seen in the movie "20,000 Leagues Under the Sea"? Why did anyone care about Rick and Ilsa and Victor? Couldn't anyone else spot the fake scenery? And that fake airplane?

As a preadolescent, I clearly failed to grasp the characters, story line, and historical context of "Casablanca." But it did launch a new era in TV entertainment, one that would now include popular movies that until then had only appeared in theaters. Perhaps the formerly restrictive movie studios finally agreed with the television networks that there was money to be made from advertisements for toothpaste, soap, and cigarettes.

Fast forward a year or two to Friday, October 4, 1957. I sat at home that night, perched alone before our TV set, watching either "The Adventures of Jim Bowie" or "Zane Grey Theater. Suddenly, the show switched off and the word "Bulletin" appeared on the screen, the first time I can recall that sort of thing ever happening. A stern voiceover quickly followed, announcing that the Soviet Union had successfully launched the world's first space satellite—"Sputnik"—and it was now in orbit around planet earth. I sat there breathless, in a state of shock, as the announcement was followed by audio that played the beeping signals coming from Sputnik.

That news proved to be a shock to the nation as well. The show I'd been watching resumed, of course, but that news bulletin and Sputnik's launch propelled the space race between the U.S. and the U.S.S.R. to a new level of intensity, with the United States apparently now in second place.

A year earlier, Chet Huntley (in New York) and David Brinkley (in Washington) had changed the face of television news, bringing serious, measured, comprehensive, and objective coverage of important events nationwide and worldwide into American homes for 15 minutes every weeknight on NBC. To compete with NBC, CBS moved Walter Cronkite to the network's nightly news broadcast. He was a versatile and popular reporter and the former host of, among other programs, a weekly retrospective news show called "You Are There." By the early 1960s, "The CBS Evening News with Walter Cronkite" would grow from 15 minutes to 30 minutes. Within weeks, "The Huntley-Brinkley Report" also expanded to 30 minutes.

When the 1950s ended, most families in Garrett Park, like most families across the country, owned a television set, and some lucky families owned more than one. Our RCA Victor 10" table model eventually was replaced by a 17" Muntz console. And today, of course, what was once only available in homes like the Walkers and ours on four channels from a small black and white screen on the front of a heavy wooden box can be seen on a hand-held device, providing access to thousands of full-color videos, images, and other forms of communications from around the world anywhere anytime.

Play Ball!

Author's Note: What follows has been largely reconstructed from memory, going back some 60 years, supplemented by contemporaneous stories that appeared in various issues of the Garrett Bugle from the mid-1950s. I can only hope the information is reasonably accurate and aligns with what other people remember from that distant time. The opinions offered, of course, are mine alone.

When the game ended, the game was over, and we all moved on and once again were friends. My memory of those days, from this distance, reminds me of the closing line from of the 1986 movie "Stand By Me": "I never had any friends later on like the ones I had when I was twelve. Jesus, does anyone?"

Athletic ability was a key defining factor for me and my male friends when we were growing up in Garrett Park in the 1950s. To a large extent, performance on the baseball field, football field, and basketball court and in the swimming pool and even at the bowling alley governed your status within our peer group. For the better athletes among us, that peer group extended up two or three years and down, maybe, a year.

Our skill levels varied, of course, and some of us were better at some sports and games than at other sports and games. Benny Gieser and John Guernsey, two of my friends and classmates at Garrett Park Elementary School, ranked at or near the top across most sports. Benny in particular, unlike John and me, excelled in just about every sport, earning him the label "natural athlete."

Often, when it came to the three of us, the two who ended up together on the same team had a competitive advantage over the third's team, regardless of the particular sport or game or contest. The one left on the opposing side faced an uphill—and usually unsuccessful—struggle to emerge with a win.

Our athletic pursuits varied by the season. In the fall, it was football. In the winter, it was basketball. And in the spring and summer, it was baseball. Interspersed were what we considered lesser sports such as softball, kickball, soccer, golf, dodgeball, tennis, badminton, and wiffleball (with a tennis racquet for a bat), along with games such as tag and white flag. That latter game, unlike most of our other games and athletic contests, was open to female participation.

During the winter, in addition to basketball, we even made occasional attempts to play ice hockey, with the iced-over swampy (and safe) areas along Rock Creek serving as our hockey rink and our leather-soled shoes serving as skates, tree limbs serving as hockey sticks, and a smooth stone serving as the puck. The annual Fourth of July festivities featured an adult softball game between Garrett Park and Garrett Park Estates, which the comparatively young Estaters usually won. It also featured egg-throwing contests, turtle races, and other events before darkness fell and fireworks lit up the sky.

In those days, youth athletics were much less organized and formal than they are now. Most of our contests consisted of pickup games of our own making, played on the baseball field, basketball court, and playground adjacent to Garrett Park School and the Community Center. We played tackle football without any protective equipment. On one occasion, an opposing player who was a year or two ahead of us showed up for one of our pickup games wearing a plastic football helmet with a single bar across the front as a face guard. When he made an attempt to run with the ball, Benny Gieser grabbed the bar and tossed him to the ground—a move I'm sure we didn't know at the time was a violation of the rules.

Most of our baseball, too, consisted of games we organized ourselves, without any adult involvement. Instead of two opposing teams, we played something called workup. Under the workup rules, three players would take turns at bat. Each remaining player would start, say, in right field and work his way around the outfield and the infield, one position at a time, as each of the players at bat, one way or another, got out. Then, after working his way around the outfield and infield positions, the player who had started in right field would eventually get a turn as one of the three batters. When, or if, the batter got out, he would start the cycle all over again.

We would play workup during recess at school as well as after-school or during our school-free time over the spring and summer. There was no real age limit or other requirement, including athletic ability, or lack of it.

But the games typically involved kids of roughly the same age or grade. The typical number of players was 12, with nine in the field and three at bat. When fewer people played, we made adjustments to the rules, such as two-field hitting, or left field and center field for right-handers, and center field and right field for the rare left-hander.

All of the baseball bats in those days were made of wood, usually Louisville Sluggers. When one split or broke, as often happened, we would tape it whenever possible and keep using it. Many years would pass before durable aluminum bats replaced those brittle wooden bats. Our baseball gloves were made by Rawlings or Wilson and bought at places like the Bethesda Sports Mart and Sears Roebuck and even McIntire Hardware or passed down to us by our older brothers. We would treat our gloves, whether new or used, with neat's-foot oil to soften the leather and make them—and us—better at catching fly balls and grounders.

Over the summer, Montgomery County sponsored recreation centers on Mondays through Fridays at locations throughout the county. Garrett Park's was based at the Community Center and included baseball along with other activities such as arts and crafts, all designed to keep kids busy and out of trouble during the summer break from school. The rec center also sponsored baseball games against teams from other rec centers around the county. Most of us, however, considered rec center baseball a sideshow once formal youth baseball arrived in Garrett Park.

What is still referred to as "Little League" baseball became popular and widespread during the 1950s. My first participation came in the spring and summer of 1955, between my 4th and 5th grades. Garrett Park's team was called the "Gnats." I don't know who came up with that name, but it sounds like something that may have originated with George Payne. Mr. Payne and his wife, Norah, weren't sports fans, and they had three daughters, who, because of their gender, weren't eligible to play baseball with us boys. But he was a clever wordsmith and town activist who went on to serve a term as mayor of Garrett Park in the 1970s. Or maybe it was Tom Wilson, the initial force behind youth baseball in Garrett Park, who came up with the name.

Steve wearing his Gnats t-shirt and hat

Wherever it originated, that play on words for Garrett Park's baseball team at once paid homage to Washington's professional baseball team, popularly called the Nats back then as now, and the pesky insects that swarmed around our heads every summer, even during our baseball practice sessions and games.

Coaching the Gnats that season was Bill Julian. It was his second year in that role. He had led a talented Gnats team to the championship of the Lockwood Little League the preceding year. He was married to or about to marry Shirley Stottlemyer, the older sister of Billy Stottlemyer, who was one of the players on that championship Gnats team in 1954.

Billy also played on the 1955 Gnats, along with other veterans such as Johnny Walter, Tommy Gironda, Richard Dupree, Terry Brown, Brian McLaughlin, Todd Pendleton, Tom Richter, and Tom Wilson's son Jimmy, along with his younger brother Tam. Although I somehow made the team, as did Benny Gieser, I saw little action. The age range was technically 12 and under, but if you were 12 on January 1 and turned 13 after that date, you were allowed to play. That meant that many of the players were 13, when Benny and I were just 10 and the youngest members of the Gnats. So on the bench I sat for a good part of the season, while the big boys took the field. And that cutoff date would come back to bite me a couple of years later.

The Lockwood Little League consisted of teams from the Kensington-Wheaton-Silver Spring area. Besides the defending champion Gnats, other teams in the league included Parkway Cleaners, Kensington Kards, and Kensington Boys Club. That last team consisted of players from the black enclave of Ken-Gar, located along the north side of the B&O Railroad tracks leading into Kensington from Garrett Park. A few kids on the Kensington Boys Club team didn't have baseball gloves, so some of us Gnats would leave our gloves on the field for the opposing players to pick up and use when the Gnats were at bat. With players like star pitcher "Toe" Waters, slugger Howie Davis, and the outstanding hitter and fielder Butch Christian, they may have been short on gloves, but they were long on talent. I don't remember ever beating that team, and they went on to win the league championship that year.

According to official Little League rules, the games lasted six innings. The bases were 60 feet apart, and the pitching rubber was 46 feet from home plate. Stealing a base was allowed but not leads off base. You could only take your foot off the base once the ball had left the pitcher's hand. Unlike our pickup games, each Little League game had a single umpire assigned by the league. Wearing a facemask and inflated chest protector, the umpire crouched behind the catcher and called balls and strikes. If a batter got on base, the umpire would remove his mask, push the chest protector aside, and take a position behind the pitcher, where he had a better view of the infield to decide whether baserunners were safe or out. The downside, of course, was that he was farther from home plate, making it difficult sometimes to distinguish between balls and strikes.

Our home field, located on the Garrett Park School playground, was rough and uneven, especially the infield. The bumpy and eroded condition of the infield, with pebbles of various sizes scattered across it, would invariably send ground balls bouncing unpredictably. The successful handling of a ground ball by an infielder seemed to depend almost as much on luck as on the skill of the player. The other baseball fields we played on weren't much better.

Our uniforms consisted of baseball caps and T-shirts with "Garrett Park Gnats" across the front. When we each took our turn at the plate, we wore a primitive version of a batting helmet. It was horseshoe-shaped and made of plastic and covered both ears and the back of the head. And we only wore it when at bat. If we got on base, we left the helmet behind for the next batter. As for shoes, we weren't allowed to wear metal cleats and could only wear rubber ones. But shoes with rubber cleats were a little pricey and offered no real advantage in terms of traction. Instead we wore what we called tennis shoes, or sneakers, consisting of Keds or PF Canvas Shoes or the more upscale Converse All Stars.

Even though I saw little game time that first season, I got to practice with the team a couple of times a week, as did all members of the Gnats. We each would get a turn at bat, giving us a chance to work on our skills at hitting the baseball. In addition to batting practice, we would work on our defensive skills. As an outfielder, I would catch fly balls hit to me and the other outfielders by one of the coach's helpers, often the father of one of the players. While we outfielders shagged fly balls, the infielders took turns catching ground balls hit by Coach Julian or Tom Wilson, who was the official head of Garrett Park's Little League and Junior League baseball teams at the time. When not coaching, Mr. Wilson often could be seen around town proudly wearing a sport jacket from his alma mater, Princeton University, Class of 1927. Once, when a practice session had to be canceled because of the weather, Mr. Wilson invited the team members to his house at 10811 Kenilworth Avenue, where he taught us how to keep a box score.

During the games, the players' parents, siblings, friends, and neighbors would watch from the sideline. The field had a backstop and had two benches for the players, one along the third base line for the Gnats and one along the first base line for the opposing team. But there wasn't any seating for the spectators. Instead, they sat on the ground or on folding chairs to watch the games.

The next year, 1956, brought with it some significant changes. For one, Mr. Wilson took over the coaching duties from Bill Julian. In addition, the Gnats joined what was called the Rockville City League, playing teams from in and around Rockville. With the new league came another important change: The Gnats left the Little League and some of its rules behind and became part of what was called the Midget League. The 12-and-under age limit remained, as did the six-inning length of the games. But rather than 60 feet between bases, the distance grew to 70 feet, and the pitching rubber was 52 feet from home plate, rather than 46 feet. With the expanded distance between bases, players could take a lead off base, as in the majors, rather than having to wait for the pitcher to throw the ball. These changes brought our game closer to the way the professional game was played.

The age-related departure of the older kids opened up things for me and for the other younger players from the preceding year. I became the starting left fielder. Unlike my teammates Mike Ofenstein, Tom Guernsey, John Hall, Tom Pinkson, and Benny Gieser, I wasn't skilled enough on defense to take an infield position. Despite my fielding deficiencies, we worked well as a team. The Gnats did much better than they had the year before, ending up near the top of the league standings with a winning record. Throughout the 1956 season, I kept a running account of my batting average, which ended somewhere in the mid-.400s. I usually batted second in the lineup. I don't remember getting any extra-base hits, so the divisor for that average consisted entirely of singles.

The arrival of the 1957 season brought with it a new coach—Owen "Obbie" Williams, who lived at 11006 Montrose Avenue. Like Tom Wilson, he was a skilled baseball player and experienced coach. During our batting practice, Coach Williams liked to take a turn at the plate, where he'd blast line drives deep into the outfield. John Hall came up with a special word to describe the turns at bat taken by Coach Williams: "bragtice."

Another change saw the Gnats join a new league, this one called the Montgomery County Boys Baseball Association. Most of the teams in our division of the league came from the Bethesda-Rockville area and included community-sponsored teams (like the Gnats) from Potomac and Burgundy Knolls, as well as teams sponsored by local businesses such as Carrier Drug, Bethesda Sports Mart, Lloyd's Sporting Goods, and Bethesda Builders Supply. And, on the defensive side, I moved from left field to first base.

We entered the new season with high hopes, but they quickly evaporated. The first sign of trouble occurred when we got our new Gnats T-shirts. The company that made the shirts misspelled Gnats, and instead the shirts read, "Garrett Park Knats." On the field, our optimism met reality when we played our first game, against Bethesda Builders Supply at Ayrlawn Park in Bethesda, where we suffered an 18-1 loss. Our only score came in the second inning, on a solo home run by Benny Gieser. At the time he was small for his age. Sensing that size was related to hitting power, the opposing left fielder and probably the other two outfielders as well moved in to positions not far from the infielders. Benny responded by sending the ball sailing high over the left fielder's head. By the time the left fielder managed to run down the ball, Benny had circled the bases and scored the Knats' only run.

The next few games ended with losses as well, although by lesser margins than that opening game. Our pitching crew seemed to excel at giving up hits and runs to the opposition. Early in the season, I approached

Mr. Williams about possibly serving as a pitcher as well as the first baseman. Unknown to my teammates, I had worked on my pitching by playing catch with my friend and neighbor Donald Lamb and my brother Andy. They both gave me tips and coached me on pitching speed and control and how to throw a curveball.

A year or so earlier, I had played in a rec center game against the Kensington rec center, whose pitcher, Pete Crook, was an excellent curve-baller. My first time at bat against him, I saw the ball coming straight at me. Instead of stepping back, in an attempt to avoid getting hit, I stepped forward, just as the ball arched across the plate, striking me directly in the chest, for what would have been a strike. After that experience, I was determined to learn to throw a curve. It took a long time and many lessons and attempts, but it finally came to me.

About a month into the season, I got my chance as a pitcher, against Carrier Drug. I managed to hold the Carrier Drug batters hitless into the fourth inning before my arm got too sore and too tired to continue. A reliever closed out the game, with the Knats at last coming out on the winning side.

My experience as a pitcher opened up a whole new perspective on the game of baseball. I liked the fact that I was continuously active on the defensive side, rather than waiting in left field or at first base for something to happen. I also liked the mind-game element associated with pitching, or trying to outwit the batters. For example, I could try to throw the ball so fast that the batter either would swing at it and miss or would not have time to decide whether to swing or let it pass, leaving it up to the umpire to decide whether it was a strike or a ball. Or, if I thought the batter was expecting another fastball, I could throw him a changeup, which could disrupt the timing of his swing. And added to my pitching arsenal was a curveball, something only a few pitchers in the Midget League knew how to throw. With the curveball, I could either aim it at the batter and see it break across the plate and into the strike zone, like the pitch that hit me in that earlier rec center game. Or, for right-handed batters—as most of them were—I could aim it at the plate and then have the ball break to the left, while the batter swung at a ball that veered away from the end of his bat.

During the games, I was on my own when it came to deciding what pitch to throw. Unlike the major league teams, we didn't have signals from the catcher to the pitcher. But now and then, Coach Williams would send me a signal from his seat on the bench, telling me to throw a curveball by making a twisting motion with his right hand.

Not all of my pitching outings were as successful as that first one. I remember one game in particular against one of the Bethesda teams where I got pounded and yanked from the game after a couple of innings. So it goes in baseball at all levels.

The Knats ended the 1957 season near the bottom of the standings. The season closed with an "all-star" game, with one division playing the other division. Coach Williams selected Benny Gieser, Frank Cady, and me to represent the Knats. Missing from the all-star selection was Timmy Honey, who played shortstop, the most difficult position in the infield. He was a rising sixth-grader, a year younger than Benny and I were and two years younger than Frank. When the season ended, Timmy was, arguably, the best player on the team both at bat and in the field. Several other players and even some parents objected to his absence from the all-star selection, believing that he should have been chosen instead of Benny, Frank, or me.

The resulting sting hit me particularly hard. Timmy was perhaps my best friend at the time, and I felt I had somehow ended up in a spot that he should have occupied. Coach Williams, to his credit, defended his decision by saying that he had to pick the players who had performed best throughout the season, rather than at the end.

I remember little about that all-star game, other than it was played on one of the baseball fields at Meadow-brook Park on Beach Drive in Chevy Chase, and I was put in the game for one inning at first base. I can't remember who won and don't remember getting a turn at bat, although I may have. After the game, each player got a white patch that looked like an oversize baseball, complete with stitching, that read, "MCBBA [Mont-gomery County Boys Baseball Association] All Star, 1957." The intent, I suppose, was to have it decorate our uniforms for the upcoming season.

A week or so later, we players, along with our siblings, parents, and friends, gathered on our home field in Garrett Park to close out the Knats' season. During the ceremony, Timmy was awarded a trophy that honored him as the team's "Most Improved Player." I remember telling him at the time that his award and his trophy were a bigger honor than getting selected as an all-star. A month or so later, he and his family—parents Jack and Mary, sisters Martha and Margaret, and their dog Bunny—moved from Garrett Park to Westport, Connect-icut, where Tim's athletic achievements continued through his days at Staples High School and Cornell University.

With the approach of the 1958 season, I found myself facing ineligibility for the 12-and-under Midget League. My 13th birthday, on December 31, meant that I was too old, according to the league's rules. I made an appeal to obtain an exception, saying that I missed the cutoff date by a mere 6 hours and 48 minutes. To support my case, I even provided a contemporary notation from the attending physician, stating that I was born at 5:12 p.m. But rules are rules, and my appeal was denied.

That denial meant that I had to move up to Garrett Park's nameless 15-and-under Junior League team while my peers and classmates and 1957 Knats teammates got another year in the midgets. The juniors were coached by Paige Linton, who lived in a Chevy house on the corner of Montrose and Clermont and whose son, Carey, also played on the team. Mr. Linton would later open a golf practice range on Rockville Pike, on land near what is now the White Flint Metro station. Tom Wilson, who had presided over the Gnats, was coaching a Jun-ior League team sponsored by the Co-op grocery store in Wheaton.

I'm not sure why I didn't elect to join Mr. Wilson's Co-op team rather than Garrett Park's junior team. My guess is that Garrett Park's roster was a little thin, meaning that Mr. Linton would have to play me somewhere, while Co-op had more players and more talented players than Garrett Park's team.

I was by far the youngest player on the team and, given my birth date and its proximity to the Midget League cutoff, probably the youngest player in the league. I found myself perched back in left field, wearing metal cleats, as allowed by the Junior League rules. As for the baseball field itself, the bases in the Junior League were 90 feet apart, and the pitching rubber was 60 feet from home plate—or the same dimensions as in the major leagues. It was a huge adjustment for me. Many times at bat, I'd hit a ball that would have gone for extra bases in the midgets but in the juniors would barely make it out of the infield. And I'm sure I didn't hit the ball that often. The opposing pitchers at the junior level were much better than those I'd faced in the midg-ets and included at least two who went on to play in the minor leagues.

My defensive play suffered as well. With my experience as an outfielder in the midgets, I was okay at re-trieving ground balls and could judge and catch flyballs. But line drives were a problem, not just because of the size of the field and the distances, but also because of the age-related strength of the batters. Most were in their mid-teens, meaning that they were much more powerful hitters than the Midget Leaguers. I could never seem to judge—or guess—whether a line drive hit in my direction would drop in for a single or sail over my head for a double, triple, or home run. And I seemed to have a knack for guessing wrong. If I moved forward to catch it, the ball would keep rising and fly over my head. If I thought it was heading over my head and moved back, it would drop in front of me.

Mr. Linton was constantly calling to me and signaling from his position along the sideline for me to move to the right or to the left or forward or back. He paid more attention to my location in left field than he did to all the other eight players combined. Perhaps he sensed a lack of concentration on my part. It's true that while in the field, I found it hard to concentrate, especially after my experience as a pitcher during my last year in the midgets, when I was always active. For me, that 1958 season couldn't have ended too soon.

When the 1959 season arrived, I decided not to participate in organized baseball. The trauma of that first year in the juniors, coupled with an interest in Whizzer motorbikes and visits to Garrett Park Pool, kept me off the baseball field.

In 1960, I was finishing ninth grade and decided to give baseball another shot. I joined a team sponsored by McIntire Hardware, a local family-owned chain now long gone. The team was based in Kensington and included players mainly from the Kensington-Wheaton area. I have no idea what became of Garrett Park's hometown junior team. The only other Garrett Parker I remember who played that year for McIntire Hardware was Eric Harris, who was a good friend at the time and who probably encouraged me to sign up.

The coach quickly assessed what I could do and couldn't do. I remember him telling me, "I have to play you because you can hit, but I need to put you somewhere in the field where you'll do the least damage." That somewhere turned out to be right field, the position that coaches and players alike thought required the least skill on defense. I also occasionally served as a relief pitcher. That summer, at the age of 15, my physical development was on a par with the other players in the Junior League, and I had adapted to the scale of the baseball field that had proved so daunting just two years earlier. My batting average, as I recall, was somewhere in the .300s. But I managed to compile an on-base percentage of nearly .500. At the time, on-base percentage—hits combined with getting on base by other means such as walks and fielding errors—didn't get the recognition it does today. Still, my ability to get on base helped the team compete, a fact that the coach recognized and valued.

The end of the 1960 baseball season brought my baseball "career" to a close. I was headed for the 10th grade at Walter Johnson High School, named after the former star pitcher for the Washington Senators who once lived in a house about a mile south of the school on Old Georgetown Road. In mid-August, I tried out for WJ's junior varsity football team. I ultimately made the team, playing linebacker on defense and running back on offense for what turned out to be a championship season. The action on the football field, coupled with the physical nature of the game, proved much more appealing to me at that age than baseball.

Another intervening factor involved the fate of the Washington Senators. During the 1950s, I was a huge fan and remained loyal to the team despite its losing seasons and seemingly perpetual occupation of a spot at or near the bottom of the American League. I would listen to the games on the radio, watch them on TV, and occasionally make the trip to Griffith Stadium to watch the Senators play live and in-person. Once, I saw Mickey Mantle, of the hated New York Yankees, hit three home runs in one game against the Senators. Another time I almost got beaned by a foul ball hit by another Hall of Famer, Ted Williams, of the Boston Red Sox. At one game I attended, probably in 1956 or 1957, I noticed that the members of the grounds crew, usually clad in a mix of shabby work clothes, were all dressed in crisp white uniforms. Shortly after the game started, the P.A. announcer said that President Eisenhower was in attendance. The president then stood up from a box seat along the third base side and waved to a cheering crowd.

Then, in 1959, it looked as if the Senators finally were about to turn things around. Outstanding young players like Harmon Killebrew joined veterans like Roy Sievers, promising a bright future at last. Then, seemingly out of nowhere, Calvin Griffith, the owner of the Senators, announced at the end of the 1960 season that he was moving the team to Minneapolis. The Washington Senators of old became the Minnesota Twins and would go on to win the American League pennant five years later. Adding to the misery, Washington got an expansion team, named the Senators,that, predictably, replaced the Senators of yore at the bottom of the American League. My loss of interest in playing baseball, combined with the trauma of losing that promising hometown professional team, would push the game of baseball aside for nearly 50 years.

Now, when I look back on my baseball days and the other sports we played while growing up in Garrett Park, I value the lessons from that experience as much as or more than the memories themselves. My friends and I were intensely competitive. We played hard and played to win. But we also played fair and followed the rules. We had an expression that frequently popped up when we participated in games or talked sports: "Cheaters choke." We didn't cheat or flout the rules or try to take any unfair advantage over the opposition during a game.

Team sports were played as a team. That meant no one bragged or claimed individual credit, whether earned or not, over the collective contributions of the team as a whole. During my working career, I found that experience and legacy particularly useful, even though some of my colleagues, and perhaps too many, never seemed to have learned that lesson. It was in that environment that I really grew to appreciate and value my experience in Garrett Park playing team sports like baseball.

Finally, and perhaps most important, we kids may have been enemies on the baseball field or football field or the basketball court or other athletic venue. But we were friends again once the game ended. I don't ever remember anyone getting angry or pouting or holding a grudge after a losing a game or other contest, no matter how painful it may have been at the time. When the game ended, the game was over, and we all moved on and once again were friends. My memory of those days, from this distance, reminds me of the closing line from of the 1986 movie "Stand By Me": "I never had any friends later on like the ones I had when I was twelve. Jesus, does anyone?"

(Written by Steve Sonner)

GARRETT PARK ELEMENTARY SCHOOL, 5th Grade Class

Top row: Judy King, Gary Lamson, Mrs. Ellerbe, Todd Miller;

Second from top row: Carol Ann Deblois, name unknown, Darlene Krouse, Mark Richter, Linda Offutt, Steve Sonner, Ellen Gordon;

Third from top row: Paula Wrench, Brad Sherfey, Benny Gieser, Priscilla Shaw;

Fourth from top row: Martha Honey, Harry Pitts, Nancy Miller, John Guernsey, Jan Fetchko, Carl Pope, Jeannie Fletcher;

Bottom row: Karen Hubbard, Ellie Berman, Erica Mortland, Beverly Schrieber, Sandy Freer

JUDY KING POPE

The town set a model in my mind of community, the idea that people should join together to make something happen. The closing off of the streets was so important to keeping that special character...That spirit of fierce defiance, that feistiness and stubborn individual nature of the town, thumbing your nose at the rest of the world, it's very endearing.

I feel incredibly fortunate that my parents chose to move to Garrett Park instead of moving to one of the many suburbs that were beginning to blossom outside of D.C. Because they chose Garrett Park, I grew up in a small town. It was a very unusual small town, since most adults commuted to Washington for work. But when they were home they created a real small town, run by its own town council, with plays and Fourth of July parades, picnics and fireworks, a library and swimming pool all in easy walking distance, and a post office that served as a meeting place for the whole community. I remember the long-serving postmistress who knew all of our mailing addresses, so that when I moved across the country I could still send a letter to Mr. and Mrs. James E. King, Garrett Park, Md. and know it would end up in their mailbox.

My parents were Barbara Crosland King and James E. King Jr. I was born in 1945 in Lakeland, Fla., and because my dad was working for the American occupation forces in Germany, my parents moved to Germany when I was one year old. My brother David (who currently lives in Port Townsend, Washington, and served two terms as mayor there) was born in Germany in 1948. We returned to the United States when I was seven or eight, and soon after that our family moved to Garrett Park. I think I was in second grade. My dad was an arms control and disarmament expert, working for a series of think tanks. My mother was an unhappy, stay-at-home mother for quite a while. Later, when I was in late elementary school or junior high, she got a part-time job at the National Institute of Health in Bethesda, which made her much happier. I grew up in Garrett Park all the way through high school, and my parents lived there until they died, so I kept going back for many years.

Our neighborhood was nicknamed Richterville, after Al Richter, the architect who had designed almost all of the houses on Weymouth Street. We lived at the bottom of Weymouth Street. The Friedmans were right next door to us, and the Kennedys were across the street. Our family was close with the Kennedys, and I stayed in touch with Elaine Kennedy for a while after I moved away from the town. Karen McLaughlin and I were good friends, and we played together a lot.

Our house was right up against the woods. Growing up, I played in the woods in all seasons of the year, spending so much time there, I don't know why I didn't die from the poison ivy. Those woods were my introduction to the natural world, and when I came home from school one day to find them being bulldozed to build Parkside Apartments, I cried. I don't think I've ever completely gotten over that first experience of losing a natural place that meant so much to me. In later years I have found that lots of people my age or younger have had this same experience because our country was developed so fast. A lot of people talk about having that painful, dislocated, lost feeling that the place we've grown up in and feel connected to has been wiped off the earth. Everybody needs wild spaces.

I remember this one time when I was in elementary school. It was an early spring day, and the weather was just gorgeous - that wonderful weather you get when you've gone through a long winter, the air is like wine, and it just makes your blood bubble. I came home from school, and I was wearing a dress with buttons down the back, a dress that my mother, who sewed a lot of our clothes, had made for me. My mother wasn't home, I couldn't play in the woods in my school clothes, I couldn't reach the buttons on this dress, and I was desperate to get outside. So I took her long, sharp sewing scissors, and I cut the dress open, got into my play clothes, and went racing out into the woods. Needless to say, my mother was not at all happy about this. That was how intense that connection was that I had with the woods.

I have many wonderful memories of playing in those woods with the neighborhood kids. There was a big rock, which in fact we called "Big Rock", and it was sort of a marker in the woods. Rock Creek Park was not very far away, and we could play in the creek, so we didn't need to wander very far into the woods. It was quite idyllic. We formed a sort of pack and played there all the time, and I remember that at one point there was a vine that had broken off, which we used to swing out into the ravine. Finally one day the vine broke and dumped some kid into the ravine, but I don't think anyone was seriously injured.

When we were out of school we just went where we pleased, forming gangs of kids who flowed from one house to the other, raiding the refrigerators as we went. Sometimes we jumped rope, and I remember that we liked to use broom sticks for pretending to be riders on horses, galloping around. We roller skated a bit on those awful skates that attached to your shoes but came off constantly. They came with a skate key that was used to tighten the clamps that held the skate onto the shoe. I have really special memories of summer nights - capturing fireflies and playing White Flag with the neighborhood kids. We played until it was too dark to see the flag, while our parents stood around outside drinking gin and tonics.

We could walk to anywhere we needed to go, we could even walk around at night if we wanted, and nobody checked on us. Our parents knew we would come home eventually, and we did. Dogs, too, had more freedom than they do now. I remember neighborhood dogs, including my collie dog, Prince, running loose. When I was young there was not yet a leash law, though that changed later.

I remember when I was just learning to ride a bike. I hopped on, right at the top of the Weymouth Street hill, and then, because I didn't know how to stop, I crashed at the bottom of the hill. My mother came running out to find me howling, the skin scraped off one side of my body. Not deterred, I learned to brake, and then I rode my bike all over town.

I knew the town as my territory, and I felt safe there. I have a feeling that all the kids in Garrett Park felt safe that way. The way that we were just left on our own to play was quite different from how it is today. This was especially true before the arrival of air-conditioning, which I think brought about unfortunate changes. People, including children, became more sealed into their houses, which I think was a detriment. Once people stopped spending so much time outside, they stopped mingling with each other outside. Today kids spend too much time indoors, and they are constantly supervised when they are outside. I am very concerned about how we are over-coddling our kids.

Softball was popular with a lot of girls, and I tried to play but I was never any good at it, or at any team sport. I much preferred to stay home and read, or play in the woods by myself. I was also into dolls, creating doll dramas with my friends based upon books that I had read - books like *Little House on the Prairie*. I had a small doll collection, and some of them were from Germany – a baby doll that looked real and a girl doll with real hair, which in retrospect seems pretty creepy to me, given that this was only shortly after the Holocaust, and we had just come from Germany. The last doll I ever had was one of those large walking dolls.

When you live in close proximity to the natural world, the seasons have a strong impact on you. Springtime was really amazingly beautiful in Garrett Park; in the spring I became ecstatic, and I still do. My dad had a beautiful garden, and it was just spectacular in the spring. He planted our back yard with azaleas and dogwoods and we had a hedge of forsythia. I used to be so excited when the crocuses and the forsythia would bloom, because that would mean the beginning of spring. The Friedmans had a beautiful magnolia tree in their yard, every year we would hold our breath to see if the tree would blossom or if it would be blighted by late snow. When it did bloom it was just gorgeous.

In the summer, I spent lots of time at the swimming pool, and I can still remember the exciting day when it first opened. There was this huge thunderstorm, so we just jumped in, and then we had to get right back out of the water. We could walk to the pool, and I remember that there were all these raspberries growing along the road to the pool and also along the railroad tracks. Huge bushes grew there, covered with big, juicy, delicious berries, and I used to pick as many as I wanted for pies. Of course I remember the Fourth of July parade with the picnic, the games, and the fireworks. It was great that Garrett Park had these kinds of small town activities.

In the winter, I remember attending Christmas parties at the town hall. A couple of times we had ice storms, and one time it iced so thoroughly that we could slide all the way down Weymouth Street on pieces of cardboard. Then my dad, who had to get to work, came out and shoveled sand on the road and I was so mad. Sometimes Rock Creek would freeze over and I remember sliding in our boots on the frozen creek. When it snowed, we could sled on Weymouth Street and a few times we went to St. Angela's hall. One time when I was in high school, Carl Pope took me sledding at night on that hill on the other side of Strathmore (Donnelly's Hill), and we were the only ones there. It was very beautiful out in the snow at night.

Probably the most remarkable thing about the town was the fact that it closed the streets to the surrounding developments. When I tell people that story, they can hardly believe it, and I can hardly believe it, even now. It was Ed Friedman and Donal McLaughlin who made it possible for Weymouth Street to be closed off from Parkwood Apartments. Ed was the lawyer and Donal was the architect, and they worked together to make that happen. The town also fought to keep the post office absolutely pivotal as the town center. I remember going there with my mother to get the mail, and people were exchanging news with each other and making plans. It was where people met, and it played a major role in the town's unique community identity.

Because I was such a huge reader, the library was a major part of my life. I was petrified of Mrs. Bunker, the gorgon librarian lady, who told me I couldn't take adult books out of the little library. The first book I tried to take out was the most innocuous book – a true account of a woman who had tuberculosis and had to stay in bed for a year. When my mother heard this she marched to the library and told Mrs. Bunker in no uncertain terms that her daughter was allowed to check out books from the adult section.

I have fond memories of Marguerite Murray, who was also a librarian. She came to one of my elementary school classes, and she read us the riddle chapter from *The Hobbit*. It was only later in high school, when Carl Pope introduced me to *The Lord of the Rings* books, that I realized they must be by the same author.

When we first moved to Garrett Park, the addition to the school had just been built. Oxford Street wasn't completely paved, and I walked to and from school partially on a dirt and gravel road. I remember meeting Mrs. Duey for the first time. My mother was very impressed with her, and thought she was a wonderful teacher. When the elementary school first started serving lunches, they were prepared by mothers in the town, resulting in unusually high quality cafeteria food. Parents often substituted for absent teachers, which was mortifying when it was your parent's turn. My mom substituted at the school at one point, and she was a Girl Scout leader, but once she started working, she didn't volunteer as much. As more women started going to work, the volunteer pools gradually began to dry up.

I had Mrs. Sutherland for two years in a row, for both third and fourth grade. The first year she was wonderful, but the second year was terrible for me. She terrified me, especially about math, and she ruined me for math to this day. She used to give us quizzes where we would fold over our paper and add columns of numbers. I was so scared that I couldn't do it at all, and I just made the answers up. One time she called on me and made me read my answers out, which upset and humiliated me terribly. I actually developed symptoms of being sick, and I stayed home for days. I think my mother knew what was going on and she wisely let me stay home. I remember this other teacher from another year, a younger woman who couldn't control the class. The class that year was just chaos, and even her physical classroom was chaos. We moved that year into a new room, and I thought maybe the new room would be nice and orderly, and I told her so. She said she hoped so.

After Garrett Park Elementary, I went to Kensington Junior High and then to Walter Johnson. I had good

experiences in both junior high and high school. I had Mr. Abel for civics, and he was a wonderful and a very creative teacher. At one point, when some kid in class stole some other kid's shoe and tied it to a desk, Mr. Abel stopped everything and had us have a trial. He did things like that all the time. But what was really special about him for me was that he recognized something in me. It started when he gave us a test, and when he gave the graded test back, he held back my paper and read it to the whole class, saying, "Here's an example of how it should be done." I had not only given factual answers but I backed them up with evidence. I was so happy that I didn't sleep that night. He then gave me an extra assignment: he had me read the poem by Stephen Vincent Benet, "John Brown's Body" and write a report about it. This really gave a big boost for my confidence in school, and in this way Mr. Abel probably changed my life.

I started attending Walter Johnson in autumn of 1960. This was a time when the county was spending more money on education than any other county in the country except for maybe Scarsdale County in New York, and Walter Johnson High School was one of the beneficiaries of that spending. I was very lucky to grow up in Montgomery County when I did.

I graduated from Walter Johnson in June of 1963, and Martin Luther King's "March on Washington for Jobs and Freedom" took place in August of that year. Towards the end of our senior year, Carl Pope had given me flyers to distribute about the coming march. For putting the flyers on people's desks in my English class, I was sent to the principal's office. Because I was such a good girl, this was the only time I was ever sent to the principal's, and I felt righteous about what I had done. I didn't think I had done anything wrong, and Carl came and defended me. The principal had no idea what was just about to come down on him and other authority figures who were trying to protect the status quo.

Of course I attended Martin Luther King's march, though we were too far away to really hear the speech. My dad had been very nervous that we were going that day. He was worried that there would be riots, and he gave us instructions about how to get away from a mob.

I left Garrett Park in fall of 1963, when I went off to college. First I attended Oberlin College, and then I transferred to Brandeis University, majoring in English. I married Carl Pope (also from Garrett Park), and then we returned briefly to the town and went into the Peace Corps right after college. We were in India with the Peace Corps for about a year and a half, and when we returned to the U.S. we lived in D.C. for a time before moving to the San Francisco Bay area in California, where I have been ever since. I was a consultant for many years, working for foundations and collaborative social service programs, childcare programs, and senior programs. For years I have done volunteer political activism, first with the single payer health care issue and now with climate change. Being in California and working to address climate change issues gives you some hope, because California is a leader in the country for addressing climate change.

I think Garrett Park did influence my political leanings and activism. Living in Garrett Park was like being nurtured politically. The adults around me were almost all liberal. I can remember seeing our neighbor, Sylvia Lichtenstein, getting off a bus and talking about going to a peace march, and in my memory she is always wearing high heels. Being in this place where people were so political and so liberal, it was just kind of in the air. Though my parents weren't particularly politically active, during the time when I was growing up everyone was intensely interested in politics, probably because we were living so close to Washington. Later, when I lived in Capitol Hill during the summer of the Watergate hearings, we were friends with people who were staffers to key congressmen and senators.

There's a funny story that tells you something about that Weymouth Street neighborhood. At some point after I had left for college, the Adlers, who lived in the house next to the McLaughlins, sold their house to an African American family, a mother and her grown daughter. They were the first black family to live in Garrett Park. That was a big deal, and the Weymouth Street liberals were so excited, because Garrett Park was at that time not diverse. The whole street gathered for a welcoming party. They wanted to welcome these new neighbors with open arms, and when they got to know them, they were surprised to discover that they were Republicans!

The thing that was so incredible about Garrett Park was that it had this small town ethos, and people were pouring time and energy into making it a community, but because it was really so close to D.C. it didn't have that hermetically sealed, small-minded quality that small towns can develop. It wasn't a little place separate from a bigger world. You could get away and go to the city, you could spend time there. And while I'm sure Garrett Park was rife with infidelities and scandals, just like any other community, I was a kid living in a kid's world, and nothing like that ever came to my attention.

To this day, doing things together with other people is very important to me, and I think that comes both from my parents and from growing up in Garrett Park. The town set a model in my mind of community, the idea that people should join together to make something happen. The closing off of the streets was so important to keeping that special character. Back when Garrett Park was first being incorporated, the town refused to join the county sewer system, and they wanted to keep their septic tanks. That spirit of fierce defiance, that feistiness and stubborn individual nature of the town, thumbing your nose at the rest of the world, it's very endearing.

I know the town is different now; it was already changing over the years as more and more women went to work, and there were fewer volunteers available to maintain the town activities. I wonder if any of what made Garrett Park so unique is still true. I hope it has diversified, although I'm sure the housing costs are astronomical, which creates a real barrier to families of color.

It was such a great gift to grow up in Garrett Park. The woods, the freedom, the time spent exploring and playing outside - these things definitely shaped me and gave me the beginning of that link to the natural world that has always been so essential to me. I was able to grow up in a place that had the best without the worst of a small town. The city was right there. It was exciting, stimulating and safe.

(Parts written by Judy Pope)

SALLY BROWN

Garrett Park was really a great place to grow up. I'm sorry that other kids don't get to grow up that way. I loved it when the streets were not paved; it was so wonderful to have that feeling in my bare feet of walking to the post office on soft mud. Now you can pay money for people to take you into the forest and you can stand there in your bare feet. "Forest Bathing" they call it. I'm not paying for it! Today I live in the town that is surrounded by country, and I love that I can just take a bus to the wilderness area. So even though it is very different from the town I grew up in, at least I can still get away into nature.

I grew up in Garrett Park from the beginning, living there from birth to when I was about twenty one. I was born July 3, 1945, in a hospital in D.C. I had two older brothers, Tom and Terry, and two younger sisters, Rosemary and Kathleen, so I was right in the middle. Tom was four years older than I was and Terry was three years older. Rosemary was four years younger and Kathy was about five years younger than Rosemary.

My mother, Ann Brown, was involved with Montgomery County politics and my father, George Brown, worked for the Department of Labor. Prior to moving to Garrett Park, my family had been living in D.C. in an apartment, and my parents wanted to find a place to raise a family and build a home. The lot in Garrett Park was being sold to railroad employees, and I think my father was an ex-employee of the railroad in some capacity. My parents built the house we lived in, and moved in as soon as it was built. My second brother, Terry, was born during the building of the house. When they built the house, they thought the street was going to run where it is now the back of the house, so the part that was designed as the front ended up in the back. This made the house a lot more interesting.

When I was little the Sanders family lived in the house next door just above us. They had the first TV in the neighborhood, and I remember that we used to watch Howdy Doody at their house. This was around 1950, and it really was an event to watch TV. You had to promise to be good and behave and walk in quietly and sit down and watch the program. Later, when I was in about fourth grade the Pope's moved into that house. In the house on the other side of us lived the Wagners. He was a sign painter and they had five daughters. The Powells and the Normans lived cattycornered from us, on the corner of Clyde and Rokeby, and the Antosz family lived across the street. Down at the very end of Rokeby was a wooded area, and Mr. and Mrs. Wells lived there.

My early memories are of a lot of kids and a lot of work. We all had chores. Mine was cleaning the bathroom. We had a schedule for who did dishes and a certain way we had to do the dishes. I usually ended up helping my mother in the kitchen. My father had a big vegetable garden in the back. I have lots of memories of picking the vegetables, bringing them back into the kitchen, cleaning them and getting them ready to cook.

Every weekend my father was out there gardening. We helped him, not because we had to but because, I at least, liked doing it. I babysat my younger siblings a lot. We raked lots of leaves, since there were so many trees.

The streets were still dirt and they felt really soft on your bare feet. It was a lot wilder than it is now; there was a lot more woods, which provided lots of places to explore, so that is what I did. You usually told your mother before you left where you were headed, and you were expected home at a certain hour for dinner, but other than that, you were free to roam. There was hell to pay if you were late for a meal. We always had the dinner hour at a certain time.

Boys and girls played together as long as the girls could keep up. We used to play in the woods across the track before they developed it over there. We had regular little paths, and we could catch crawdads and play in the water and gather water crabs and build bridges and play. At first I would go over with my brothers and their friends, but after being "treated like a girl" I would start going over by myself. Those were times of just being by myself in the woods, looking at bugs and exploring paths in the woods. The paths weren't real trails; they were kind of minimal. I got lost a number of times, but I always got myself out of it. I look back at it now and I think, "My God, no parent today would allow their child to do that." I don't know if my mother knew what I was up to. That just isn't a possibility these days - children just don't do that. I don't know what they do! I remember when they brought the bulldozers, and how this woods that seemed so endless was suddenly gone. Randolph Hills replaced it.

I was a tree climber, and dogwoods were among my favorite trees to climb. I always thought of climbing trees as a boy thing to do, and that's why I did it. Boys seemed to be having a lot more fun than girls in those days. There were no sports teams for girls to join. Boys could play baseball and girls couldn't. The Little League was boys only and so was the Rifle Club. I wanted to join, and my brothers said you can't, you're a girl. I think later on they opened it up and I didn't still join it, because my brothers told me I wouldn't be wanted. I never joined the Girl Scouts, and somehow I never fit it to those organized groups. But I did enjoy the activities offered at the town community center.

In the old days we really did know everybody in the town. I was a very curious child, and I had to know everything about everybody. I just got out and found people in the town to play with. I had to go out to look for girls, because there weren't many girls close to my age in the immediate neighborhood. One of my best friends was Kathy Murphy. She lived on Montrose, where it branches off from Argyle, in a big old house at the top of the hill there. She was about my age, and she had an older sister. Both of them were hell- raisers, and their mother was really neat. We used to do things that would just make her older sister scream like tying up a bed sheet on the four-poster bed with her sister's scarfs to make it really nice. Her sister was always yelling at us. I remember her mom painted the kitchen floor black, and then she spattered paint all over the floor in different colors, and I thought that was wonderful. When it snowed we made snow cones; we'd go out and get the snow and her mom would put syrup on top. And we pulled taffy there for the first time in my life. That was a fun place to be.

The people across the street from Kathy had another big house with beautiful, beautiful gardens and a gazebo. If you asked permission from somebody in the yard you could sit in the gazebo. It was just a little gazebo, but it because of it, I always knew what a gazebo was and I always thought they were great to sit in. You find people who don't even know what gazebos are, much less have the experience of sitting in one. I don't think I was ever in that house, but the yard was beautiful.

Joyce Reynolds lived up on Kenilworth, and she was a good friend. I had a nice strong connection with that family and ended up always showing up for dessert. Dinners were timed in those days, so I knew when to show up. If I finished my dinner, did my chores fast, and zipped out of the house, I could make it to the Reynolds in time for dessert. We laughed a lot about that. The way you entered someone's house is you opened the door and you yelled, "Is anybody home?", and you waited and if you heard a response, then you'd say, "Is Joyce home?" or they would say, "Who are you?"

I also visited with adults. Amee Booth lived in a little white house on Albemarle with her husband, a great big man named Jack. I remember that she had this little dog that had some kind of skin disease. I would go visit with Amee and she would make me drinks. I would always have coke or something and we would sit and talk about stuff, and she would smoke like a chimney.

Then there was the lady with the goose, who lived just down the street from us on Rokeby. Well, I think the lady who owned the goose was Lucy, or maybe that was the goose's name. She and her husband, they were two nice people. It was thought that he was an Indian (American) or part Indian. I never knew what an Indian would look like, but now that I know, I think, yes, he could've been an Indian. He was a very strong, big man, and she was a nice lady, and they hung a flag out Fourth of July all the time. The kids in the neighborhood were all terrified of that damn goose because it bit. So we never really went there a lot, because first you had to get past the goose.

Marie Young lived in a house at the top of Argyle. If you stopped off there when you were sledding on Donnelly's Hill, she would make you hot chocolate. Marie was a good buddy of mine, and I used to hang out with her a lot as a kid. I'd stop in to see her regularly; she was one of those people I could sit and talk with. She used to sit out front on that porch, or actually it's more of a cement slab, and I would sit and chat with her, and you could watch flying squirrels from there. She always had a candy dish. She would always tell me, just take candy if you want it, but my mother would always say, you may not have any candy unless it's offered to you – it was a contradiction to a young child who was trying to figure out how to get the candy. I remember the house had these big smooth polished wood floors. They had Chesapeake Bay Retrievers, and Mr. Young was a photographer or artist or something and she always used to make fun of him. He was a nice guy though. He had a studio upstairs and it was always neat to go peak at something, and there were pictures of naked people - it was exciting.

I remember when Clyde Hall started the Bugle. It was a one-sheet that he pretty much wrote. But then he got a bunch of us kids to be reporters and to go out and sell it. We would sell it door-to-door for a nickel, and we got to keep three cents. Clyde went broke, but us kids had plenty of money! Lee Chisholm lived up on Kenilworth. He started a garden club for children, and he had kids that would come over to his house. He was a nice man who had nasty Dalmatians. They would just bite you at the drop of a hat, so he would always have to put the dogs away when the kids came over.

Haile Chisholm also lived on Kenilworth. I remember that one time my dad had a fight with him over something to do with the oil business Haile owned. He was a big, bodacious man. When his daughter started wearing nail polish he had a fit about it. She said she was going to do it anyway, so he painted his toes with red nail polish and walked around town barefoot just to give her a hard time. He wanted to embarrass her.

I knew Lina Penn and I knew Mr. Penn. They lived next door to the general store and the post office. You would go in the store and there was a candy counter, and it opened up into this wood stove. Mr. Penn would sit in a rocking chair next to the wood stove and he was pretty old. He wasn't a frightening character. To me, he was sort of something of interest. He didn't hear very well and he would talk to you and you would talk to him but he couldn't really communicate very well. But this is the story I love to tell: You would go and buy Bazooka bubble gum, and it had two little marks in the bubble gum. I decided that was because Mr. Penn bit the bubble gum before he sold it to us kids. That didn't seem reasonable but that was about the only explanation I could think of. After Mr. Penn died, there weren't any marks on the bubble gum, so it proved it.

Right near the post office, there's a road that leads across the tracks. You weren't supposed to go down there, but finally, I was so curious, I went down a couple of times and there were always a lot of automobiles and some men hanging around who lived there. Mr. Dove, the old, old man who lived down there, whose son's relatives lived there too, was the school crossing guard at Strathmore. He was ancient. I can still remember him to this day. He had big feet, you know, hard shoes and he was hunched over and skinny and wore a cap and would slosh out there and cross the kids and slosh back, and he did it forever. He was an old guy but he had bright eyes and he wasn't like Mr. Penn. You could talk to him and sometimes he didn't hear you too well, but he would talk back. He was related to the people who lived directly across from the post office up the hill. He was very old, just a bag of bones. That was old Mr. Dove.

I remember when they decided to build the swimming pool. There was a lot of talk about doing it and they decided to do it but they wanted to save money. As I remember it, we would all go on Saturdays to dig the hole for the pool. I remember going to do stuff, and it being a big muddy mess and the guys digging. Maybe they were just leveling it off or something. I can't imagine that the town actually dug the actual hole, but that's how I remember it. When they put the pool in it became known very quickly by my brothers, and then by me, that the quickest way to get to the pool is down the track. The question was could you make it down there when the trains were coming. I did it once or twice but it felt real uncomfortable.

I started going to the pool when I was eight. I was on the swim team, which was one of the first teams girls could join. Pam Payne and I were the captains of the swim team. I remember getting up early, early in the morning on summer mornings and jumping on my blue and white bike with fat tires, peddling down with a towel around my neck. I would ride down and around the post office and around on Montrose and down the hill that swooped and up by the Day's house. My first job was at the swimming pool. I was twelve or thirteen years old, working at the desk, making sure everybody signed in. I was good at being efficient. We would also clean the bath houses. As I got older I got to be a lifeguard.

One place I remember going to was the town library, located next to Garrett Park Elementary. Mrs. Bunker, the librarian, coughed like you wouldn't believe because she was such a heavy smoker. She wouldn't let us take out certain books. I remember a girl named Cassandra Kelly wanting to take out some books which Mrs. Bunker didn't want her to read. Mrs. Bunker was always pretty nice to me because I read a lot, and I never questioned her right to tell me not to read a book. She didn't frighten me, but she had authority, and I respected her authority.

Of course I remember community events. The big event was the 4rd of July, which was the day after my birthday. As a kid I just thought "This whole thing is for me." On the 3rd we started getting our bikes ready for the parade, and it was a really big deal. As kids we did our own decorating. No adult did it for us or even helped us. We had to figure out where to get stuff and what to do with it. You would get up early in the morning and you would go down to the parade. I don't know where it started but it seemed to me we would start at the top of Rokeby and make our way down to the post office or to the park for a while. After the parade we ended up at the pool and then we would go to the recreation center where they had all these activities and games, and a big town potluck. I was certain that all those cakes at the end were my one day late birthday cakes - two days of birthday celebration for me! It was just great, and the games were fabulous.

Halloween was another great event. You didn't go buy a costume, and your mother didn't make one for you. You just put together your own costume, found some people to go out with, and went door to door getting candy. It was just fabulous. The whole town was the neighborhood, so I just found a friend and went all over town. Joyce Reynolds had a birthday right around Halloween, and her family turned their house into this really scary place.

The center of activity was Garrett Park Elementary, but I didn't go there, I went to Holy Redeemer, in Kensington. This made me a bit of an outsider. I don't remember having any friends in the town who attended Holy Redeemer. After Holy Redeemer, in ninth grade I went to Holy Cross for a year and then I put my foot down and said "I'm going to public school."

The first thing I had to do was figure out how to get to school – my mother wasn't going to drive me. I took the bus. I remember that first day, taking the bus and being scared as hell, and I remember arriving at the office, terrified, not knowing what was going on and what I was doing, and Andy Sonner came along and said "What are you doing here?" and I told him I wanted to go to school here and I probably broke out in tears.

Anyway, he got me through it, and it was at Walter Johnson, in tenth grade, that I started to have more fun, because that's when I started getting to be friends with more people in Garrett Park. We had a very closely knit group in high school, kids who lived in Garrett Park. Pam Payne became a friend, and Joyce Reynolds, Chris Woodwell, and Susan Kizer, who were all a little older than me. I was friends with John Hall and John Guernsey, and there were people who weren't from Garrett Park but who hung out with that group. We loved ourselves, as many teenagers do. We partied and we would go down to Washington for music and entertainment. I also became friends with Carl Pope who lived next door, and who used to help me with my Latin.

After high school, I left home searching for adventure. I wanted to see and do everything in the world. I went to the University of Maryland for a while, and I went to the New School for Social Research in New York City for a year or two. After that, I moved to Washington and worked for a political activist priest for a while. Then I took off for Europe, the smallest of the Balearic Islands in the Mediterranean, to find a friend, and found one and decided not to go back. I came back to the states and went to the macrobiotic school in Boston and then I moved back to Europe, and opened up a macrobiotic restaurant in Nice. Next, I went to Istanbul, met a man, had a baby and moved back to Montana which was where he was from. We started a natural food distribution system here, long before anyone else was doing it, starting out in Whitefish, Montana and ending up in Missoula. I am still living in Missoula. In Montana you do whatever you can to make a living. I found work with an international science firm, and I became an indexer. I've been doing it for three years.

A little over twenty years ago I began to practice Zen Buddhism. I've stuck with Zen and with yoga as a physical activity. I think this is more my way of being of service, by starting with myself. Because my mother was so very politically active, so involved with the Democratic Party and activist causes, I grew up stuffing envelopes, going door to door, making phone calls. I have memories of being in a picket line at Glen Echo to oppose segregation. I was ten or twelve at the time, and my mother made me join the picket line. We succeeded in getting Glen Echo integrated with our picketing. Later, I was also politically active on my own, but I was conflicted about whether I was doing it because it was expected of me and my family, or because I really believed it is the best way to change the world. I still volunteer for political causes, but I don't necessarily believe it is my way to go. I have had to learn who I am, to discover my own form of giving back to the world.

The world I grew up in has really changed, as has the town, of course. It's really spiffy now and it takes a lot of money to live there. It used to be that people from all kinds of economic backgrounds could live in Garrett Park, at least as long as they were white. Back then there were no black people in the town. In my memory, black people came in on the bus to work and went home on the bus at night, though one of my closest relationships was with the woman who came to work in my mother's house. I loved her and formed a very close bond with her.

Garrett Park was really a great place to grow up. I'm sorry that other kids don't get to grow up that way. I loved it when the streets were not paved; it was so wonderful to have that feeling in my bare feet of walking to the post office on soft mud. Now you can pay money for people to take you into the forest and you can stand there in your bare feet. "Forest Bathing" they call it. I'm not paying for it! Today I live in the town that is surrounded by country, and I love that I can just take a bus to the wilderness area. So even though it is very different from the town I grew up in, at least I can still get away into nature.

(This narrative is excerpted in part from an interview conducted by Barbara Shidler on July 7, 1995, courtesy of the Garrett Park Town Archives, and in part from a phone interview conducted by Lee Pope.)

CARL POPE

No doubt I was impacted by the experience of enjoying all those wild places as an eight year old in Garrett Park, and seeing how they had completely disappeared by the time I was eighteen. I think my awareness of the environmental narrative of overdevelopment came from watching these old farms vanish and become suburbs.

My parents were Barbara and Roger Pope. They met and were married in Ann Arbor, Michigan right before my father shipped out with the Navy during World War II. I was born in San Francisco, in 1945, right after the war, and my younger sister, Lee was born in Michigan in 1947. Our family moved to the D.C. area from Michigan when I was three or four, and we lived in Silver Spring until the spring of 1954, which is when we moved to Garrett Park. My father, a research lawyer, worked for the federal government, and my mother did clerical work for various organizations that were connected with higher education.

When we first moved to the town, we lived in a small rented house on Montrose Avenue. We were only there for about six months. I have this first memory of the time when we had just moved in and were fixing up the house: I remember lying on the porch and reading a newspaper, reading about how the French had just surrendered their fortress at Dien Bien Phu, in what was the beginning of the Vietnam War.

Roger and Barbara Pope - 1941

My first impression of Garrett Park was "bucolic", though I probably wouldn't have used that word at the time. In Silver Spring we had lived in an apartment on a big highway. It wasn't in a real city or anything - there was park across the road - but by comparison, Garrett Park felt like the country. You had single family homes, the town was very shady with lots of big old trees, and the streets were very quiet. I remember we had a mulberry tree in the back yard and as it was late spring the tree was in fruit, and I went out back, and we were actually able to eat mulberries from that tree, though many of the mulberries had little white worms in them. But I remember eating mulberries in my back yard and this was the first time I had ever eaten fruit from my own house, my own back yard.

We moved there at the end of the school year. I went to school on my first day, and was introduced to Mrs. Sutherland. I remember walking into the classroom and Mrs. Sutherland had her students working extremely hard. For the first time in my life I was having a hard time keeping up in school, and I was having nightmares, and insomnia, and I had a lot of anxiety about school for the next six weeks, although later on, when I had her the following year for fourth grade, I got along very well with Mrs. Sutherland. For example, at the school I

Third Grade

had come from we were only half way into learning cursive handwriting, while at Garrett Park Elementary, everybody was basically prohibited from using block printing. I had to learn cursive in a week, which I have since used as an excuse for my terrible handwriting. So I really struggled with school at first.

Another early memory I have is that the Garrett Park swimming pool was opening that year, and I was very excited by the fact that we would be having a community swimming pool. Since it was a co-op pool, my family spent a lot of time there that summer, painting and doing clean-up and things like that, and I got to help. I doubt I was actually very useful, but I did whatever I was asked to do, and I was really happy to be helping out.

Soon my parents bought a house at 11303 Rokeby Avenue and we moved there. I remember two things that struck me right away about the new house. I had this big attic all to myself, and at the opposite end of the attic from where my bedroom was we had this big exhaust fan, and my bed was right under the window, so that there was a very strong breeze pulled by the exhaust fan that blew right over me in the heat of the summer. Because it was in the attic where no one ever went, I had my own private realm and I could keep it as messy as I wanted, which was pretty messy.

The second thing that I remember was discovering that there were railroad tracks and a railroad right of way right there behind our big back yard. There were also a lot of berries – blueberries and raspberries - growing back there as I remember. I used to pick the blueberries, and my mother would make blueberry pancakes on Sunday morning.

Those railroad tracks had all sorts of opportunities for mischief. At some point I began to play with my sister and other kids from the neighborhood down on the tracks. We gathered pieces of metal, things like railroad spikes that were scattered along the tracks, and periodically we would try to derail trains by putting stuff on the tracks. Of course we were down at the bottom of these steep hills on either side of the tracks, so if we had succeeded we would have been crushed along with the train, but we didn't think of that, and we didn't think of the consequences at all, in fact. I guess you could say this was a form of "pre-awareness" delinquency. We really didn't know we were doing anything seriously wrong.

In our immediate neighborhood, the Roberts family lived across the street, with two kids a few years younger than me, Suzanne and Tommy. The Lutenbergers, a Pennsylvania Dutch family, lived next door on one side, and the Browns, who had five kids (Tommy, Terry, Sally, Rosemary, and Kathy), lived on the other side. Eventually, our friends the Thomases moved in a few blocks down. Sherry and Sam Thomas were hanging around a lot.

Overall, I had a good time at Garrett Park Elementary, at least once I got used to Mrs. Sutherland. I was good at the academic part of school, but in that era it wasn't such a dominant part of what parents or the school expected. I remember when I first came to the school being very impressed that Steve Sonner was such a fantastic artist – he could draw really well. But he was also good at baseball, which made him a star. Among the boys, baseball was the main sport, and everybody was evaluated by how good they were at it. This was unfortunate for me, since I was no good at baseball. For some of the sports I was actually not so bad, but due to my lack of skill in baseball it was assumed that I was not athletic. As a result I was always picked last for any team. We didn't only play team sports though. I remember we used to play "Capture the Flag" in the woods behind the elementary school.

Something else I remember about school, since I grew up during the cold war, was the duck and cover air raid drills in the halls. I didn't take these air raid drills that seriously – it was just something adults made you do. After all, we were made to do many things that didn't make a whole lot of sense.

In the summer I remember playing out in the yard, chasing and capturing fireflies. I remember running around with other kids in the neighborhood, playing with the Roberts kids, and the Thomases. We played "hide and seek" in the yard, and after school we played football. I really liked the swimming pool, and I was on the swim team. I was good as a sprinter, but not as a long distance swimmer. I enjoyed the swim team, and I went on to become a life guard during the first or second summer of high school.

Some other happy memories are of raking leaves in the autumn, jumping into leaf piles, and burning the leaves, and the smell of smoke that was at that time a huge part of the autumn season. I also have some great memories of camping with my Kensington Boy Scout troop.

In winter the whole town went sledding on Donnelly's Hill. Sociologically and economically Garrett Park was just a suburb, in that no one actually worked in Garrett Park except for the post office and general store, and everybody else commuted. But culturally it operated like a small town, and it was tribal like a small town, and like a tribe, it was hierarchical. To us, Garrett Park was on top and Garrett Park Estates, the suburb next door with much more recently built houses, was on the bottom. And we would not let kids from Garrett Park Estates use Donnelly's Hill. My sister, Lee, doesn't remember this, so it may have been just among the boys that this happened. If they tried to sled there we would chase them away, as long as the adults weren't there to prevent this. We were the aristocracy.

Something I really liked about Garrett Park was that there was a lot of consistency, and kids weren't moving in and out all the time. It felt like a very solid and stable cohesive community. We had our own rituals and traditions, our own fire-

Carl (on left) as Bert in *All My Sons*

works, our own library, our own elementary school, our own sledding hill, town council and mayor. My father was in the Garrett Players and I got to participate in a few plays. I played the youngest brother in *All My Sons* and I think maybe I was one of the kids in *Papa is All*.

I also really liked that there were wild areas still around there. There was a patch of wineberries (a type of wild raspberry) on the way to the pool. I would bike over to the pool and on my way home I would stuff myself with these berries. But I never saw a deer in Garrett Park, and I don't know why there weren't any.

Even as a kid, I was pretty politically oriented. There were a bunch of people who were Democrats and a bunch of people who were Republicans, but you wouldn't necessarily have known who was which – it seemed kind of arbitrary. There was a brief period when I decided to be a Republican, although my parents were Democrats. When I was in second grade, I spent the summer in Old Greenwich with my aunt and uncle, and they were Republicans, and due to their influence I decided to become a Republican. And so I was the leader of the Republican faction at Garrett Park Elementary, and Martha Honey was the leader of the Democratic faction.

But it wasn't a very big deal, the difference between the two. When we got to junior high school things began to heat up a bit, but it wasn't until we got to high school that politics became a big deal.

I remember just after we moved to Garrett Park and the McCarthy Era was going on, and Joseph Welch denounced Joe McCarthy, and my mother made me come in and watch the hearings. While I had no idea what was going on, obviously it was important to my parents. In fact, the only reason my atheist/agnostic parents ever took us to church was that Reverend Powell Davies, the Unitarian minister in D.C., was one of the few people who was willing to publicly denounce McCarthy. So just during that period in American history our parents took to attending the Unitarian Church, and we attended the Sunday school there. This was the only time we went to any church. Actually, we had a number of friends in Garrett Park who were on one of McCarthy's lists. But at the time, I had no real awareness of what McCarthyism and that side of the 1950's was about.

I do have the following memory: One afternoon, when I was about twelve, I was home alone raking leaves in the back yard. This FBI agent came along and asked if my parents were home, and I said they weren't, and he said "Ok, I'm doing this security check on one of the neighbors and we'd like to interview you", which I thought was kind of peculiar. And he proceeded to ask me how well I knew this family, and I explained that I only knew them because I had walked their daughter to school one year. And then he wanted to know if I had any reason to doubt their loyalty to the United States, and I said "No…" He wanted to know if I knew if they ever had parties where communists were present, and I said "No…" Then he wanted to know if I knew of any parties where homosexuals were present, and I said "No…." Clearly I wasn't going to know anything, and I thought the whole thing was absurd, but I supposed he had to get an interview and earn his quota.

The changing political times were very much an influence on me as I grew up. When I was in high school, in the early days of SNNC (Student Non-violent Coordinating Committee), my parents hosted a fund raiser at our house featuring Marion Barry. At that time he was an organizer for SNNC, not a particularly well-known person. This was around 1962, I think. Andy Sonner, my high school history teacher, was very big on the Mexican Revolution, and he had a definite radicalizing effect on me. A few years later, when I was in college, I spent most of the summer of 1965 volunteering for SNCC, registering black voters in West Helena, Arkansas.

I graduated from Walter Johnson High School and went off to college in 1963. After college, my first wife

(Judy King, also from Garrett Park) and I joined the Peace Corps, which was probably partly due to the influence of growing up in the Washington D.C. area, during the 1950s and 1960s. We were stationed in Bihar, in north eastern India. After the Peace Corps I worked in D.C. for "Zero Population Growth", and then, when I was hired as a lobbyist for the Sierra Club, we moved out to Oakland, California with our two young sons. I was with the Sierra Club for forty-three years, and eventually became the Executive Director there. Today I am still working on environmental issues, primarily as a consultant on clean energy and economic development. No doubt I was impacted by the experience of enjoying all those wild places as an eight year old in Garrett Park, and seeing how they had completely disappeared by the time I was eighteen. I think my awareness of the environmental narrative of overdevelopment came from watching these old farms vanish and become suburbs. So I think that is one way that Garrett Park had quite a bit to do with what I ended up doing with my life.

Garrett Park was always kind of an ornery place. It was not at all a conformist kind of environment. So I have to assume that it had a significant impact on pushing me further in the direction I would have gone in anyway. I was last there a few years ago. I went to see the house I grew up in, and the house was gone, had been torn down and replaced. But Garrett Park was still Garrett Park. The guy

Pope house after addition

who had torn it down had done so because my parents, in adding on to our house, had constructed the addition so that the living room intruded on the lot next door. This meant that the lot next door could never be developed. And so his response was to tear down the house. He wanted to build two houses, but the city wouldn't give him the permit to build on the second lot. So he put up one very large house instead, but he didn't get away with crowding that second house in there, so that shows that Garrett Park is still Garrett Park.

ROB FREER

It's crazy that kids are no longer allowed to walk around by themselves. When we were kids, adults weren't continually managing our time, and we had lots of freedom to direct our own lives and to figure things out for ourselves. I think that kind of childhood freedom, which is so rare today, provides kids with a really important and valuable learning experience. For me, growing up in a town like Garrett Park played a huge role in preparing me for life.

My parents, Charles and Ruby Freer, moved to Garrett Park in April of 1950. Our house, built in 1888, was at 10934 Montrose Ave. Back in 1950 the area surrounding the town was still quite rural. It was understandable that my grandparents, who lived in N.E. Washington D.C. near Catholic University, couldn't believe that my parents were moving so far into the boondocks.

My father had grown up in Washington, D.C. and my mother was from South Carolina. Her family had moved to Washington in 1931 when she was eighteen. My father's father worked for the Bureau of Engraving and Printing for fifty years, which I always found to be an incredible accomplishment. He had told my father that he would pay for him to go to college when he graduated from high school, but if he didn't go to college then, later he would be on his own. My father didn't start college right away, and so he had to pay his own way, finally starting at Georgetown University before the war. When the war started he went into the Navy and picked up at Georgetown when he got back. At that point he was married and had two children and was working, so that was a pretty tough row to hoe. My older sister, Sandy, was born in September of 1945, and I was born just over a year later in D.C. on December 5th, 1946. My brother, John, was born in 1952.

My father worked for a theater chain, and then in 1952, like so many others in Garrett Park, he went to work for the government. He became a budget officer in the Navy, working at the Pentagon, where he worked for his whole career. In 1974 he had a heart attack and retired early at the end of that year. My mother was at home when my sister, brother and I were growing up. Later, when I was in high school, she started working at the post office. Mrs. Parsons was the postmistress, and our neighbor Mrs. Newhall also worked there, as well as Mrs. Ofenstein.

The real bonus about growing up in Garrett Park was that you could just roam around wherever you wanted. When I was a kid we liked to play behind the house across the street from our house on Montrose, in this vacant field. The house belonged first to the Planks and then to Mr. Hardesty, who let us play in the field, and so we spent a lot of time playing there. We played baseball and this other game called "six grounders, three flies". One person would be up, and a couple of people would be out in the field, and you would just hit. If you caught three flies you were up, or if you caught six grounders you were up. Behind the field was a creek and behind that a woods that went all the way to the railroad tracks. We weren't allowed to go up there, and we didn't go out of our way to play on the railroad tracks, but at some point we would end up on the tracks and then someone would call your mother and tell her that they had spotted us playing there.

We played a lot at the tennis courts, sometimes playing tennis, sometimes playing a form of baseball there with tennis rackets. And we also played basketball at the basketball courts. At some point, when your parents gave you permission to cross Strathmore by yourself, there were all these baseball and softball games you could play. We could walk to the community center, where there was a coke machine with cokes for five cents. Or we would go to the library, which had air conditioning, which was a big deal on hot summer days.

I was pretty close friends with Timmy Honey, who lived on the other side of Strathmore prior to Timmy's family moving to Westport, Connecticut around the beginning of his fifth grade year. There was a whole group of kids – the Sonners, the Lambs, the Wilsons, the Honeys, the Modines, and the Wilpurs, who would play White Flag in the Honey's big yard. We would use the whole yard, and sometimes the whole neighborhood for the game. Across the street from the Honey's and next door to the Wilson's lived a lady named Miss Rucker who had a cow in her yard, so at that time Garrett Park still felt a little bit rural.

I became really good friends with Tam Wilson, who was about eighteen months older than me. He was like a big brother to me, and that's who I mainly hung out with. I also liked playing on the basketball court with Ron Horn, David Crichton, and Mike Garrett, although they were all a grade below me in school. I played Little League Baseball with the Gnats, and as I got older I played with the Co-op Team (sponsored by the Co-op supermarket in Wheaton) coached by Tam Wilson's father, Tom.

The Fourth of July was always a lot of fun, something kids really looked forward to. The day started with a parade, which began at the school grounds and ended at the tennis courts, where I remember that they handed out free popsicles to all the kids. In the afternoon we got to watch dads from Garrett Park and Garrett Park Estates play softball. As you got older, around high school, you might even be invited to play in that game, and I remember that it was a big deal when Benny Gieser played in that game with the dads. Once it got dark we had the fireworks. There was a maintenance man from Parkside Apartments who sold firecrackers to us, and we would set them off throughout the day. The adults didn't sanction that, but we did it anyway. The Fourth of July was such an important yearly event, it always seemed like people from Garrett Park would try to get home at least twice a year, once for Christmas and once for the Fourth of July.

I believe that Garrett Park was the first community in Montgomery County to build a community swimming pool. My father was on the town council at the time and we became charter members of the pool. That was just a huge bonus for the neighborhood, to be able to have the pool. All the kids had swimming lessons at 8:30 in the morning and I still can remember what it felt like to jump into that freezing water. We could walk to the pool, down Clermont and then up an old road between these houses. I remember that the house on the left had a cow pasture for a back yard. I think the family who lived there was named King.

Though I really liked the pool, I wasn't much for being on the swimming team. But once I got to high school, my mother suggested that I take this water safety course at the pool, which turned out to be a really great thing for me. Ron Horn, Mike Garrett, David Crichton, and Brian Sherline were in that course with me. Later, when I had just finished my first year of college, Barbara Modine, who was at that time the pool manager, wrote me a letter asking me if I would work at the pool as a lifeguard. It was the summer of 1965, and Mike Garrett, Dave Crichton, Ron Horn, Karen Modine, Nancy Abrams, and I all worked at the pool. I worked as a life guard the first year and then I became an assistant manager.   Mrs. Modine moved on to manage a complex of pools in Glenmont, and I ended up working as assistant manager at the Glenmont pools. This was a really great experience for me.

I was able to earn my own money from a pretty early age. In third or fourth grade I had a paper route, first delivering a paper called *The Daily News* and then moving up to *The Washington Star*, which was an evening paper. Then I delivered *The Washington Post* one summer for somebody. I also cut grass for people in the neighborhood. Between shoveling snow, and delivering papers, and cutting grass, you could earn some spending money, and you could spend it at the little general store, where they had coolers filled with cold water with drinks in them. Having your own money, and going down there and getting a candy bar was a real treat.

Louie Karsh, who ran the store with his wife, took over the store, when I was about seven. When they bought the store they had a celebration right in the street in front of the store. I remember that it was early in the evening, and there were free hot dogs. My mother would send me to Louie's store to get the proverbial milk, eggs, and bread. They had a notebook with a page in it for keeping track of charges, and they would record your purchases in the notebook, and you would pay up once a month.

I could also earn money by babysitting. I inherited some of my sister's babysitting jobs as she moved on to other things. I babysat for Rusty Penn, who was the grandson of Lina Penn, the postmistress before Olive Parsons. Rusty lived above the store with his father. I would babysit for him though it really wasn't real babysitting – he was older and he would just do his homework and go to bed, and I would just watch TV.

That house had to be twenty or thirty feet away from the railroad tracks at the most, and whenever a train would come through, it sounded like the train was coming right through the house, and it scared me to death. Rusty would sleep right through it because he was used to it. My mother used to say that when we first moved to the Park the trains would keep her up all the time. I remember when friends who were not from Garrett Park would come home with me and they would hear the trains, they would say, "My God, how do you put up with that?" and I would say, "Put up with what?". At some point you just got used to it, it was just like background noise and you didn't pay attention to it.

We built tree forts in our back lot. Here's an interesting piece of trivia: we had a huge oak tree in our back lot, and it was very conducive to building a tree fort, which was really only a platform nailed up in the tree with some boards. One day I noticed something sticking up out of the ground under the tree, and I thought it was a nail, tried to pull it out, starting digging around it, until I was finally able to get it out. As far as I could tell, it was a Civil War bayonet. I cleaned it up, chipping the rust and the dirt off of it, and over time I would look at books, and it matches up with picture of Civil War bayonets. This was a big old tree with a good leaf cover, and at some point General Jubal Early, a Confederate general, marched with his unit from Frederick, Md. towards D.C., I thought (and I still think) that this would have been an ideal place for people to camp out. Of course there was no town there at the time. I was very excited to make this discovery.

A lot of landmarks in the town had names that we had given them. The school crossing guard at Strathmore and Kenilworth was Mr. Dove. We thought he was about one hundred but he was probably only sixty or seventy. We called it "Dove's Corner" just like we called the sledding hill "Donnelly's Hill". We would say, "I'll meet you at Dove's Corner or at Donnelly's Hill."

My sister was a year ahead of me in school. In one of my earliest memories, I remember being so sad when my sister went off to school, leaving me home by myself. I stood in our yard, which was a very big yard with an extra lot with apple trees on it, and watched her leave. A year later, I started kindergarten. I was only four at the time, as I did not turn five until December. There was no kindergarten in Garrett Park at that time. You got on a D.C. Transit bus, paid a nickel, and you went to kindergarten at Kensington Elementary.

From first grade on, I attended Garrett Park Elementary. Mrs. Duey, the principal, was my first grade teacher. I had someone named Mrs. Simon, whom I fell in love with, for second grade, and then Mrs. Sutherland, who was very strict. At the time I couldn't stand her, but later I realized that she was probably a very good teacher, like a coach that you didn't like when they were coaching you but later you see them as having been pretty good for you. She taught third or fourth grade. I think in fifth grade I was in a combined fifth and sixth grade class which they were trying out. The teacher might have been Mrs. Miller, but I can't remember for sure.

I went to Kensington Junior High, and for high school I attended Walter Johnson. At WJ I played basketball, and I was on the team in my last year of high school. I attended University of Maryland, graduating in 1968, and then I joined the Army. The Vietnam War was on and America had a draft at this time. At first it was fairly easy to get a student deferment, and then they were going away. I didn't want to wait to be drafted, and instead I enlisted so I could go to OCS (Officer Candidate School). I spent three years in the army - at Fort Benning, GA, Fort Carson, CO, and on the DMZ (de-militarized zone) in Korea. After the military, I attended law school at the University of Miami. Then I went into the Army as a JAG officer, and spent three years in Charlottesville, VA, before finally leaving the army. My wife and I moved to Fort Lauderdale, Florida, where I worked for a small law firm for a year and a half. In 1981, my wife and I moved back to Charlottesville, and I was hired as the assistant investment officer at the University of Virginia to help manage the university's endowment. I was there for thirty-six years, retiring as a managing director in 2017 of the University of Virginia Investment Management Company.

I currently keep active with my own investment entity, Keswick Associates LLC and I am on the Investment Advisory Committee for a group called 10Talents Investors LLC. I think my childhood experiences in Garrett Park helped me develop valuable life skills. For instance, from a very early age I started delivering papers. It was something you had to do every day, and at the end of the month you had to collect from people and you had to pay the bill, and whatever was left was what you made. And then there was cutting grass and shoveling snow - all these things helped me develop a sense of responsibility. If you don't keep your commitment to deliver the paper or cut the grass, people will want to know why. I think that has always served me very well.

Unfortunately, I think it's harder nowadays for kids to have these kinds of practical learning opportunities. I've noticed this with my own kids. I used to say to people "Don't handicap your children by making things too easy for them." But as a practical matter, it isn't so easy to create opportunities for them to learn responsibility. We live in the historic part of downtown Charlottesville, in a house that was built in 1888. It has virtually no yard, and I didn't own a lawn mower, because I didn't need one – I just shared it with the next door neighbor. My son did start his own business, where he would collect people's mail and newspapers and take care of their plants for them when they were out of town, or he would sometimes shovel snow, stuff like that. So he had that, and later when he was in high school, he worked at a local ice cream store. My daughter worked there too, though not quite as enthusiastically as he did. So they did manage to get a little experience with real work before they grew up.

Today, parents have, rightly or wrongly, developed into helicopter parents. In Montgomery County a while back, some kids were walking home from a park and someone called the police, and said, "These kids are just walking around by themselves!" and the police picked them up drove them home. It's crazy that kids are no longer allowed to walk around by themselves. When we were kids, adults weren't continually managing our time, and we had lots of freedom to direct our own lives and to figure things out for ourselves. I think that kind of childhood freedom, which is so rare today, provides kids with a really important and valuable learning experience. For me, growing up in a town like Garrett Park played a huge role in preparing me for life.

Rob with his wife, Kathy, his son, Walker, and his daughter, Hallie

14

JENNIFER MURRAY LAPP

One thing I really loved about Garrett Park was the sense of community. It seemed different from anywhere else. You knew everybody in town, and you were comfortable walking around. I used to like to go out and puddle around in the water looking at crayfish, and it was really gorgeous when it snowed. When it snowed, it was nothing to me to put on warm clothes and go out into the woods near my neighborhood. You can't do that these days, you can't let kids run like that, because you have no idea who is in the woods. Back then, it was so safe and free.

My mother, Marguerite Murray, was originally from Chicago and my father, James Murray, came from Iowa and Indiana. My parents moved to the Washington area in 1935. My father had taken a civil service exam and had gotten a position in the government printing office. When my father secured this job, my grandfather went down to the University of Indiana, where my father was, gave him a ticket and $5.00, and said, "Go to Washington, you've got a job!" It was the middle of the depression, and so my father went to Washington. My mother had earned her library degree at Carnegie Tech in Pittsburgh, and she was hired as a children's librarian at the D.C. public library.

My dad was already in the service when my parents were married in March of 1944. He landed at Normandy on D-day plus 30 (July of 1944). He was also supposed to be going to the Pacific, but as he had one battle point over the limit, he didn't have to go back. Mom had gotten this little efficiency apartment they could live in. My dad's job was repairing the teletype machines that they used to send messages to the front lines. Though he was never on the front lines, he saw enough of Germany and the concentration camps so that whenever he heard anyone using anti-Semitic speech, he would really light into them. Dad had very decided opinions about things, and wasn't always the easiest person to get along with.

My father worked for the IRS for forty-one years, and my mother ended up as the head of Children's Services for the Montgomery County Library System. In 1949, my parents built our house on Keswick Street, and we moved to Garrett Park. I was three when we moved there. My brother, Alan, was born in 1950, and my sister, Cilla (who started out as Priscilla and was known as Beebee when she was little), was born in 1952.

We were a family of readers. Because of my mother's work as a children's librarian, she was introduced to *The Hobbit* when it first came out, and we all grew up with it. I also remember mom playing the piano while we would stand around it and sing together. Every summer Sunday afternoon we would get into the car and drive out into the country and have a picnic. My parents had bridge parties with other families from the town, the Popes, the Paynes, and the Johnstons. After my parents built the addition in the back, they put a ping-pong table in the downstairs, and we used to play ping-pong. My father was a really good cook over charcoal. He made wonderful ribs, and so my parents liked to have summer parties in the back yard. On summer evenings we played "Kick the Can" and once we had a television set, we liked to come inside in the afternoon and watch Mickey Mouse Club.

Our class started kindergarten at Kensington Elementary while Garrett Park Elementary was under construction. Before that, the whole school was housed in a two-room schoolhouse. Because Nancy Abrams and I both had birthdays in December, we started school when we were only four and a half years old. Most days we were picked up by either my mother or Mrs. Abrams but one day, because neither of our mothers could get there to pick us up, we were given instructions on how to ride the D.C. Transit bus home to the top of Keswick Street. However, when school let out, Nancy and I decided it would be more fun to ride one of the orange school buses than the D.C. Transit. We rode around and around Kensington before finally being returned to the school and two very panicked mothers! We never got the chance to do that again!

Mrs. Duey was the long-time principal of Garrett Park Elementary School, and she was also my first grade teacher. Since my family read a lot, I had learned to read by first grade. Usually I would read the entire reader by the first week. We were supposed to work on *Weekly Readers* and fill out worksheets. Often I would get sent off to the office because I didn't want to re-read the book.

In the spring of 1956 I contracted nephritis, a strep infection of the kidneys. I missed the last month of school, a class trip to Annapolis (I guess we were studying Maryland history) and I spent most of summer lying in bed being dosed with penicillin. Each week during that summer, Mrs. Bunker, the town librarian at our tiny library, would come spend the day with me and let mom take the other kids out or go shopping. Mrs. Bunker taught me to play Mah-Jong and she would read to me. Later on, Nora Payne took over the library.

When I think of Mrs. Bunker, I remember her sitting at her desk at the library with the clouds of cigarette smoke rising from her yellowed fingers. I also remember that she didn't approve of some of the books that I wanted to read. I went home and complained about this to "my" librarian, who promptly called Mrs. Bunker and told her I could read anything I wanted to try, making it very clear that if I wanted to read something, I could read it. If I didn't like it I could return it. Yay Mom!

I remember sometimes during the winter waking up to a white and silent world outside; without the forecasting we have now, this was such an exciting event! We would listen to the radio to find out if we were going to be off school. Sometimes the lower part of Montgomery County would be going to school while Gaithersburg and further north had the day off. If it was a big snow and we knew we weren't going to be attending school, we would eat breakfast and bundle up to get outside. We would wander down the street and into the woods. During one big snow we were out walking around and discovered that a snow plow had tried to go down or up Strathmore hill with predictable consequences. It was wedged into the bank at the end of the bridge over Rock Creek and no one could go up or down for quite a while. Of course, as we got older, we would go sledding over at Donnelly's Hill when it snowed.

We lived across the street from the Weavers; Mrs. Weaver's mother was a Diffendorfer and an original resident of the town. They lived on the corner of Keswick and Oxford and they owned all the land from Keswick to Clermont. Behind their house was a spectacular wildflower garden and if you were very, very good, Mrs. Weaver would take you on a tour of the garden. She was very fond of my mother and would give her cuttings to plant in our backyard. She had a yardman named Guy, a black man who had been born in a former slave cabin down by the side of Rock Creek. He never learned to read or write but he was so kind to all the children.

Guy had been drafted during World War II. They took him away, and the Weavers didn't hear anything from him for a long time, and people just figured he had died. But one day he just showed up again. It turned out they never did send him to Europe because he couldn't read or write. They really couldn't put him in any kind of position where he had any responsibility, so they sent him over to the Eastern Shore and for the whole war he peeled potatoes. So that was Guy. He was pretty old, and I'm sure his parents were slaves. He lived down on Rock Creek.

When we were in elementary school, Oxford Street ended about half a block from Keswick. There was a dirt road through the woods and up the hill and about half a block from Montrose it was paved again. We walked to school on that road for years. Clermont Street was paved from Strathmore Avenue to in front of two or three houses. Eventually both of those roads were extended, and then Oxford was paved over to Montrose. The hill was very rocky; the first or second time I rode my bicycle down it I came to grief and flew off. Guy came out of the garden and picked me up, dusted me off and sent me on my way. Our house was three or four blocks from the school and before they gave us a cafeteria, we did walk home for lunch. My grandma, my mom's mom, Ruth Myers, lived with us from 1952 on, and she would be there. She lived with us from September to June, and then she'd go off and visit the rest of the family. When the weather became too cold or inclement, we would bring our lunch and eat at school. Milk was free, thanks to a government program.

Garrett Park Brownie Troop, 1946 birth date

Front row: Jill Howard, Kathy ?, Lynne Hill Storm, Nancy Abrams, Jennifer Murray, Linda Paul, Suzanne Roberts, Jan Fetchko, Lynn Mc Cracken
Top row: Glinda Long, Jewell Grinnell, Susan McCamey, Lois Werner, Debbie Chisholm, Barbara Wintberg, Sally Zanelli, Kathy Holmes, Carol, Jeanne Thrasher, Patsy Murray

In 1956 the school was enlarged and when I came back in the fall we had a cafeteria! I was a picky eater and I particularly didn't like broccoli. I still don't like it. One day I rebelled and put my broccoli into the milk carton. Mrs. Sutherland caught me, made me take it out of the trash, out of the milk carton and eat it. Could a teacher get away with that today? After that, my mother made sure I didn't get Mrs. Sutherland as a teacher. In my sixth grade year, they were switching her to sixth grade, but there were two sixth grades, and I had Mrs. Strayer, the other teacher.

I remember that the school used to show films on Saturday. They would start with the WWII newsreels, move to cartoons, and then we'd get to see a movie. Though I have no memory of what we saw, I do remember that it was fun.

I had this bicycle. It was a wonderful bicycle, a small bike, not a 26 inch bike. My father had been in France during the war, and he had met this family who had a son about my age. At some point in the 1950s, they sent me a French bicycle. It was painted cream, and the fender and all the other pieces were aluminum. It had hand brakes, not foot brakes. When I got old enough, I rode it to school one day, and when I came out it was gone. So I went to Mrs. Duey's office, and I said, "My bicycle is gone." As it turned out this boy named Jimmy, who lived on the other side of town, had fallen in love with my bicycle, and he had stolen it. Of course his parents brought it back and he had to apologize. One day Nancy and I were riding up and down Keswick Street, which has quite a hill, and we decided to ride each other's bicycles. As we were coasting down Keswick Street, this stupid Chesapeake Retriever came strolling out into the middle of the street. We were flying down the hill, and I couldn't remember where the brakes on Nancy's bike were, because they were foot brakes and I was used to hand brakes. I hit the dog going full speed, and the dog went flying, and I went flying. I have never liked Chesapeake Retrievers since.

I was in the Girl Scouts, and later the Mariners, until dropping out in tenth grade. Mrs. Abrams, was the leader for both the Girl Scouts and the Mariners. The reason that I quit was that we had been selling Girl Scout Cookies, and Mrs. Abrams decided we would sell more, and we weren't allowed to just sell them in the neighborhood, we were to sell them in the federal buildings downtown, and I had done all I was going to do selling Girl Scout Cookies. I was done, and so I quit the Mariners. But I doubt that I would have lasted much longer.

I was friends with Mary Winegarden, who went to Catholic school, and Nancy Abrams. Later, in junior high, I was also friends with a girl named Barbara Kameras who lived nearby. I played with Jack Pendleton, who lived across the street, and Robin Mason and I were good friends. I also remember a little girl who lived around the corner that was a dreadful child; we spent a good time tormenting her.

I grew up during the cold war. We spent many a night listening to the air raid siren which had some faulty wiring or something, and it would go off by during thunderstorms. We would hear it and be under the bed. This must have been when I was in fifth or sixth grade. I think that impacted the way we lived, worrying about "a red under every bed" or whatever, and worrying about a nuclear attack.

And then there was the Kennedy assassination, such a shock! I was in twelfth grade when Kennedy was killed. I had been absent on class picture day, and Patsy Murray and I got on a bus and rode downtown to get our pictures taken, and everyone on the bus was crying. I've never forgotten that.

The very first television I ever saw was at the Wood's house next door. They had a television set, and we watched the 1952 or maybe it was 1956 political convention. It was Adlai Stevenson against Eisenhower. I remember watching that. I marched in the civil rights march of 1963, and I was there for Martin Luther King's speech. Civil rights did really impact me, and I'm still as left wing as I can be, but I'm not as starry-eyed, not as optimistic about the future, as I was back then.

One thing I really loved about Garrett Park was the sense of community. It seemed different from anywhere else. You knew everybody in town, and you were comfortable walking around. I used to like to go out and puddle around in the water looking at crayfish, and it was really gorgeous when it snowed. When it snowed, it was nothing to me to put on warm clothes and go out into the woods near my neighborhood. You can't do that these days, you can't let kids run like that, because you have no idea who is in the woods. Back then, it was so safe and free.

The town had a feeling of being enclosed from the outside world. We might take an expedition to the grocery store, but we didn't go out of town to eat and people weren't eating fast foods then. We walked to the post office every day, and we could buy stuff to eat at the general store. Because the people were interesting, it was an interesting community. We're talking about a whole town full of people who mostly worked for the government.

The only thing I can think of that I didn't like about Garrett Park is the same thing you don't like about any small town. There was this time, it must have been when I was in high school, when my friends and I were standing at the top of the street, at the corner of Keswick and Strathmore, waiting for the bus, and it was really cold, and the bus was late, so we got a pile of leaves together and made a bonfire. And Betsy White came along and started screaming at us. You couldn't get away with anything in such a small community.

I graduated from Walter Johnson in 1964, and attended Montgomery Junior College. I met my first husband in a coffee house in D.C. It was a great coffee house with fantastic music. We saw Roberta Flack there one night. We were married in 1966. We lived in Rockville while he was in school full time at Montgomery College, and I was working as a teletype operator. Then we moved to Rochelle, Illinois, a tiny town, a community of mostly farming people. They rolled up the lights at dusk, and there wasn't anything happening. He was from Ottawa, Illinois, but I was completely out of my element. He got a job offer at a printing plant in Bladensburg, so we moved back to Maryland, living in Prince Georges County, in Riverdale. I left my first husband after ten years of marriage to him, and I moved to Alexandria. I had learned to be a typesetter in Northern Illinois, and a typesetter I have been for the rest of my life. Now I am retired.

I moved to Alexandria in 1976, and remarried a man I had met in college. I lived there with my second husband until his death. I live a short walk from the Potomac River, just half a mile. I have found that I can't live where I don't have water.

My mother lived with me for eleven years before she died. Mom was slightly deaf and had developed macular degeneration. She had gone over to have dinner and ring in the New Year at Kitty Barclay's, along with the Gootenbergs and some other people, and she said to me the next day, "You know, I was driving home and I discovered I was driving on the left side of the highway". At that point I realized she shouldn't be living alone, and that is when I arranged for her to move in with me.

Marguerite Murray

Growing up in Garrett Park definitely gave me some special opportunities. While I never ended up being a librarian, I think that having that small town library made a big impression on me. I worked with my mom setting up the town library, and later I got to help her when she was asked to go over and set up the library in

D.C. for handicapped children. That library was spearheaded by the Kennedys, because Rosemary Kennedy was mentally handicapped.

I think that being comfortable working in the library, using those skills, gave me a sense of myself as someone who was competent in a new skill. It gave me an opportunity to do something real. So I knew I had the competence and basic skill to do something later on, because I had done this kind of work under my mom's tutelage. I am grateful for that.

(Parts written by Jennifer Lapp)

Marguerite and Jim Murray with Jennifer

15

KAREN MCLAUGHLIN GALLANT

Our childhood was extraordinary. Mary Winegarden, Jessica Myers, and I have often talked about how it was something very special. I think there was some kind of energy vortex right there on Weymouth Street. I had many friends in the neighborhood because of the post war baby boom…And we have remained friends our whole lives, particularly Jessica, Mary and I. We were friends through high school, through college and into our adult lives, sometimes losing touch for a while but always reconnecting. We are still very current and our families are friends; these are lifelong friendships, and I find it to be one of the most precious things in our lives.

My parents, Donal and Laura McLaughlin, moved with our family to Garrett Park in 1951. I was four years old, my brother, Brian, was eight, and my sister, Coille was twelve. Prior to that, we had lived in Takoma Park. My dad and mom had sold our house in College Park, because they were building a new house, a house my dad, who was an architect, had designed. Because it wasn't ready for us to move in, we had to live in these apartments in Takoma Park for about nine months. So moving to Garrett Park was a very happy time.

Because Al Richter was the architect who had designed most of the houses there, our Weymouth Street neighborhood was called Richterville. It was a remarkable and very tightly knit community. My dad was very active in the town - he was involved with getting the swimming pool established, he helped with the Garrett Bugle, and he was involved with the town's acting club, the Garrett Players – and he was also active in the neighborhood. Together with a couple of other neighbors, Dad and Henry Myers (who lived across the street from us) formed the Weymouth Street Golf Association, which meant they got together to golf a lot.

There were many neighborhood parties, and people often dropped in on each other for a visit. Henry Myers was famous for dropping in at dinner time and helping himself to whatever was on the table, which we thought was really wonderful. I remember that at least once we went on vacation to the outer banks of North Carolina with the Richters, the Myerses and the Franzes.

McLaughlin house

Coille McLaughlin (lower left) with BCC cheerleaders

Our childhood was extraordinary. Mary Winegarden, Jessica Myers, and I have often talked about how it was something very special. I think there was some kind of energy vortex right there on Weymouth Street. I had many friends in the neighborhood because of the post-war baby boom. There was Jessica Myers across the street, Ellen Bortman next door, Judy King down the street, Ann Lehman, who later moved away, and Mary Winegarden over on Keswick Street, who moved in when I was five. And we have remained friends our whole lives, particularly Jessica, Mary and I. We were friends through high school, through college and into our adult lives, sometimes losing touch for a while but always reconnecting. We are still very current, and our families are friends; I find these lifelong friendships to be some of the most precious things in our lives.

Jessie and I, in particular, played dolls, absolutely passionately, for hours and hours. I had quite a doll collection, and once when we were in our forties or fifties, Jessica came to visit, and I got them all out. Mostly my mom got my dolls at thrift shops, but they were always quality dolls, and I also had a couple of new ones. I had several Madam Alexander versions of the Ginny Dolls, as well as Tiny Tears dolls and many others. We played with our dolls a lot – washing and dyeing their hair, putting them in different outfits, and they always needed repairs, new wigs and so on. There was a place in Bethesda, Helen's Doll Shop, where we loved to go. Helen was this old woman who made a lot of the doll clothes as well as repairing dolls. My grandmother, my mom, and Jessica's mom also sewed outfits for our dolls. My mother made this prom dress for my twelve-inch

doll and another for my Ginny doll, so I had little sister and big sister dolls. We had romance dolls, pioneer dolls, tomboy dolls, and baby dolls, and we would say, "What kind of dolls should we play with today?" As I watch my grandchildren play, I am reminded that a child's world of play is so different from the adult world.

We also spent many hours playing in the woods at the bottom of Weymouth Street. There was a creek, and these vines that we loved to swing on, and one day when Jessica was swinging, she fell on her back so that the breath was knocked out of her. We panicked and ran up the street to get her father, Henry, who was a doctor. Of course by the time we got back she was ok. There were these big clumps of vines growing on

Karen McLaughlin, Mary Winegarden, Jessica Myers

the ground there, and we would hollow out inside of them and play "poor people". That was our name for when we imagined ourselves as children living in the woods. We would bake cakes out of dogwood berries and nuts, and create little mats of pine needles where we pretended to sleep.

When the weather was not so good for playing outside, we played board games like Monopoly and Parcheesi. When we were about eight or nine we were all into the Narnia books. Sometimes one of us would go to the bathroom, and then come running out and say, "Oh, you're still here! I've been to Narnia, I've been gone for three whole years!" We thought if we just wished enough we could fly. We would jump off Jessica's front steps, and say, "You know, I think I really was flying!" and we would try to fool each other. We were on that cusp where we knew it couldn't happen, but we still wanted to convince ourselves that it was possible.

In the summer evenings, when there were enough of us, we would band together with some younger kids in Judy King's yard, which was nice and big. We would all play Capture the Flag, and Freeze Tag, and other games. As it became late and the fireflies would come out, we would hear our parents calling us, and we would have to go in - we would hear the screen doors and a mother calling, "Karen…you have to come in now!" and as they heard their mothers calling them, the children would run home; I just get washed over with the preciousness of it all – it was like "Our Town". It was such a beautiful, innocent time; Jessica and I still talk about it sometimes.

The swimming pool was the major thing in the summer, and we could walk to the pool on our own. From the beginning of the summer I would be barefoot, and walking all the way to the pool would hurt my feet, but by the end of the summer my feet were tough and nothing hurt them. We would spend the whole day at the swimming pool, walk home for lunch and then go back, and our eyes would get red from the chlorine. At the pool we would lie on our towels in the sun, play games, and pretend to do water ballet. We were on our own there, without our parents. As an adult living in Garrett Park, I took my own children to the swimming pool, but my children were never so independent the way we were. Things have changed so much.

I have wonderful memories of winter and especially of Christmas. Jessica lived across the street and our house had a bay window. She had a frosted storm door which she could open. So I would call her up (they were on our party line), and I would say "What did you get?" and she would say, "I got a Tintair Doll!" (a doll made by Effenbee, with hair you could dye) and I would say, "Oh, I got a Tintair Doll too!" and we would hold up our dolls so we could see them. Our mothers must have colluded on that occasion.

When it snowed, we could go sledding on my driveway or down Weymouth Street, but the best thing to do was to go to the big hill at St. Angela Hall. One time when I was sledding there, I went so fast my sled went into the creek and I almost got wet. I went home crying, and it was a long walk. Another time, when we went ice skating on the swamp in the woods at the bottom of Weymouth, Judy King fell through and soaked her feet. She was afraid she would get frost bite. I remember that older kids would go sledding on Donnelly's Hill, but I never went there – it seemed like a scary place where the big kids sledded.

This was such a different time. When I was seven or eight, we could walk to the post office without any adult supervision, and we would buy candy like Necco Wafers, Skybars, O'Henrys, or Bazooka gum (and read the comics). Judy and Jessica would want to put nickels and pennies on the railroad track when a train was coming so the train would squash them flat. I was terrified that they were getting too close, because we thought that if you were too close the wind would suck you under the wheels. They would tease me because I was afraid, and I would start crying. I remember riding bikes in the summer and riding them to school, and roller skating with those skates that had skate keys. Keswick Street was very smooth, so it was the best for skating.

First Grade

And then there were the fireworks and the Fourth of July parade, and Halloween and the Girl Scouts. I loved Brownies and later Girl Scouts, which I thought was so much fun. We had Mrs. Thompson for a troupe leader, and then later we had Mrs. Boehm. I have so many memories of Girl Scouts. I remember loving the Camper's Stew with macaroni and corn and tomatoes. I also remember that we had horseback riding lessons, and feeling scared on the horse, because I couldn't trot.

We had a project in Brownies one Christmas. We each were given a candle, and we had to cut out about forty pieces of crinoline with sequins on them into zig-zag shapes. They got smaller and smaller and, when stacked together from largest to smallest with the candle in the center, eventually it made a white Christmas tree. I remember when we were doing it that some part of me knew that this was not "good taste", not my mother's taste. When I gave it to her, she said "How nice". For me, that was the beginning of understanding that some people were looked down on by people like my parents, that there was this social hierarchy in the world. Nothing was ever said to me, but children start to know these things very early. I remember we didn't think much of Garrett Park Estates. We thought those were the dull people, while Garrett Park was cool because it was progressive and professional.

All the kids in the neighborhood walked or biked to the community school, and nobody ever thought about going to a different school. In first grade I had Mrs. Duey, who was a nice teacher. She was also the principal, and whenever she had to go to the office to do something, she had this assistant with pointy glasses who would come in and read to us. In second grade I had Mrs. Bratley, who was wonderful. I was a bright student with many good girlfriends, and I was very happy there. I loved going to school, and I never thought twice about it. It wasn't until adolescence that I began to criticize, and even so, I'm much more critical now than I was then. As an adult looking back, I realize that mid-century American public education wasn't all that suited to me, and that while I was a good little girl, I wasn't encouraged to be myself. But that's a later perception.

In 1959 I graduated from Garrett Park Elementary and started at Kensington Junior High, riding the school bus to school. After that, I attended Walter Johnson High School from 1962 to 1965. It was in high school that I became aware that Garrett Park was where the beatniks and "artsy-fartsies" lived, the cool place to live. Just because of where we lived, we were cool and so much more advanced. I was at the right place at the right time, the place and time for me to believe in being a progressive and creative American. In this way we were quite elite, though I didn't think of myself that way. My husband, Frank, who lived in Garrett Park for a while, he got it. He said "You grew up in a very elite group" but he meant it as a compliment. It was so different from what most Americans experience. It's made me feel frustrated with the rest of my country my whole life. It's so evident that we could do better than we do.

I remember the Cuban Missile Crisis and how we went downtown and protested in front of the White House. Parade Magazine published a picture of the protesters and I was in the picture. I remember coming back from that and having hysterics, true hysterics, screaming and crying and pounding my fist on the floor out of terror that we were about to be killed by a nuclear bomb. And I also remember in elementary school, when we had to file out into the hall, kneel down and cover our heads, that kind of thing. That was scary.

My friends and I were involved in civil rights activities. We attended SNCC and CORE meetings with Ray Popkin and Hyatt Bache, and I remember doing some things with the Washington Ethical Society. The summer when I was in eleventh grade I was a counselor for a camp for underprivileged kids in Triangle, Virginia. It was an overnight camp and I had a cabin of girls. That experience was very hard. I read them *Charlotte's Web*, and I don't know if they liked it but at least they went to sleep.

After graduating from Walter Johnson in 1965, I attended Antioch College in Yellow Springs, Ohio. After college, I moved first to Boston, then San Francisco, and then to New York City, where I attended Pratt Institute to study painting. During that time I summered in Cape Cod, which is where I met my future husband, Frank Gallant. We got married and moved to Kennebunkport, Maine, where we had our two sons, Ben and Nick. When Frank got a job in Washington, D.C., we moved back to Garrett Park. We originally planned to only stay in the area for a year, to live with my mom and dad for a while until we had saved enough money to move back to Maine. However, we ended up living with them for eight years, so my two little boys got to spend the first part of their lives growing up in Garrett Park. Eventually we bought a house in Takoma Park, where we lived for twenty-two years. In 2009, we moved to California and built a house for ourselves just south of Santa Cruz in Soquel. We've been living there since 2012, next door to our younger son, Nick, and his family. I love this house, and in many ways it reminds me of the house I grew up in. My son, Ben, lives nearby, and I have four grandsons. My heart brims with gratitude, to have my family so close and to be able to share in their lives. Community and relationship have always been so important to me.

The Weymouth Street neighborhood has slowly changed over the years as neighbors have changed. Still, a lot of the neighbors - the Richters, the Myers, the Baldwins, the Bortmans, the Kennedys, the Lichtensteins and the Kings all stayed in their houses to the end of their lives. Both of my parents died at home in the house my father designed, which is exactly the way you want it to be.

My mom died in 1998, eleven years before my dad, who died in 2009, shortly after Frank and I moved to Berkeley. We wanted to keep the house in the family, but as things unraveled with my dad it became impossible to hold on to it. Selling the house was extremely difficult and painful. It was very meaningful to me to have lived so much of my life in the house my father designed for us in Garrett Park. It is still there, though it has been remodeled. I loved that house, and I have never since lived in a house I really liked until we built our current house in Santa Cruz.

Karen, Coille, and Brian

Karen with her grandsons - Milo in back, L to R in front: Rory, Caspar, and Nolan

I think I owe my idealism to growing up in Garrett Park. It was a community of good people, and overall, the American culture worked for us there. Of course there were some problems. I remember when the Adlers sold their house to a black family, and one morning there were crosses burned on their lawn! This utterly stunned the neighborhood and the whole town. It was really shocking, not something we could ever imagine would happen in our neighborhood. The new family lived in the neighborhood for ten years before moving away. Actually, unlike most (or maybe all) of the other people who lived on Weymouth Street, they were Republicans, which probably made it hard for them to connect with their progressive neighbors.

Garrett Park was a wonderful place to be growing up as a kid in post-war America. I remember hearing a lot of positive comments from the adults about what a great town it was, and I remember my mom and dad saying how much they liked other families. I grew up surround by this feeling that people liked each other; it was a community, and people did things together.

Karen with her sons- Ben and Nick- and her husband, Frank Gallant

16

LEE POPE

Growing up, I felt thoroughly embedded in the natural world and spent as much time as possible outdoors. I lived in anticipation of each season, and every season had its own wonderful flavor. Summer nights were magical, a time for all the kids in the neighborhood to come together. After dark we would play shadow tag under the streetlights until bedtime, or hide and seek, or we would catch fireflies in jars and let them go in the morning. The fireflies added a special kind of magic to those warm, humid summer nights. We don't have them here in California where I live.

My parents, Barbara and Roger Pope, met at the University of Michigan and were married right before my father was shipped out by the U.S. Navy to do his bit in World War II. My older brother, Carl, was born in San Francisco in May of 1945, and two years later in November of 1947 I was born in East Lansing, Michigan. When I was a year old, my father was hired to work in D.C. as a research lawyer for the Department of Agriculture, and we moved from Michigan to Maryland. We lived for some years in an apartment complex in Silver Spring, moving to Garrett Park in the spring of 1954. I was six and my older brother, Carl had just turned nine. My parents had for some time been looking for a house to buy, searching out an area where schools were good and conditions perfect for raising a family. I remember how elated they were to discover

Garrett Park, this wonderful little town with big trees and big yards, a town council and mayor, and a school you could walk to. When we moved there towards the end of my first grade year, it felt like the beginning of a wonderful new adventure. In fact, it was.

I started at my new school, Garrett Park Elementary. My new first grade teacher, who was also the principal, was Mrs. Duey. I remember her quite vividly as a grandmotherly, plump woman with warm brown eyes who wore her iron gray hair in an old-fashioned bun. With her soft pillow-y chest in a gray flannel dress, she was rather like a bard rock hen. The children were friendly, and I felt safe and comfortable at this school right from the beginning.

At first we rented a Chevy House on Montrose Avenue. It had a big back yard with trees and a hammock. My mother helped me plant my very own garden, a small circular one with marigolds, petunias,

Lee and Carl around 1950

and pumpkins. Almost right away my brother and I joined ranks with a small group of neighborhood kids. We could walk to the general store, just a few blocks away, to buy candy and "Lick-i-made" from Louie (the guy who ran the store) and his wife. All summer my left palm was permanently died red or purple or green from the

Rokeby Avenue house

Lick-i-made. All kinds of candy and other supposed "food" began to play a huge part in our daily lives. I particularly remember loving those red lips, buck teeth, mustaches, and pan pipes (made of flavored paraffin!) that we used to buy and chew up like gum. While feasting on this stuff, we explored the tree-lined streets barefoot and carefree. This new-found sense of freedom and unlimited possibility was intoxicating.

Soon my parents purchased a permanent house for us from Al Sanders at 11303 Rokeby Avenue. The back yard was wonderfully large, and in a deep gully just behind it ran the railroad tracks, with a forest on the other side of the tracks, waiting to be explored. Black raspberries grew wild along the railroad right-of-way. The mournful whistle of the passing trains in the middle of the night became a signature sound of my childhood.

I remember the very first time our parents took us to see the house. We walked down to the very end of the street, and I discovered that in an unspoiled wooded area there was a huge tree with a branch growing straight out of the trunk which then turned up in a perfect right angle. I immediately fell in love with this tree and made up a song about it called "The Turn-Up Tree". I just knew that this new neighborhood would bring me many adventures.

There could not have been a more ideal place for a child to grow up in the whole state of Maryland. The town was tiny – you could easily walk from one end to the other in less than an hour. There was no reason to lock your door, and no one bothered. Many of the houses were fairly old, and almost all of the lots were large and shady, with no fences between houses. Dogs back then ran free, as did the children. There were lots of children in the neighborhood, all ages, and not only did we have plenty of freedom to explore the world in safety, but we also enjoyed the richness of growing up in a strong community. Everyone knew everyone.

Because the meandering streets were lined with huge trees, there was plenty of shade in the summer. There was no need for sidewalks on any but the main road (Strathmore), because there wasn't much traffic and no one drove fast. A wild cousin to the raspberry (which I recently have learned is called a wineberry) grew in the vacant lots – red and shiny and sticky and more delicious and juicy than anything you could buy in a store. A short walk away, at the south end of Rokeby near the train station, was a playground (later named "Wells Park") with a creek running through it. Mom and Pop Wells lived in a small house in the woods where Rokeby dead-ended just down the street from my house. They were kindly old folks who welcomed visits from neighborhood kids. Shortly after we moved in, Suzanne Roberts, who lived across the street from me, took me there to visit them. They offered us M & Ms from a candy dish and showed us their garden, which even had a scarecrow. I remember a little Japanese style bridge that went over the creek near their house.

We began to meet the neighborhood kids. They roamed the streets in a clump, older and younger often together. Suzanne and Tommy Roberts lived across the street and Timmy Powell (whose father was the mayor!) lived on the corner of Clyde and Rokeby. Next door was the Brown family – Timmy and Tommy and Sally and Rosie, who was a year or two younger than me. They had a double-seated glider swing in their yard, and I like to swing on it with Rosie.

An early childhood friend was Sherry Thomas. We had been friends and neighbors in Silver Spring before her family moved to Garrett Park shortly after mine did. Sherry and I would walk together down to the general store at the bottom of my street, buying bags of candy and stopping to play at the park on the way back. We would gorge on wineberries, and swing across the creek on the branches of willows that grew along the banks.

I was a feisty kid who enjoyed playing with boys at least as much as girls. I took pride in my tree climbing skills, and I liked to sit for long hours in a tree, doing nothing in particular. I would climb the tallest trees around, and my parents never seemed to worry about me, though my mother sometimes cautioned me not to harm the tree. If a neighborhood cat got caught in a tree, I would be the one to get it down. I was also very comfortable handling snakes. Once a neighbor lady had a snake in her garden and called on me to get it out. It was a black snake, and it bit me on the hand when I picked it up. The bite didn't hurt, but left two small holes. I was proud of my snake bite, and couldn't wait to get to school and show it to my classmates.

I remember a few times when the neighborhood children would get together to put on a carnival, and once we had one in our yard. It featured a haunted house in the dark attic with peeled grapes (eyeballs) to feel, and the shadow of a huge hand descending from overhead – a thrillingly scary special effect. We created a ride in a tin tub that someone dragged by a rope along our wire clothes line. We made lemonade and popcorn to sell, and my friend Carolyn was the "fat lady", stuffed with pillows. There was another carnival at the Guernsey's house, with a very rickety, makeshift roller coaster, which I think entailed sliding down some boards on a card-board box. Tom Guernsey, who was three years my senior, praised my courage and skill on the roller coaster, which made me very proud.

I especially delighted in playing traditional games, such as hopscotch, with neighborhood kids. I had this definite sense that children had been playing these games since time immemorial and that by playing them we were carrying on a great and ancient tradition. I felt the same way about jump rope, tag games, hide and seek, and roller skating. On our block, Rokeby Avenue had a long hill that was perfect for roller skating, with few cars and just the right amount of steepness. Skating provided an opportunity for us all to get together with no regard for age or social standing.

Where Clyde and Kenilworth intersected, there was a wooded area that the neighborhood kids called the "Bad Boys Woods." Rumor had it that there was a gang of teenage boys who would capture hapless children and strip them, roll them in poison ivy, tie their hands so they couldn't scratch, and then let them go at mid-night. There was a path through that woods that I often took to visit friends who lived in Garrett Park Estates. The Bad Boys legend added an exciting thrill of fear to the experience of walking alone on the path, though it was not a particularly pleasant thrill.

Once a group of us got together to go to the dump that was in this woods and search for treasure. We took an old red wagon with us to transport the loot. We came back with a rusty saw, some old bottles of various colors, and other treasures that I don't recall. Then, right there on the path before us, was a small dagger of some sort (a toy?) with red nail polish painted on the blade. Susanne Roberts, whom I remember as having a vivid sense of drama, picked it up and exclaimed, "Look! It's a dagger, and it's got blood on it!" We carefully hid the dagger under the treasures from the dump, and headed on down the path. Suddenly about five big boys emerged from the woods with their faces covered by t-shirts pulled up over their heads. Somehow we were able to recognize one of them as Lance Antosz, the older brother of Candy Antosz, who lived across the street. We screamed and Suzanne pulled the dagger out from the wagon. One of the boys snatched it from her and said, "That's my dagger! See, there is blood on it! I killed a man with it!" We talked about the incident for many weeks after. "He almost cut off my head with that dagger!" Suzanne would say.

Perhaps under the influence of a TV show called *Brave Eagle, Chief of the Cheyanne*, Suzanne Roberts and I decided to be Indians, and she picked the Sioux tribe for us. We rode around the neighborhood on sticks that we had carefully peeled and given names to – our Indian ponies. I'm sure we had Indian names as well, but I can't remember what they were. This was when we were in third and fourth grade. I'm sorry to say that you don't see kids of that age playing that way anymore. I had an alter-ego as a young Indian boy, and as soon as I arrived home from school I would change into an Indian costume my grandfather had sent me, climb the dog-wood tree in our yard, and sit there for hours just communing with nature. At some point I made a teepee in the back yard with poles I had collected from the woods and an old bedspread. One summer night I tried to sleep in it with no mattress or top blanket, but it was too uncomfortable, and I eventually ended up in my own bed.

From the beginning, Carl and I played on the railroad tracks with our parents' full knowledge. They must have trusted we would know to get out of the way if a train was coming, and we always did. We also liked to explore the seemingly endless wooded area on the other side of the tracks. One day, while playing by the tracks, we encountered a shabby looking teenage boy, who said he was heading towards Rockville. He asked us if we knew where there was a bathroom and we told him no, he would have to use the woods. Then we set out ourselves to explore the woods, and on our way back we saw him again, a short distance away through the trees. He called to us, asking us if we didn't want to come and play with his "Little Willie" and Carl, not un-derstanding what it was he was suggesting, started to walk in his direction. Grabbing him by the arm, I pulled him back and told him what the boy had said.

When we returned to our house, Carl told my mother about what had happened. To our surprise, she called the police, who came and interviewed us about the incident, asking us to describe the boy. A few hours later they returned and stood outside our screen door with a young man they had picked up on the streets of Rock-ville. But he was not the same one, and I felt terribly guilty about this, that we had caused this innocent guy to be picked up by the police. The next day at school, a rumor had spread that Carl and Lee Pope had been kid-napped.

It seemed to happen almost overnight that the endless forest across the tracks was razed to the ground to make way for a new housing development, "Randolph Hills". All around us during this time, wooded areas were being clear cut, the precious wild spots destroyed to make room for development. The Bad Boys Woods shrank to nothing as Garrett Park Estates expanded. The woods at the bottom of Rokeby was shrinking too, and I can remember when a G.E.M. store popped up over by White Flint, so close we could easily walk there. I was in junior high by then, and my friend, Patty Keenan, and I were excited to think we could walk to the G.E.M. store and buy lipstick. But as I got a little older, it began to sink in what we were losing to all this de-velopment.

Growing up, I felt thoroughly embedded in the natural world and spent as much time as possible outdoors. I lived in anticipation of each season, and every season had its own wonderful flavor.

Summer nights were magical, a time for all the kids in the neighborhood to come together. After dark we would play shadow tag under the streetlights until bedtime, or hide and seek, or we would catch fireflies in jars and let them go in the morning. The fireflies added a special kind of magic to those warm, humid summer nights. We don't have them here in California where I live.

The Fourth of July was the crowning glory of the summer season. The day before, every child in the town was busy with red, white, and blue strips of crepe paper, decorating bicycles, wagons, scooters and even tricy-cles for the big parade. The parade ended at the tennis courts where the town mayor would hand out popsicles to all the kids. In the afternoon there was a huge community celebration followed by a picnic over on the field next to the elementary school. We had all kinds of fun activities - three-legged races, an egg throw, and even a turtle race. Later, as we waited for the dark to come, Clyde Hall would lead everyone in singing American folk favorites – "I've Been Working on the Railroad", "Oh Susanna!" and of course "The Star Spangled Banner". Finally it was time for the fireworks, which were always spectacular, though a bit too loud for my taste. After we got home, we had our own fireworks. Sparklers, fountains, and other kinds I can't remember the names of. You had to be careful not to step on hot sparklers in your bare feet.

One summer when I was about eight, I found a tortoise in the woods and brought him home. He was very fast for a tortoise, and so I decided to name him "Flash" and enter him in the turtle race on the Fourth. I proudly painted his name in red nail polish on his shell. I was very excited, certain that Flash would win the race. The big day came. This is how the turtle race worked: A large circle was drawn with chalk, and a smaller circle in the center. All of the turtles were placed in the small circle under a box. When it was time to begin the race, someone blew a whistle, and someone lifted the box. The year I entered Flash in the race, some older boys came along and asked the name of my turtle, and decided to root for him. The whistle blew, the box was lifted and the race was on! Flash made a promising beginning, and it looked like he would live up to his name. But though Flash might have been fast, he wasn't used to all these people waving their arms and cheering him on. Every time he started in one direction, he would see the faces of excited fans and hear the cries of "Go Flash, Go!" and he would turn around and head in the other direction. The fastest turtle was also apparently the shyest. So Flash lost the race, and may have even come in last.

Autumn was the most delightful season. Banks of dead leaves on the side of the streets made a wonderful crackling noise when we scuffled through them, kicking them with our feet on our way home from school. Raking leaves was one of the few mandatory jobs I remember, but jumping in the piles before they were burned made it fun. On weekends you would see all the neighborhood families out raking leaves into big piles, and as the day progressed, the tantalizing smell of burning leaves would fill the air. I was indignant when the burning was eventually outlawed. I remember waking up on crisp, cool Saturday mornings feeling certain that some wonderful adventure awaited me. I could hear the cawing of the crows and the wind in the trees; the sky stood out a bright turquoise blue against the vivid fall foliage, and a wonderful smell of leaf mold filled the air. Best of all, there was always someone to play with in the neighborhood.

Then there was Halloween. Back then the costumes were handmade and not particularly gruesome – Indians, cowboys, and princesses, ghosts and witches. Kids went out alone – no parents worried about kidnappers or razorblades in apples. Some of the houses were elaborately decorated, and some families invited us in for cider and cookies, or some other kind of treat. Most people don't seem to recall this, but Halloween was really kind of a two-day affair back then. The night before Halloween was "Trick or Treat Night". If you didn't hand out any treats, you would regret it on Halloween, the following night. That was the night of tricks, when the ghosts and goblins were having their last hurrah.

Right before Thanksgiving, the year I was in second grade, Old Mr. Dove, who was both crossing guard and janitor, brought in a huge live turkey to our classroom. He introduced the turkey as "Tom", and I was so impressed that I insisted that year that we name our Thanksgiving turkey "Tom" as well. On Thanksgiving Day, when my mother innocently invited me to come and say goodbye to "Tom", as he was going into the oven, I burst into tears. Naming Tom had caused me to bond with him, in spite of the fact that he had arrived from the supermarket headless, plucked, and wrapped in plastic. I could not stop crying until my mother applied her favorite method of consoling an upset child – she made up a story. It was something about a little turtle who had to earn its spots by doing a good deed. I have been a vegetarian my whole adult life and I guess the tendency was there from the beginning.

Snow days were both rare and exciting. After sitting around the radio waiting to hear the news that school had been cancelled, we would stuff ourselves into our winter clothes, grab our sleds, and head over to Donnelly's hill. Someone would have already built a fire there, and we would spend the entire morning sledding down and trudging up, until our feet were frozen and numb and it was time to go home to lunch. If there was enough snow, we might stay home to build a snow fort, or make snow statues. One year when there was an especially deep snow, Carl and I built a snow alligator and a snow statue of George Washington. When it snowed I loved to go alone to the woods at the end of the street, where I would find a completely transformed world: the honeysuckle vines that grew in mounds had become magical snow caves. I loved the sharp, clean smell of the snow, the deep silence, and the blue shadows, and I reveled in the opportunity to be alone in it.

The town was never more beautiful than in the spring, with new leaves on the trees, so many different varieties of song birds singing their spring chorus, and the blossoms – forsythia, dogwood, cherry, and other flowing shrubs and trees. My mother and I had a ritual of looking for the first crocuses in the yard. Later it was narcissi, daffodils, tulips, and iris, and of course azaleas. When the weather started to get warm in the spring, you could hardly wait to take your shoes off, though the ground was still very cold at first. Those first barefoot days were so special, with the songs of the birds, the smells of damp earth, and the promise of warmer, sweeter days to come.

I remember these middle years of childhood as blissfully happy. I had many friends in the neighborhood or within walking distance. If there wasn't anyone to play with I would explore the woods on my own and lie or bounce in the springy beds made of honeysuckle vines, make tiny people out of acorns, write plays to be later performed with friends, or play alone in my room, orchestrating long stories involving stuffed toys.

I wish that every child could have such a childhood as I was blessed to have. My vivid imagination was enhanced by reading. I was especially fond of fantasy books and horse stories. I read and re-read the Narnia books, *The Black Stallion* books, and many others. My blue English Racer bicycle was a horse to me, and I would ride it through vacant lots and over logs, pretending to jump it. Though we technically lived in the suburbs, the forces of nature were all around us in their full-blown glory, and I found endless enchantment and amusement in that world.

It was not long after we moved to Garrett Park that the local swimming pool was built. My parents had asked Carl and me whether we would rather have a TV or join the pool – apparently it was an economic impossibility for us to do both – and we wisely preferred the pool. As a result, I was fully nine years old before my family succumbed to the TV habit, and even then in a very limited way.

Swimming lessons followed and soon I was a good enough swimmer to be allowed at the pool without my parents. I remember those early morning swimming lessons. The water was always freezing cold in the morning. One of my swimming teachers was a dark, handsome lifeguard named Slugger, and another lifeguard, Bunny, was pretty and slender with long blonde hair. I idolized them both for their good looks and perfect tans; they looked like they had stepped out of a Coppertone commercial. Once when I was a new swimmer, I jumped from the diving board into my mother's arms, immediately began to clutch at her and pull us both down. It was Slugger who rescued us.

We could walk to the pool alone and did walk there every day all summer, except of course on the rainy ones. I can still remember the pleasant meandering streets that led to the pool – this house on Clermont had a sweet smelling mimosa tree with blossoms that looked to me like tiny fairies wearing silky pink tutus, and there were concord grapes that grew along a path that finally led us to the pool. We ate a lot of those grapes, starting from when they were small and green and very sour. As children we would spend the whole day at the pool. We would buy popsicles or Good Humors and stayed in the water until our lips turned blue and our fingers were wrinkled up – a phenomenon my mother told me was called "washerwomen hands."

I joined the swim team for a while, but I was not a fast swimmer and never really liked the competition, so I dropped out. When I was in about sixth grade I took diving lessons, which I loved. Andy Sonner was my diving coach. He was a wonderful teacher then, and again later he was a wonderful teacher when I took U.S. History from him at Walter Johnson.

The elementary school and public library were adjacent to each other, a short half-hour walk away. I remember one time when I was about twelve, I road my bike to the library to find a book. I was searching the shelves for a teen romance like *Seventeenth Summer,* when the librarian, Nora Payne, asked me if I had read *The Five Children and It*, by E. Nesbit, and in this way she redirected me to my favorite author of children's fantasy literature. From many small episodes like this I arrived at the belief that the world was friendly and adults were available to take an interest in me and assist me when needed.

My shy, retiring father joined the Garrett Players and performed in a number of plays, including a musical comedy where he was cast in the role of a very dopey gangster and actually sang, though he couldn't really carry a tune. I guess for that part being a bad singer worked just fine. Some of the plays were serious dramas, such as Arthur Miller's *All My Sons* – my brother had a small part in that one. There was a play called *Papa is All* featuring Harry Dubinskis as a temperamental Pennsylvania Dutch patriarch. I remember that the Players put on *Night Must Fall* - a thriller which featured a severed head in a hatbox. I didn't see that one, but the hatbox spent some time in our house for a while which greatly disturbed me. When I was in high school my father had a part in *The Thurber Carnival.* I loved seeing the adults in my community doing something creative and fun together.

Most of my school experiences were positive, though third grade with Mrs. Sutherland was a bad year for me. She was known to be a good teacher, but for me she was not a fit. She obviously found me a disappointment after having taught my brother, and she seemed to find me both lazy and sloppy. It seemed to me that I could never measure up to her expectations even if I tried, and I spent my third grade year trying in vain to avoid being singled out by her. Still, looking back, there were some things I can appreciate about her. She made sure every child in the class could jump rope, boys as well as girls, and she taught us all to knit. I believe that these skills, in addition to being fun, are important ones for a child's overall development and today most children never learn them. She also brought in clay for us to work with, and even arranged for the pieces that we made to be fired. I clearly remember the remarkably ugly stoneware ashtray I made and proudly presented to my mother for a Christmas gift. I had pressed my forefinger into the clay to make a dent on each side for the purpose of holding the cigarette, and I had lovingly scratched her full initials into the bottom – B.L.E.P.

The teacher I remember as my favorite was Mrs. Murray, my fifth grade teacher. She was also the school librarian, and she loved to read aloud to us. She read us *The Hobbit* when it was a new book. She was one of those teachers who made a point of encouraging every student in the class, and I felt very safe with her. Later, when I became a teacher myself, she served as a model for me, as did Andy Sonner with his use of stories to bring history to life.

Sixth grade with Mrs. Strayer was a year of transition to more worldly preoccupations. Students joined the safety patrols, wearing white belts with silver badges over our khaki uniforms. Once a month we were visited by a police officer named Sergeant Seek, who inspected our uniforms. If he found our belts dingy or our shoes unpolished, we would get a demerit. For some reason, I found it really hard to keep my patrol belt clean, and was always having to soak it in bleach. Still it remained a dirty-looking beige instead of white. It was my responsibility to escort a group of kindergartners from the school over to Garrett Park Estates. I took this job very seriously. Giving kids this kind of responsibility seems to be out of fashion now.

My whole class attended ballroom dancing lessons one evening a week. The dancing teacher was Mr. Clark, a short, square-faced man with a pockmarked face. He was also our P.E. teacher. He taught us to jitterbug, fox trot, and waltz as we shuffled around the auditorium accompanied by songs like *Green Door* and *Elmer's Tune*. We all made "love lists" of our crushes in the order of preference and shared them with each other. I was invited to my first boy-girl party, and the year ended with an actual dance.

Mrs. Strayer encouraged creativity and initiative. I loved it when she let me work on a mural in the hall with other students, depicting everyday life in the Middle Ages. When one of my classmates, Paul Davids, single-handedly wrote a play of *Jason and the Golden Fleece*, Mrs. Strayer turned it into a full-fledged production, starring Paul as Jason. To this day I vividly recall my Greek page-boy costume, sewn for me by my mother, the one line I had in the play, and the song that Paul wrote for the court bard to sing, a ballad recounting the story of the origins of the Golden Fleece.

That May we planned our "graduation" ceremony. Mrs. Strayer, good sport that she was, thought it would be fun if we wrote a song for the ceremony as a whole class, so we did. Amazingly, I still remember both the words and the tune to the song we wrote. It went like this:

> We're the class of '59
> For a change we're here on time
> We don't know how to fill our pens
> We're noisier than a flock of hens
> We give the teachers dirty looks
> You'd think that we were dirty crooks!

Mrs. Strayer even consented to let us sing *The Battle of New Orleans* (which was then at the top of the pop charts, sung by Johnny Horton) for the graduation. It had nothing to do with any kind of graduation theme, but we begged her to let us sing it, and let us she did. We were at the end of our elementary years. I had, for the most part, been blessed with teachers who seemed to really understand me and take an interest in my well-being. My whole childhood had been spent in a truly safe and supportive community. I could hardly realize at that age how fortunate I was.

Junior high and high school were times when our world grew larger and began to gradually merge with the adult world. At Kensington Junior High I made new friends, including Karen McLaughlin. She lived in Garrett Park, but because she was on the other side of town on Weymouth Street, and she had almost always been in a different class than mine in elementary school, I had not known her well before. With other friends, we began to take buses into D.C. to see movies or sometimes eat lunch.

By high school our group of friends was volunteering to usher at Arena Stage theater (so we could see the plays for free), visiting art galleries downtown, going to parties where getting very drunk was the main activity, driving for hours all over the place while we smoked forbidden cigarettes and listened to pop hits on the car radio, and at one point, when they had a concert in Baltimore, implementing an unsuccessful scheme to meet the Beatles. We discovered Schwartz's Drug Store, an old-fashioned drug store near Dupont Circle, which became a kind of home-away-from-home for us in high school and beyond. My friends and I spent hours at Schwartz's drinking coffee, smoking, and watching the world go by. When Sam Cooke was shot and killed, we headed straight to Schwartz's to smoke cigarettes and grieve together.

My parents encouraged me to live my ideals and to volunteer. In the summer, several friends and I volunteered at a day camp for inner-city children in Anacostia, and continued as a volunteer tutor for the same children during the winter. The following summer we volunteered for Project Head Start. These were formative experiences, and from them I learned the rewards of being of service to others. I

Barbara and Roger Pope - 1963

am grateful that I lived in a time and place where these opportunities were so readily available. I was at the March on Washington, and I remember when Martin Luther King gave his famous speech there, though I don't remember the actual march or who I was with at the time. I also remember a Bob Dylan concert where he introduced one of his new songs, "Who Killed Davey Moore?"

My friends and I were very political. My small group of cronies included Ray Popkin, (who had recently moved to Garrett Park). We used to gather at my house after school to sing protest and labor songs, or listen to *The Peat Bog Soldiers*, a scratchy old 78 rpm Paul Robeson record that belonged to Ray's father. One time we gathered outside of Benjamin Franklin College in D.C. to picket their admissions policies, which were reputedly discriminatory against blacks, and we regularly drove downtown to attend CORE (Congress on Racial Equality) meetings. I was surprised (and secretly thrilled) at one point to learn that the administration at Walter Johnson had me on a list of suspected subversives that needed to be watched. Since my parents had always condoned my political activities, it had never occurred to me that my idealism could be construed as anything but virtuous. Perhaps growing up in Garrett Park had insulated me from the mainstream conservative views of the time.

After graduating from George Washington University with a degree in English Literature, I lived for a time in the Maine woods, working at an alternative school for delinquent teenagers. In my mid-twenties I moved out to the small town of Mendocino on the north coast of California. Actually, the original impulse to move to Mendocino had come from our Garrett Park next door neighbors, Don and

Splitting logs in the Maine woods

Sally Shook, who had moved to California around 1968 and ended up in the town of Albion, just south of

Mendocino. I had been a frequent babysitter to their three little boys, and the winter after they moved, they made a trip back east and paid my family a visit. When I saw how healthy and colorful the whole family looked, the boys with long hair, headbands, and tie-dyed tee shirts, I decided that Mendocino would be my future destination. It was early 1975 when I actually followed through with this plan, and it was in Mendocino that I met my husband, David, a year after moving there.

Eventually, we ended up moving to the foothills of the Sierra Nevada mountain range, and raising our three daughters in an intentional community there. In the mid '90s I became a classroom (Waldorf) teacher, where I worked hard to foster community in my classroom. When my class was in fifth grade, I was inspired by my childhood memories to have my students collaborate in writing their own play – it was "The Golden Fleece" of course, and in my opinion it rivaled the one that Paul Davids wrote back in 1959. My wonderful childhood memories, most of them a gift of the town I grew up in, have influenced me in countless immeasurable ways.

I took the essence of the experience of growing up in a town like Garrett Park with me into adulthood. I have always sought out places to live which offered abundant natural beauty and a strong sense of community, things I experienced and learned to think of as essential in childhood. I can't really imagine how differently my life might have unfolded had I grown up in a conventional suburban housing development.

A few years ago I discovered that the modest house I grew up in had been torn down and replaced with a very large Victorian-style house. I admit that I was dismayed – it didn't seem right that someone would dare to do this to a place that held so many precious memories for me. Occasionally I have dreams that I am wandering the streets of Garrett Park, trying to get "home" again. I have lived in many beautiful places, I've felt supported and connected to communities of like-minded, interesting people, and Garrett Park will always be the standard against which I measure them.

(Written by Lee Pope)

Pope-Daum Family - Caitilin, Lu, Gaea, David, and Lee with Cassie the Cat

TIM POWELL

The town, for the most part, is physically still there. If you walk around you still get the feeling that it's Garrett Park. It was a version of small town America that got created in the image of an English village in the 1890s, and here it is 2017, and it's still pretty much the same place. From an urban planner's perspective, the town is special in its own right, not just because it's the place where I grew up. The problem is, it's so hard to create it. What is it that's there, and why can't you recreate it? What is it and why is it so special?

My parents, Sam and Iris Powell, both grew up in Washington near Capitol Hill. In 1943, they built their home at 4700 Clyde Ave. and moved to Garrett Park. I vaguely recall them indicating that in addition to the benefits of living in a home with a yard and being part of a community, my mother saw buying a house in the suburbs as an investment. She ended up buying a few more lots in the neighborhood and then later selling them.

I was born on March 12, 1947 at Sibley Hospital in Washington, D.C. I have one brother, Tom, five years older to the day. My father ran, and then owned, a custom engine and auto parts company at 14th and W. in NW Washington. My mother had worked at AT&T before we were born, and up until when I entered high school, she was a stay-at-home mother, returning to work at AT&T when I was a teenager.

Living in Garrett Park really offered my father what he needed, giving him unbelievable opportunities to show his leadership skills. He could become an integral part of a community, something that would have been much harder if he had stayed in Washington. He was politically active in the town, rising up through being on the town council to becoming mayor and chairman of the Garrett Park Pool Association, and he was an active, enthusiastic participant in the Garrett Park Players.

Right from the get-go he was part of a small group of people who used to cut down trees. There were so many trees in Garrett Park, and when people needed to clear a lot for house-building purposes, this group would come and cut them down. They cut down gigantic old oaks of huge diameter with hand tools - giant saws with handles on each end, sledge hammers, and wedges, and they had to figure out how to drop these enormous trees. I used to go with him and watch them at work. In fact, one time I put my hand down at the wrong time on a wedge, and somebody brought down a hammer and smashed my finger.

It is noteworthy that neither of my parents had any formal education beyond high school, something my father was very self-conscious about. That explained to me why he was such a voracious reader, and why he encouraged me to do the same. That was a very big thing in our house, the fact that he didn't have the education that so many of our neighbors did. But he was able to keep up with people, and I heard this from so many of our neighbors, that "Your father is so well-read". I learned early that reading was very important. I was always asking people what they were reading, and then I would think, "Well, maybe I should read that book".

On weekends our parents took us in to Washington to visit monuments, museums, or the zoo. My father had been a cab driver in the 1930s, and he really knew the DC area well. My parents also hosted frequent fancy cocktail parties and dinners prepared by my mother. I was allowed to attend these parties in my later years in elementary school, and my parents' parties provided my first lessons on how to socialize with older people, lessons which became very valuable to me during and after college.

My mother raised me to be responsible for all household chores. My brother and I shared the house and yard chores until he left for boarding school in the ninth grade. From that point on, I essentially became an only child, which meant I had to do all the yard chores except during summer and vacations. We also had a maid (Margaret Hawkins) who did the house cleaning work during my younger years, cleaning for us three to five days a week, and in later years, one day a week.

The big yard job was leaf raking. I can vividly recall both dreading raking leaves and enjoying some side aspects of doing this chore. I used to develop a pattern of how to rake them up, thinking of an efficient way that would lessen the task. Burning the leaves (allowed in our younger years) was always a fun task, creating great smells. Sometimes, before we burned them, and if the leaves were piled on soft ground, running and jumping and burying oneself in the pile was fun. Shoveling snow was always an event, depending on the severity of the snow fall. I saw it as a challenge to keep up with shoveling it before it became too deep, and how to address dealing with it after an all-night snow fall.

The Normans, who lived directly across the street from us, were like an extended family to me. The Norman kids were Paul and Storry. Peggy, in later years, became a second mother, and Storry, a little sister I never had. George Norman was an inventor and creator and an eccentric character. He had a fascinating job at the David Taylor Model Basin, and one year he took me there for an open house. I was truly fascinated and have never forgotten the experience. George was always building things - the fort in their back yard, his Styrofoam boat in the garage. From the fourth grade, since my brother had gone off to private school, I was the only child at home, so I played at the Norman's house, and our parents socialized to a certain degree. Peggy took me on some summer trips with them. I will always remember going to Kitty Hawk one summer with their family. I have so many "family" memories that include the Normans.

The Brown family consisted of cigar smoking George and his wife, Ann, and their daughters, Sally and Rosie, as well as their older sons, Tom and Terry. They lived catty-cornered from us in an interesting house with a dark paneling wood interior.

The Popes lived next door to the Browns. Carl Pope, who was two grades above me in school, tried to get me into Boy Scouts, but I did not have the discipline. I was friends with his sister, Lee, who was my age. I thought that both Lee and her friend, Sherry Thomas, were smart, and this influenced me to want to be good in school and looked upon as a smart kid.

The Halls lived next door in a stone house that was like an historic English cottage inside and out. They even had an earthen vegetable cellar off the patio that was a wonder to me. They also had a croquet "court" in the upper yard that we used for years but surprisingly I never became an accomplished croquet player.

Our rear neighbors were the Booths. They took me in when I was young and challenged me to do crossword puzzles. I was the child they did not have.

The Borrors lived next door on Rokeby. Marty and Bunch were the parents, Christy was the daughter, and Buddy was their son. I spent a lot of time next door playing with Christy.

My main group of friends consisted of Ron Horn, David Crichton, and Chuck Reynolds. With my friends, playtime was simply outdoor time, sometimes doing things at one of our homes. My mother had the rule that if the weather was nice, you had to play outside, no TV. Back then simple things were sufficient. We just did "stuff". You just did stuff all the time and when you look back on it, you are somewhat puzzled about what you were doing. You were just doing whatever. The town itself was our playground, and we would roam over a great part of it on our bikes or on foot. Garrett Park was full of opportunities; we had the presence of so many trees, and we were surrounded by good neighbors. The playground that later became known as Wells Park was ground zero of hours of play during our elementary school years, and once the pool was built, we spent most of our summer hours there.

Ron Horn and Tim Powell

The adjacent portion of Rock Creek Park was always good for exploring, as was the railroad, especially the steep "cliffs" just northwest of Wells Park. We played on the railroad tracks all the time. We had this game where we would wait on the tracks when the train was coming, to see how close it would get before we would jump out of the way. Or right where it gets real steep down on both sides of the track, we would go there and see if we could shield ourselves when the train went by. When you think about it, it was kind of stupid and not really safe. The old railroad station was a symbol of the past, and I was sad to see it torn down.

There were some woods at the end of Clyde where we liked to go before they built Garrett Park Estates. There was a path where you could go right on up into the woods, and there were a couple of areas where we had cleared out the brush and we used to sit around and talk and fool around; who knows what we did? We also liked to hike in the Christmas Tree Woods over where the Wellses lived at the end of Rokeby. Beyond that was the White Flint Golf Course, and we used to sleigh ride on the golf course because there was a nice long hill there. They had a little shelter there for the golfers, so we could go there to get out of the wind when we were sledding in the winter.

That is where they built the mall, which, believe it or not, was the absolute state-of-the-art mall when I was in high school, or maybe it was college. It became one of those malls that got passed over, and I think by now they have torn it down. They had all the high end stores there, but it failed. I remember going over to the toy store over on Rockville Pike. You could walk there by going through Garrett Park Estates, and there was a Tonka toy tractor that I wanted to buy. I was only eight or nine, and I saved my money and walked all the way over there. My parents weren't very happy with me. Another time David, Ronnie and I walked all the way to Kensington on the tracks. My parents weren't very happy about that either.

I remember winters playing in the snow, sledding on Donnelly's Hill. I can recall years of sledding on the hill during the day and sometimes at night. The best part of a good snowfall was seeing how fast we could go on our American Flyer sleds, how far past the bottom of the hill or down into the playground park. We rode double deck on sleds, having "wreck races" against each other, and built big fires (which melted the asphalt) at night at the top of the hill. All were such great times.

In the summer, my parents rented homes at Rehoboth Beach, and later, when I was a senior in high school, they purchased a vacation home there. Except when we were vacationing at Rehoboth, the swim team consumed most of my summer from the time I was six or seven until I left for college. It was my focal point for five to six days each week. In the early years, I also worked at the swimming pool, first at the ice cream concession stand, and later as a life guard. Playing baseball was another sport I enjoyed. Other activities included being a Safety Patrol crossing guard in elementary school and working at the post office in my high school years.

I attended Garrett Park Elementary, and I liked it. School was an extension of the neighborhood, an integral part of Garrett Park, and a safe place. Going to school seemed just part of life, not a chore, and I don't recall ever dreading it. I was an average student who wanted to be smarter. I took some ribbing when I had to start wearing glasses in fourth grade, and kids took to calling me "four eyes", but it wasn't a big deal. At a recent Walter Johnson High School 50th reunion, I had the opportunity to be one of four (Becky Hodges, Kathy Offutt, Ron Horn, and myself) that had known each other since first grade. Somehow, that seemed special, all good feelings.

Mrs. Sutherland was a memorable teacher. I recall having her two times, as did my brother, so she had a lot of experience with my family. I always wondered whether she was the mother of Donald Sutherland as I recall one time she spoke of her actor son. I really liked her and wanted to please her, though she was hard on me.

Mrs. Reynolds (Dorothy - Chuck's mother) was head of the cafeteria and always friendly at lunch time. The school auditorium became a special place for me, as I remember taking dance classes there, trying to pair up with Pam Croom, a girl that I liked at the time. These were all fun things that made life interesting.

The cafeteria was the place that the Garrett Park Players performed theater productions. These provided my first exposure to theater, fostering an interest which has lasted throughout my life. My father was an actor in some of the performances, all serious dramas, not musicals, and I got to be the concessionaire, selling drinks from the ice cooler during intermission. Taking part in theater was another of the many of the wonderful opportunities that Garrett Park gave my father.

Due in part to living in the Washington metropolitan area, I had an awareness of national and world events. My friends influenced me to want to stay up to date on current events. Sherry Thomas and I were supposed to go to a "Peter, Paul and Mary" concert downtown, but that was the weekend when President Kennedy was shot, and it didn't happen. That was such a traumatic event. I will always remember driving down to Washington to stand on Pennsylvania Avenue to watch the Kennedy funeral procession, the riderless horse with the boots in the stirrup. It was all happening just a short drive from the safe haven of our town.

Overall, I lived a life of innocence: no drugs, limited alcohol consumption, great parents, and a charmed life, though as I got older, I remember a few minor "dumb" things that caused some temporary consequences. While home from college one summer, I got drunk at a town party and made fun of some important town officials. George Payne, who was town mayor at the time, overheard me and scolded me severely, and I felt quite embarrassed about the whole event afterwards. Once with a childhood friend, we broke into the swimming pool to go skinny dipping together with his girlfriend. We had to climb over the fence, and I was quite drunk, so I did not do very well, and I landed in an awkward position on top of the lower wooden entryway fence. Apparently, either due to some noise we generated or local gossip spreading very quickly the next day, I was outed by my brother. Both my parents were quite angry with me for being drunk, as well as for skinny dipping and breaking into the pool at night. My father was still involved in the Pool Association and my brother was the pool manager, so it was a sure thing that it was not going to go over well.

I graduated from Walter Johnson in 1965 and went to Clemson University for seven years, obtaining my undergraduate Architecture and Masters of City and Regional Planning degrees. From that time on, I only came home for holidays and summers. I married my first wife in 1970 while I was still in college, and we lived in Clemson. Upon graduation in 1972, we moved to Tampa for my first full-time job as an urban designer with the City County Planning Commission. My daughter was born in 1974. I divorced my first wife in 1981, and in 1983 I married my current wife Sandy, who had two sons from her first marriage. Both of our former spouses have now passed away, and our three children all live in Tampa. We have a vacation home in Ponte Vedra, Florida, which has been our permanent residence since 2003. My land development consulting company, which I started in 1988, is still in business today. I have commuted weekly to Tampa for the last fourteen years for my business. My oldest son joined the company a year ago and will eventually take control of it as I transition into retirement.

It's hard to express what Garrett Park was and how much it meant to me. It was such a safe haven, a protected little cocoon that you could live in. Because of the quality of people, I always felt like I was struggling to keep up with the neighborhood kids, who all seemed so smart and nice. And I am really thankful to Garrett Park for providing me with a stimulating environment. It really gave me an incentive in school all the way through high school and into college. I always give lots of credit and want to thank the kids who lived in Garrett Park, and the parents as well - there were a lot of smart parents in Garrett Park.

My involvement with the Garrett Players really influenced me a lot, and at WJ, I was involved with the theater group. My mother ruled my life, and she basically said, "Look, you can do theater, but if your grades start to suffer, you are out of it." Ironically, the more I did theater and the less I studied, the better grades I got. I think I learned how to study in a more concentrated manner because I so desperately wanted to do the theater. We had some unbelievably talented people in the theater at WJ, and while I wasn't on the stage, I got to see all that. What I was doing in theater, planning all the details for the final production, was similar to what I had to do in architecture. When I went to Clemson, I had to make a decision between theater and architecture, and obviously I chose architecture. But to this day, I am fascinated by live theater. I'm an avid theater fan, and we used to have season tickets in Tampa for the big traveling Broadway shows.

Growing up in Garrett Park has influenced me in so many ways. Being around "land development", including trees and the cutting of trees, I was always intrigued by houses and lot development. I remember playing in my front side yard with a neighborhood friend, building small houses and showing how they would fit on the land. When I was in high school, I once drew a rendering for the Thomas's, showing an addition to the back of their house. I was probably trying to impress Sherry, though I also liked both of her parents. I was in an architectural drafting class in Walter Johnson at the time, which led to my studying Architecture and City and Regional Planning at Clemson, and then specializing in land development. Was playing in the dirt, pretending to develop house lots, a precursor to what I ended up specializing in my entire life? Maybe. Was Garrett Park as a planned village an influence? Maybe. Was living and growing up in close proximity to one of the most interesting cities in the country an influence? Maybe.

The railroad was another influence, and it was so much a part of our lives. I remember David Crichton sometimes saying he had been up most of the night because a train had gotten stuck at the station near his house, and it would blow its whistle all night long, waiting to go forward. How many communities have a train running right alongside where the houses are like that? If we had that in a community now it would be the kiss of death on a new development, and people wouldn't like the noise. Yet it was a positive feature that attracted people to Garrett Park. When my wife and I drive to Tampa and back on weekends, portions of the highway run right beside the railroad track, and I still have the habit of rolling down the window to hear the train whistle at crossings.

In so many ways Garrett Park seemed like classic small town America. Garrett Park was a totally self-contained community containing the self-sustaining "town" elements of its own train station, commercial center and post office, elementary school, community center, library, swimming pool, all the ingredients of a "village". The town had its own holiday traditions, such as the July 4th parade down by the post office, events at the swimming pool, and fireworks at the community center. The residents formed the entire spectrum of society from the farmer, small business owners, an author, high level government workers, teachers and a lot of just plain good people who sensed that Garrett Park was "their town", something to nurture and protect, which obviously is still in play today.

Over the years I found myself being part of the land development industry in Florida, trying to create communities that captured the essence of Garrett Park. In doing this I learned the difficulties of recreating such a community, and the unique set of influences that went together to form what I had grown up in.

My oldest son had the Garrett Park experience for a year, when he lived with my parents and took care of them. We moved my parents out of the house in the 1990s, renting the house until 2001 before selling it to the tenant. This was a time of very mixed feelings for me, as it was an end to my physical connection to the house. However, I still think of myself as both "from" and "a part of" the town, as it made so much of an impression and had so much influence on me. My memories all merge when I consider how the town, my childhood home, my parents, my friends, and my education have all contributed to who I am today. Garrett Park was as formative to my life as were my parents, and I have only good memories of growing up there.

My last visit was during my fiftieth Walter Johnson reunion in 2015. Ron Horn, my wife and I drove through the town. There were some obvious changes. New homes had replaced several of the original homes, others had been expanded, and we saw homes on lots that we had always thought of as permanently wooded. Otherwise, the town still had the feel of the Garrett Park of my childhood memories. I could still picture myself playing in the neighborhood, in Wells Park, swimming at the Garrett Park Pool, going to the elementary school, being an elementary school crossing guard. The town, for the most part, is physically still there. If you walk around you still get the feeling that it's Garrett Park. It was a version of small town America that got created in the image of an English village in the 1890s, and here it is 2017, and it's still pretty much the same place. From an urban planner's perspective, the town is special in its own right, not just because it's the place where I grew up. The problem is, it's so hard to create it. What is it that's there, and why can't you recreate it? What is it and why is it so special?

(Parts written by Tim Powell)

Tim and Sandy Powell, Portugal 2016

18

DAVID CRICHTON

Garrett Park was a real community. I got so much joy just from reading the Garrett Bugle, especially when Clyde Hall was the editor. He would write the "Christmas Epistles" and name every family in the Park, wishing them a good Christmas. I remember that Clyde had nicknames for a lot of the people in the town. In the old Garrett Park Bugle there used to be a brief history of the Park that somebody would write, and I would be so fascinated by that, and I liked to find some of these places that were mentioned from back in the 1890's. I was always interested in the history of the town, like how the Wilbur's house was the first school house. As a boy I liked riding my bike all around and the feeling of knowing the town real well.

My parents were J.C. and Lizanne (Elizabeth Anne) Crichton. Dad worked for the State Department, and after being a stay-at-home mom when we were young, mom went back to work for what was then known as the Department of Health, Education, and Welfare. So they were both government employees. I was born in 1947, the oldest of their four children. My sister, Anne, was born two years after me, and two years later my brother, Mark, was born. Laurie, the youngest of us, was born about '53 or '54.

We moved from Prince George's County to Garrett Park in 1952. My brother Mark was a toddler, and I was just ready to start kindergarten. I think my parents moved there primarily because of the Montgomery County school system. Turk Stevens, our next door neighbor, was an architect, and he and his brother, who was a home builder, had built a spec house there, and I think Dad was looking for a place where he could commute easily on the train to Washington. Somehow they stumbled on to this spec home in Garrett Park.

We lived at 11016 Rokeby Avenue. I had any number of friends in the neighborhood, as the town was teeming with baby boom kids. At the time the railroad station still existed, and the park (Wells Park) was right across the street with swings and a slide. We played all kind of games in the park, games like White Flag. It was a very exciting place to live, so close to the railroad. The steam engines were still running in the early '50s, and on more than one occasion I remember the excitement when there were leaf fires in the park, ignited by sparks from the steam engines. Can you imagine anything more thrilling than coming home from kindergarten and finding twenty fire trucks in front of your home?

My father was a big rail fan; he loved trains. He encouraged us from an early age to take the train into Washington and get on the street car. He would meet us for lunch, and you could catch the 5:15 train in Union Station to get you home. I remember the schedule of trains, because that's when you would have to be home when you were playing outside - it was when the 5:15 came. It was a commuter, and usually it was on time.

As a result of Dad's love of trains, I loved trains as a boy. He taught me to tell time by drawing a clock and saying, here is what the clock will look like when the Capitol Limited goes by. Here's what the clock will look like when the Columbian goes by. He had all these clocks – and of course he was gambling that they were going to run on time. But I think that in the fifties the railroads were running better than they did later.

We played on the tracks, though it was probably hard on my mother, because her father had been killed by a train when she was a young girl. I walked down the tracks a lot to get to the pool when I was a kid, because it was the shortest way to get there. Of course we used to put coins on the tracks and let the trains flatten them. I remember being scared when the railroad police would come. Fuel oil tank cars used to get dropped over there where Mr. Chisholm had his oil business, and we would play on those cars. Every once in a while the railroad police would show up to keep the kids off the property.

The four o'clock mail train both picked up the mail and kicked it off, and that train came through real fast. Mr. Chamberlain, who had the TV business, always caught the sack. Once in a while the sack would get kicked off the mail car, and once or twice the bag would rip open, and with the wind of the train rushing back, the letters would swirl all over the place, and he would be running around picking up all the mail.

My mom liked to have a lot of kids around the house, and she made the neighborhood kids very welcome, so our friends always felt comfortable being at our house. She loved to play cards. She played bridge with her friends, and she tried to teach us kids how to play bridge, but I wasn't very apt. I think some of the kids actually did learn to play bridge from her.

My dad was really into family vacations, and we would go away every summer for two weeks. We almost always went to New England, places like Vermont, and later, Cape Cod. He lived for these vacations, and he loved planning them. So there was lots of excitement around that, getting ready to leave, packing up the station wagon. When I was real young we went down to Rehoboth or Dewey Beach a few times, but my dad didn't actually care for the beach that much, so we didn't go often. I also remember that we took a trip to the Smokey Mountains along the Blue Ridge Parkway when I was a little tiny boy. But primarily we would go to New England, and once we found Cape Cod, that became the place we would go. We liked to rent this little house in West Dennis, in the central Cape.

The night before leaving on vacation, my dad would take us out to buy comic books. There was a journal store in Wheaton that had every magazine you could dream of – *Harpers*, *The Atlantic*, *The New Yorker* - and he would take us there to buy our comic books. The next morning, we'd all pile into the station wagon. There was a little place in the back of the car that one person could slide into. You could lie on top of everything, and that seemed really great until a few hours into the trip, and then you would want to swap with somebody else. It was a long trip. In those days you had to go through Baltimore, and you didn't pick up the turnpike until New Jersey.

I had a very good feeling about my family. We had dinner together every night. Mom and Dad hardly ever went out, and we hardly ever did either. Dad was a big reader, so after dinner he would sit and read, while we would watch TV, if we could, or play sports. I played with Mark, and Anne and Laurie played together.

David and Laurie Crichton

My parents talked me into taking Mark under my wing and kind of looking after him. I was pretty hard on Anne when she was a little girl. Laurie was born with a heart defect, so she was special to all of us. She couldn't do as much exercise as other kids, and as I got older I was closer to Laurie than anybody, though she was seven years younger than me. When I got back from the service, Laurie was still living in the house, and we spent a lot of time together.

Of course I had a lot of friends in the Park, and we spent a lot of times outdoors. I have this early memory from when I first started kindergarten that Ron Horn had a club, and I think Chuck Reynolds was in it too. He had been influenced by the Lone Ranger, and they would wear masks and ambush people. As the new kid, I got ambushed by them a few times at the triangle where Waverly branches off from Kenilworth. They would run ahead of you when you were coming home from school, hide in the bushes, and jump out at you. They wouldn't exactly terrorize you, but you knew that you weren't part of the gang at that point.

Soon after, Ron Horn, Chuck Reynolds and Timmy Powell all became good friends of mine. We played sports in the park across the street - baseball, kickball, and catch. We had baseball there even though it wasn't really laid out for that. I used to be invited up to Tim Powell's house, and we would play trains in the basement. Other friends included Donald Franz and Stanley Woodwell, who both lived on the other side of Kenilworth. Garrett Park Estates was just starting to develop, and Tim Coulter was a friend of mine who lived over in the Estates. Rob Freer, who was a little older, became a good friend later. I was friends with the Bolton's too, even though they were younger. Bill was two years younger than me, and Todd was my broth-

Mark, Anne and Laurie with Ron Horn

er's age, and they had two little sisters. My mom was very close to Mrs. Bolton, who died when the kids were very young – the little girls were probably still in pre-school. So the Bolton kids spent a lot of time at our house, my mother helping out by looking after them.

All of my friends' parents were very special. Ron Horn lived just up the street, and Mr. and Mrs. Horn, as well as Mr. and Mrs. Reynolds, were always very important to me, especially as when I was in high school and beyond. The Powell's were always very nice to us boys. I can't think of anybody that wasn't. The Stevenses lived next door and they were very sweet. Mrs. Stevens always called my mother Anne instead of Lizanne. Mrs. Parsons, the Freers, Mrs. Penn, and Louie Karsh, who ran the store, were always very friendly, and also Louie's wife.

I have wonderful memories of seasons and holidays. I remember celebrating May Day with a Maypole at school when I was young, and I also remember that there was a field day late in the school year when classes would have three-legged races and other games.

Walt Reynolds with David, 1960

I enjoyed the long, lazy summers, and the sense of coolness, the relief when you came back into the Park with all its trees, compared to everywhere else. The town had a community center in a building that was an old surplus army barracks, and somehow it got relocated there. Volunteers had to finish it – clean it up, paint it, varnish the floors, and I remember there would be work parties there, and the little library used to be attached there. My folks always wanted me to be part of the summer rec program they had at the community center, but I resisted that. In the summer, I just wanted to go see what my friends were doing. We'd go down to the store to buy some candy or a Popsicle, or we'd go to the pool, ride our bikes, or play catch. Sometimes we would invent our own dice games. We didn't belong to the pool at first, and when my parents joined it was a big deal. The pool was a great community thing. We could ride our bike there or walk on the tracks.

The Fourth of July was really fun, the parade and decorating your bike, trying to win prizes. That was another sore point between Anne and me. My father would go to great extremes to help Anne decorate her bike, but I was considered too old for that, so I had to decorate my own bike. She would have these flying saucers and mobiles hanging from her handlebars, and win first prize, and I would just have crepe paper in the spokes of my bike wheels. I remember the Fourth of July events, and that the fireworks were always great.

I always loved the fall. It was my favorite season and it still is. I love the colors. I loved the leaves, but I didn't like raking them so much – Saturday morning you couldn't do anything until you had gotten the leaves raked. I remember the smell of burning leaves all the way to Christmas time. And I loved football season. Mr. Horn, Ron's dad was the principal of Wheaton High and he would take us to the football games. I remember being excited watching the high school football games.

At Christmas, when I was young, they used to light the big tree up at the community center, and we would sing carols. Someone would dress as Santa Claus and hand out candy. I have wonderful memories of sledding, though there can't have been that many times that it really snowed that much. I remember the way they closed off Donnelly's Hill so we could sled there. And for some unknown reason, the Lightning Glider sled my father bought me was the fastest sled on the hill, from when I was a little kid, even though Flexible Flyers were known to be the best. I still claim to have the record – one time I made it all the way down the hill to my own driveway. We also made trails and sledded on the Cleveland's hill in their big yard on the corner of Rokeby and Albemarle. It was nice, that they would let us do that. And at night we would build some wonderful sled runs all the way from the Reynold's yard, through the Horn's and the Bolton's back yard and down through what was known as the Turner's house, right at the corner of Argyle and Rokeby. We had a trail that ran all through there, and we would put candles in the snow so as to see the run at night. The sled runs never worked that well, but it was fun building them.

We would cut through people's yards all the time. The Giesers lived up on Kenilworth across from the Reynolds' house. They had three boys - Benny, and his older brothers, Steve, and Jimmy. They had a basketball court on their barn, and they had these lights. Ron Horn, Chuck Reynolds, and I would go to the Giesers' house at night and ask them to turn on the lights so we could shoot baskets, and they would. Even when Benny or his older brothers weren't around, we could play basketball at all hours. It seems like it was different back then, the fact that you could go to someone else's house and ask to use their court and they didn't mind at all.

Garrett Park was a real community. I got so much joy just from reading the *Garrett Bugle*, especially when Clyde Hall was the editor. He would write the "Christmas Epistles" and name every family in the Park, wishing them a good Christmas. I remember that Clyde had nicknames for a lot of the people in the town. In the old *Garrett Bugle* there used to be a brief history of the Park that somebody would write, and I would be so fascinated by that, and I liked to find some of these places that were mentioned from back in the 1890s. I was always interested in the history of the town, like how the Wilbur's house was the first school house. As a boy I liked riding my bike all around and the feeling of knowing the town real well. I had paper routes from the time I was in fifth or sixth grade all through junior high school, and really at one time or another I had a route covering every section of Garrett Park, including Richterville.

I started school as a kindergartner at Garrett Park Elementary. My dad and mom walked me to school the first day and walked me home. I remember meeting Mrs. Duey as a five year old boy, being in Mrs. Duey's office, and her welcoming me to the school. I remember the building, and the stage, and the wooden floors, and I remember having Mrs. Duey for first grade. I think she was a great teacher. I remember the new additions being built, how exciting it was to watch those additions go up. And I remember Mrs. Sutherland, my sixth grade teacher, very clearly. She was sort of intimidating, but she was a very good teacher.

Mrs. Reynolds ran the cafeteria, but Chuck and I would almost never eat there. Instead we would ride our bikes to Louie's store and get a hot dog, which drove Mrs. Reynolds crazy. Louie could be kind of gruff with kids but for some reason he really liked us. When the big guys - Tommy Jeronda, Buddy Borror, and Donald Lamb - would be sitting on a milk crate in front of the post office, if you were a little kid you felt like you had to run the gauntlet just to go into the store. They might pretend they were going to steal your Popsicle or something, and I was intimidated by them. So I'd head up to the store, and if I saw the big guys sitting over there, I'd turn around and go home.

Overall, my memories of Garrett Park Elementary are very positive. I remember looking forward to recess, to lunch time, to playing games with my friends. But I had one experience that really set me back. In sixth grade, we took ballroom dancing classes with Mr. Clark, and there was a dance at the end of the school year. It was at the dance that I was traumatized. I had this girlfriend named Sandra Donelle, who was a cousin or something of Barbara Krouse. Though she didn't live in Garrett Park, she attended Garrett Park Elementary. At one point during the dance, I was outside with Sandy, and she wanted to kiss me. Mr. Pepsin, the chaperone, came out just at that moment, and naturally he assumed it was me that was trying to kiss her. He told her to go back inside, and he gave me hell. That set me back for years!

It was during my sixth grade year that Mike Yogi joined my class, when his family had moved from Hawaii to Garrett Park Estates. Mike and I became good friends, and we still are good friends today.

Leaving the womb of Garrett Park to attend Kensington Junior High was like shell shock for me. I remember this kid in the seventh grade class named Tommy Monte. He was kind of a tough guy, and he looked so much bigger and so much older than me and my friends from Garrett Park Elementary. When I went to the first assembly, where they were orienting the new seventh graders, and I saw him, I thought "This guy is in my class??" There were kids there from much different places than Garrett Park. I remember older kids staging fights between younger ones down by the bridge. I abhorred the notion of older guys, ninth graders, promoting fights between seventh graders after school. Everyone would go down to the bridge to watch the fight, so there was a big audience. I just hated that.

Mr. Cross was the school disciplinarian. You had to be in Mr. Cross's office at least once to say you had had a real experience of being at Kensington Jr. High. It was a rite of passage to have to go to Mr. Cross's office, and have him take his little whip and whip you. So Kensington Junior High was a less happy experience. I just lived to get out of Kensington, lived to get on the bus to Garrett Park and to go home, and I loved for the weekend to come. I'd been too sheltered and too happy in my own little world of Garrett Park.

I think I did have some good teachers at KJH. I had Mrs. Stickley for English, and I remember Mr. Abel. But the social dynamics of the place didn't work for me. I made some new friends there though, kids that weren't from Garrett Park, like Nick Bambakis, who lived in Garrett Park Estates. Actually, he was one of the hoody ones, one of the kids out pitching pennies.

One fun thing that I always remember about Nick Bambakis was the ringing of the bell at the Seventh Day Adventist church. It was kind of a tradition that got passed down as you aged that someone would get up in the belfry and ring the bell on Halloween night, and they got chased out of there. It was always something I heard about as a kid, my father would talk about how on Halloween night the big kids (the JDs, or juvenile delinquents) would always ring the bell. When I was old enough to be involved with that, Nick and I went up early that week and climbed up on the roof at night. We tied a rope onto the wheel, tied a long string onto the rope, used the string to ring the bell from the ground, and then ran away. We ran from the police and hid back behind the church. It was a lot of fun.

Adolescence was a difficult time for me. I wasn't a very good student. At Walter Johnson, I wanted to be on the football team, and I got onto the Junior Varsity in tenth grade, so I had fun playing sports a little bit. I wasn't any star but I was on the teams. But I liked going home to Garrett Park and playing with my friends. The last semester of my senior year I cut school a little with Chuck Reynolds, but we'd mostly hang out in Garrett Park. I didn't drink at that point, not until I was older.

I graduated from WJ in '65 and I went one year to American University. I didn't really want to go there, and I flunked out. I was kind of in rebellion from my dad at that time, rebelling for no reason really. It was just that time of your life when you rebelled. I had wanted to go to Montgomery Junior College where a lot of my friends went, but that would have been a disaster too, because I just wasn't ready for college.

After that, I worked for the county, raking leaves in the fall of '67. Then I enlisted in the Marine Corps. I had been waiting to get my draft notice, and so on Saturday I went down there and signed the papers, and I got my draft notice that very day. Because I had volunteered to be drafted, I would only have to serve for two years instead of four. I kept it a secret from my parents until the night before I left. It must have been quite a blow for them.

Here is how they found out: Carrie Linton, the older Linton boy, was going to give me a ride to the recruiter's office at six in the morning, and he called to check the time with my mother. He didn't know I hadn't told them. That wasn't a good thing to do to my parents. I don't' know what was going on in my mind. I was in the service from December '66 to December of '69. Mike Yogi saw me off at Dulles when I left for Vietnam, and he was there when I returned.

This was the Vietnam era, a very formative time. My parents were quiet about the war, though I remember my mother was very upset, very angry when Kent State happened. And my mom, probably more than my dad, became very much down on it all.

I became more focused after coming out of the service, and I was very sympathetic to the anti-war movement when I came home. I hadn't thought that much about it before signing up. When people asked me about why I signed up for the Marines, I would say idealistic, altruistic things to people like "I've been lucky all my life, and the people who are going into the service now haven't had it as good as me, so why should they go instead of me?" I had some naïve feelings that we were doing the right thing, wanting to help the peasants in Viet Nam, who were being put upon by the Viet Cong, who were taxing their rice and terrorizing them if they didn't support the insurgency. Of course I was disabused of a lot of those ideas because of what I experienced over there, and so by the time I came home I was much more sympathetic to the anti-war movement, and began to pay more attention to current events. Once I got to Montgomery Junior College, there was an anti-war veterans group and they asked me to join.

One time when I was home on leave from Vietnam, I was visiting Ron Horn in Pittsburg. We drove up to Ohio to see Chuck Reynolds, who had always been one of my best friends. By then Chuck was a real hippy. I remember when he saw me he said, "Jesus, Crichton, you look like such a Marine!" It was like all of a sudden this bar came down because I didn't look like everybody that Chuck was hanging out with. I think this split has carried over to how the world works today.

Another, later time, I remember going to a rally with my then future wife. We went up to Pittsburg quite a bit, and I remember a big rally there down on the waterfront, and one of the speakers was this burly older man, a carpenter's union official, and he was speaking out passionately against the war. I think maybe he had lost a son, and I remember the comments from the crowd. They were, of course, all smoking dope, and they had this negative reaction to him, like "Who is this guy?" They didn't like the way he looked, and they were really cut off from those kinds of people, ordinary working people.

Chuck Reynolds and David

After I got out of the Marines, I was finally ready to go to college, and I enrolled at Montgomery Junior College. It was when I was best man at Ron Horn's wedding that I saw and reconnected with my future wife there. She was Ron's first wife's roommate. We had met a little before that when I was still in the service, and then I saw her again at the wedding and took up with her.

She moved to Boston, and I transferred to go to Suffolk University. I got my degree there, and then I attended University of Michigan where I got a social work degree. I ended up working construction, and I became interested in labor relations. Michigan at the time was a big labor state, and I ended up going to Michigan State to study labor relations. When I graduated, I got a job with a big contractor. I worked for a number of contractors there. So I made a career in labor relations, and on and off I also worked as a brick layer. I'm retired now, living on Cape Cod, where we always used to vacation. We moved here in 2010.

David's 60th Birthday: Bill Millard, David Crichton, Ron Horn, and Mike Yogi

I'm still in touch with a few people I knew back then in Garrett Park. I still know Ron Horn, Rob Freer, and Bill Millard, as well as Mike Yogi and Nick Bambakis. Three years ago in June I had some business in Washington, and I actually stayed in Garrett Park, in Bill Millard's house, the same house he grew up in on Rokeby Avenue. I've known Bill since we were kids living a few blocks away from each other, and over time we became good friends, especially as young adults. Bill and I both came home from the military and Vietnam within a year of each other, which definitely created a shared bond.

I think the Park still feels like the Park to me, and I can still recognize a lot of things that are familiar to me, things that bring back memories. But there has been a lot of growth, remodels, knock-downs where houses have been replaced by much bigger houses. My house was first added on to and then taken down and replaced. Of course it's very expensive to live there now. You couldn't be a barber and buy a house in Garrett Park today. But it still feels like the Park to me. It's different, but it's not dramatically different. That's one of the main things about it. People have really aspired to keep it from being ruined.

Of course the whole region has really been changed completely, but I've gone back so many times over the years, I kind of saw it changed gradually. It doesn't seem as dramatic when you see the changes in small increments, routinely. Still, as I've gotten older I dislike that the whole region has gotten so expensive. The surrounding area over by Rockville has changed a lot, so much that I can hardly recognize where I am over there. The wholesale development has kind of swallowed everything up.

I always have a warm feeling about Garrett Park, and I have only good memories. I think Garrett Park in the 1950s and 1960s was a special time and place, a good time to be a kid. The community spirit was really alive after the war, and the economic situation was very different. A lot of people had blue collar jobs and yet the wives were able to stay home. When you think of how many stay-at-home moms there were, you just don't see that anymore. It made things really nice for the kids. My childhood gave me a sense that life was good, there were a lot of nice things in the world. You could go through life expecting good things to be happening instead of bad, though of course it depends a lot on the family you came from. It was hard to transition out of it as a boy, because it was so nice, so maybe in some ways Garrett Park was a little too safe a harbor for me. It was so shocking to go the big regional schools with kids from really different places, so shocking getting exposed to new things.

When I think of what I liked best about growing up in Garrett Park, it is that general feeling of well-being I had as a child there. It was a safe place, a friendly place where you had a lot of friends, as well as adults who cared about you. It was a town that promoted a good community life and a family life. And I always fondly remember the shade in the summers. With those big old trees, it was like a safe harbor.

Anne Ptak, David and Mark Crichton

19

RON HORN

Garrett Park was a strong community in the best sense of the word. That was because of the movers and shakers of the town, who were really invested in making the town a community, people like Sam Powell, who was the mayor at one time, and as far as I was concerned never stopped being mayor.

My parents, Harold and Louise Horn, moved to Garrett Park in August of 1946, nine months before my birth. My father had been working as a public school teacher since returning from serving in World War II; as a teacher he didn't make much money, and I think that my parents were only able to afford to buy their own house after my father inherited some money from his father. When my family first moved to Garrett Park, the address was 14 Rokeby Avenue, but at some later date it became 11114 Rokeby Avenue. I was born on May 3, 1947. I have an older sister, Barbara, who was born during the war in 1943.

Harold, Ron, Barbara and Louise Horn

Ron, Louise, Barbara

Ron in middle front,
Tim Powell on front right

My father taught physics at Montgomery Blair, and at some point he transitioned into being a vice-principal, eventually ending up at Wheaton High School. My mother had also been a teacher. She was a music teacher at one time, and taught English as well. When I was young she didn't work, but later, when I was in the 7th grade, she started working as a substitute teacher. I'll never forget one time when she substituted at Kensington Junior High, and I was hanging out with a bunch of terrible characters in some club. Later she taught at Gaithersburg High School. She really liked music and was into teaching choir.

I can't remember all the people that I played with when I was little, but I think I played with Timmy Powell, who lived up on the street on Clyde Avenue. The Clevelands, who lived in a house near ours on the corner of Rokeby and Abemarle, had a boy my age, and I played with him. I have a story that my father would relate to me: one time when I was really little, I went into the Cleveland's yard and somehow I triggered this mole trap that they had. I was so little that I just thought the world was going to end, and I came running home and told my dad, "We've got to move!" I didn't go to nursery school, but I think my mother had kind of a co-op where we would play with each other when we were three and four. I can remember when Dave Crichton moved into town when I was in kindergarten.

Boys growing up in the town spent a lot of time playing outside. We played in Wells Park all the time. Our parents let us run over there and we would be gone for the day and do whatever. One game we played a lot was White Flag, a capture game with two different teams. There was also an active creek, which even had crayfish in it, and it provided a sort of natural boundary for our games. The park has changed quite a bit since then.

There used to be a large swing set across from the Crichtons, and there was another swing set and a slide, I

Ron at the Bat

believe. We also had self-organized sports. When we were older, in the summer we used to play baseball with the Millards, a large family that lived just a little up Rokeby from the park. Believe it or not, we even played baseball in Wells Park. There are lots of big trees, but we would set up a home plate, and when you hit the ball, if it hit the trees, you would keep on going. One summer when we were ten or eleven or twelve, Dave Crichton's cousins came from New York, and for a couple of weeks we played baseball with the Millards every day. I also remember playing basketball down by the post office with David Crichton and Rob Freer.

The post office and the general store were right down the street from my house. At different times there were different people that were proprietors of the store, and one of them I remember was Louie Karsh. Back then you could buy a coke for a nickel. The older kids, like Bing Reynolds, would sit out there drinking cokes on that raised area in front of the store, and they would throw the empty bottles up on the tracks and break them, never returning them for deposits.

The railroad tracks were right there behind the park. The Pungas, who lived in the same house as the

Dubinskis family, had a son, Frankie, who was about three years younger than me. We used to play up on the hill that led to the track right behind their house. We had a little fort that was sort of a dugout in the side of the hill, and we would watch the trains from there. I'm sure no parents today would allow their kid to do that, but it was pretty thrilling to watch them go through. Periodically there were fires caused by the steam trains - not big ones, just little ones, when coal or something blew out of the engine, and we would watch them put the fires out, which was quite exciting, sitting in this little fort above the trains. The trains were much more regular back then. I believe that when I was fairly young we used to be able to ride clear to Kensington, to Forest Glen, and maybe even Washington, D.C. on the train. And of course, once I was about ten the railroad track provided a good route for walking home from the Garrett Park Swimming Pool.

In the summer, the swimming pool was the main focus for me. The pool was built about 1952 or 1953. The first manager was a nice-looking young man, a guy named Frank Major, and I kind of remember taking swimming lessons around that time with him. In the summertime, at least after I had turned eight, we could go to the pool on our own, and most of the summer we'd go up every day, barefoot, on the hot tar roads, and see how long we could stand it. There was a large white house on one side, the King's house, where there was just a path to the pool and you could cut down there through that.

I was on the swimming team from when I was thirteen and fourteen. Tom Powell was the coach at one time, and later it was Kay Gilson. Sherry Thomas was a year younger than I was, and she was on the swimming team, as was Karen Modine. Timmy Powell was the best swimmer on the team. Garrett Park never had the biggest membership, and we would always be in sort of an average division, maybe the B division, whereas Cedarbrook, in Kensington, which seemed to be one of the more established pools, was in the A division. I remember that Candy Antosz, who later was one of the lifeguards, was quite a swimmer, quite a water polo player. She was on NVAC, almost a national champion water polo player one time, so she was kind of like our pro.

There weren't many job opportunities when you graduated from high school, so many of us Garrett Parkers worked at the pool. I ended up being a lifeguard in '65, '66 and '67. Later, after my freshman and sophomore year in college, I was a swim coach. Rob Freer was a lifeguard along with me, and then he became assistant manager one year when Barbara Modine was the manager.

The lifeguards used to skinny dip at the pool at night, and one time when Nancy Abrams, also a lifeguard, had a party at her house, I got drunk, and we were just fooling around, jumping around, and I jumped up and made a hole in her ceiling with my head. They had this very low tiled ceiling, and it would have been impossible to fix. Being a lifeguard started that process of doing things I hadn't done before, and once you had turned eighteen, you could just go and drink in the city. I had been a real goody-two-shoes in high school, and didn't really drink at all until after I graduated.

The town holidays were really special in Garrett Park, like the big Fourth of July parade. We'd go out on the front porch to watch, and then we'd go down to the tennis courts or the basketball area. I also remember that on the Fourth of July, they would drop coins in the pool and we could dive for them. When I got older there would be the Old Garrett Park - Garrett Park Estates Baseball Game. I remember the fireworks, and the time someone got hurt and got their leg burned. They stopped them after that. In the later years, guys like Tom Guernsey and Brian Sherline would play in the band in the parade, and after the parade the band would get the use of the community center.

I remember the big snow storm we had in the late 50's. We had to stay inside and play Monopoly all the time. It didn't seem to always snow that much in the winter, but when it did, it was a good time, and we went sledding on Donnelly's hill. And when you were one of the younger kids, you'd be sort of fair game for the older kids. You would jump on your sled and then the big kids would come up behind you and try to pull the sled out from under you, or they'd chase you down the hill and wreck you. I don't think anybody really ever got hurt too much, no broken arms — maybe you'd get a cut on your hand or something. You would try to avoid them, and then when you became big enough you did the same kind of antics to the younger kids. On the good snowy days a good run would be really racing down the hill and going all the way down into the park. There also used to be fires at the top of the hill in the evening. So when we were probably ten to twelve, we would go out there at night and sled until pretty late at night and stay warm by the fire. That was, I think, a very favorite activity in the wintertime.

Most of us went to Garrett Park Elementary School. We also went to school with the kids from the Estates, so our group of friends expanded with a lot of new friends once we started school. Maybe two-thirds of the kids we played with were from the Estates. We'd walk to school, and Mr. Dove was the crossing guard. Later on we rode our bikes, still at a fairly young age. No cars were driving us to school. I went to first grade in the new building, and Mrs. Duey, who was also the principal, was my first grade teacher. I had Mrs. Bradley for second grade, and Mrs. Sutherland for third grade. She was pretty rigid, but I didn't do too badly with her, though there was one thing she did that I have never forgotten. It made a life-changing impression on me. She announced that Stanley Woodwell was the best math student in the class, and that really resonated negatively in me. I had Mrs. Greene for fourth grade and Mrs. Collison for fifth. She would keep track of the books you had read with this chart on the wall. I read all these Hardy Boy books, maybe twenty-five of them, and she said, "Oh, you can only get credit for two of those books." She said they weren't literature!

From second grade on, we played a lot of baseball at school, at recess and also at lunchtime, although many of us may have come home for lunch and then gone back again. I came home for lunch for many years. When Mrs. Reynolds became the manager of the cafeteria there was always a conflict, because she wanted people to eat there. She wanted clientele and she probably had pressure from the school district. But we still wanted to ride home on our bikes, have a sandwich and then go back and probably play during the last fifteen minutes.

Don Franz, who was my age, played with us, and also Timmy Honey, who was a year older. We played with some of the older kids who were kind of the sports people - Benny Gieser, maybe John Hall. We used to play football in the Giesers' yard. There was a hedge and if you got through the hedge, it was a touchdown. And they had a barn, and a blacktop with a basketball hoop, so we could play basketball there. I was one of the younger guys and Benny was two years older than me. The Guernseys would play too, particularly Tom, I think. Later on the games moved on into the Holy Cross area and the Garrett Park School. I always remember that the Giesers and the Guernseys, always wore good clothes playing football. They all got messed up and seemed to have no concern about it. I'm sure my mother would have been a little bit upset about it.

We had a baseball team, the Garrett Park Gnats. Mr. Wilson was the coach, and then after him, Mr. Ofenstein from the Estates was the coach. We only had one team, and you would try out to got one of the limited numbers of contracts to be on the team. It was pretty serious business: you would practice, during the try-out and then only so many people would make it. In fifth grade you were lucky if one or two fifth graders made it. And then a few more sixth graders made the team. And then the majority of the seventh graders got to be on the team. We had to handle the trauma of being selected or not selected. The last year Mr. Ofenstein's son named Tommy joined the team, and one of our friends who had been on the team as a fifth and sixth grader didn't get selected; we felt Tommy had replaced him, and it really split us apart. It was very traumatic.

We had paper routes. That was good way you got to know who was more liberal and who was more conservative, because the conservatives took *The Washington Star* while the liberals took *The Washington Post*. I had a paper route when I was in seventh or eighth grade through about tenth grade. I delivered *The Post* to that area around Montrose and other streets all on my side of Strathmore, and we had about sixty customers, so it took a good hour. I delivered papers to Ms. Ostrander, who was the subject of a later tragedy. She was murdered by a boy who was her handyman, and that really took Garrett Park to a new dark reality.

Garrett Park's not an easy place to deliver papers; in fact it's pretty tricky. It was nice to have two of us delivering papers, and we'd split it up at times. But you got to know the various people; and you had to collect. *The Post*, I remember, was $1.95 at that time, and hopefully, you'd be getting tips. You'd go around, and you'd sell calendars, and people would make a donation for whatever they thought was appropriate, so you would make maybe a dollar a person or something like that for the calendar. And a lot of times people kicked in a nickel or you got $2.25 for delivering *The Post*, so it was a pretty good deal. Of course, the paper wasn't light but it was a heck of a lot lighter than it is today. You had to throw the paper onto the porch - that was mandatory. But you'd be the first people to know whether you'd have a snow day or not because you'd be up at 5:00. I got up at 5:00 and then I'd go back to bed.

I first delivered the paper with Dave Crichton and later with John Guernsey. John's father, George was an AFL-CIO rep and he was friends with Dizzy Gillespie. I was in awe of the number of records George Guernsey had. He probably had the biggest record collection in all of Garrett Park at that time and they were probably the first people on the block to have a stereo. I can remember them having huge — I mean, hundreds, a thousand record albums, you know, tremendous. I don't think John played piano at that time, but later I think he taught himself how to play piano. John's older brother, Tom was probably a more active musician than John at that time, during the late fifties, early sixties. They became sort of the heroes of the town when they formed the Reekers, and later the Hangmen, Tom's band with Mike Henley and John Hall. I played the trumpet, and they were always encouraging me to jam with them, but I never actually did play with them. I didn't hang around with them much. I basically just played sports.

Garrett Park was a strong community in the best sense of the word. That was because of the movers and shakers of the town, who were really invested in making the town a community, people like Sam Powell, who was the mayor at one time, and as far as I was concerned never stopped being mayor. Sam was really involved with the Garrett Players, and Tim Powell and I sold refreshments, cokes and things, at the plays put on by them. Tim got the job and he got me to help him. My mother was even in one play – she liked to sing, something about "By the Pool", and she wrote some of the music, I believe.

I think Garrett Park probably is continuing in the tradition of being predominantly Democratic, as I believe it was at that time. When I was growing up, Stanley Woodwell's family lived behind the school, and I think they were active in the Democratic Party. I remember election time, that their house was kind of the headquarters for Democratic action. I can remember hanging around there, particularly being for Stevenson in 1956, and later I actually did go down with two friends, Dave Crichton and Chuck Reynolds, to attend the inauguration of Kennedy in 1960. Then there was the Vietnam War, and I remember when Dave was drafted, and he was leaving, and I thought, "I may never see him again."

I went to Walter Johnson for high school. My main activity there was playing football. I started out playing junior varsity, and then the last two years I played varsity. I graduated in 1965 and went away to college, to Carnegie Tech., where I continued playing football. I would come home in the summer and work at the pool, so I basically was engaged in Garrett Park until I moved to Pittsburgh for a couple of years. Then I got a job and moved out to the west coast, eventually attending graduate school at UC Berkeley. I have a PHD in Materials Science. I've spent more than half my life in California, and now I live in Palo Alto. My father died early, and after his death I would come back and see my mom periodically. After my mother died, we sold the house I grew up in. The house, which was originally a very small, two-story house, and which my parents had re-modeled as a sort of a project, has been remodeled again since we sold it.

Garrett Park was really a wonderful place. Dave Crichton and Tim Powell were both good friends over the years, and their parents were always friendly and open. I would go the Crichton's house and they always had cokes and made me feel welcome. Tim's parents would take some of us to the beach since they always rented a house for a month in Rehoboth, and he would take two or three friends for a week at a time. They were really generous, and they sort of made things more worldly for me. There were a lot of very smart people living in the town. I remember that J.C. Crichton worked for the State Department, and that he would always be reading whenever I went to his house. He had the job of hosting the Russian athletes for the State Department, and he was about the least athletic guy you could imagine. I also found out later that Mr. Bolton, our next door neighbor, worked for ARPA (the Advanced Research Projects Agency, an agency of the United States Department of Defense, which underwrote development for the precursor of the Internet).

I'm grateful for the experience of growing up there. There was always a sense of strong community and bonds with friends that still continue today. My sister still lives in the area, so I plan to go back and visit her again and drive through Garrett Park, showing my wife the unique town where I grew up. I hope I can visit some people who now live there and find they continue to enjoy the same special feelings I have about Garrett Park.

(This narrative was excerpted in part from an interview conducted by Barbara Miller on December 28, 1995, courtesy of the Garrett Park Town Archives, and in part from a phone interview conducted by Lee Pope.)

Linda and Ron Horn

SHERRY THOMAS

My childhood in Garrett Park has influenced me all my life. I had a lot of encouragement around writing early on that has stood me in very good stead...I've also never forgotten my mother taking us each year to pick out our dahlia bulbs to plant. Those seeds eventually led to my thriving landscape design business on Long Island. And Garrett Park left me with a template for what community can be and a strong moral compass for social justice. That's a lot for one little town to do, but Garrett Park was unique in all the Washington suburbs. You belonged there, you didn't just live there.

I was born in 1948, in Americus, Georgia. At that time my parents, Bill and Betty Thomas, were just finishing college after WWII. I'm the oldest of four children born over a period of seventeen years - three girls and, finally, a boy. My younger sisters are Susan, whose name is now Sam (born in 1950), and Lynn (born in 1958) all of whom lived in Garrett Park. My brother Will was born in 1965 and left Garrett Park as a baby when my parents moved to Thailand for work.

My mother was an extraordinary person trapped in the 1950's mold of housewife and mother. She was an excellent cook and hostess; I came home for a hot lunch every day of elementary school. My very first political memory is working at the polls for Adlai Stevenson with her. Eventually, she became the county Democratic Chair and was active in state politics. But it was only after they moved to Thailand in 1968 that she came into her own. She organized the entire diplomatic community into an Asian Culture Study Group that taught Thai language, Buddhist culture and Thai, Cambodian and Vietnamese art. She repeated this model in several other countries around the world making close friends in the countries where she lived.

When I was very young, my father went to work with the federal government, (he eventually ended up in the Office of Management and Budget), and we moved to an apartment complex in Silver Spring. There my parents met and became friends with Barbara and Roger Pope. The Popes moved to Garrett Park first, and a few years later my parents bought a vacant half-acre lot on Albemarle Avenue, just around the corner from them. My parents built a house on the lot (from plans found in a magazine) but left most of the lot in woodlands.

The Garrett Park house had a fort in the back yard made out of logs cut down in the building process. The backyard fort was important to all the kids who played cowboys and Indians there. My younger sister, Sam, was always the Indian and we liked to tie her up. I remember cooking dandelions in the fort for dinner and making paste out of roots and plants. Our house was the only house on our side of the street. The family to the east of us had a very old house on a big lot, and to the west was a vacant lot, so we had tons of space to play in and explore.

We also had an amazing sledding hill, Donnelly's Hill, just a block away from our house which was closed off during snow storms with a bonfire at the top of the hill. There were lots of sled races down that hill, with occasional falls into the creek at the bottom.

All the kids in Garrett Park bicycled everywhere. Because Strathmore Avenue was the only through street, the whole town was fair game for kids. Because everyone went to the post office for their mail, and the Post Office was in the same building as the country store and next to the train station, my friends and I would always ride home from elementary school via the store. I always wanted a dill pickle, but my friends mostly chose ice cream. We used to put pennies on the train tracks that ran through town and then collected the squashed ones.

Sherry with her prize ribbons and her Shelty named Lady

Early in our time in Garrett Park, the families got together and dug a public swimming pool for everyone in town. I joined the swim team right away and eventually was training seriously as a competitive swimmer. All the families spent summer afternoons around the pool and everyone knew everyone else. I joined Girl Scouts as a Brownie and continued all the way into high school with the Mariner Scouts. Our troop, founded in Garrett Park, was a white water canoeing and kayaking group; we ran rivers and races all the way up to Canada. And we built our own boats out of fiberglass. This was probably one of the first times that I learned that anything was possible.

One amazing thing about our street was a neighbor across the street named Ummie Booth. She worked from home as a medical copy editor and took in all the neighborhood kids. She helped me start to write, lending me all sorts of books to read, and eventually sending my young poems to the New Yorker as well as helping me to start a novel in my teens. My sister Susan used to bring all her friends over there for ginger ale and cookies, and Ummie named her Sam for a local mooching puppet character. She still goes by Sam sixty years later.

Ummie left Garrett Park when I was in high school; her husband had lost his job and they had to sell their house. The next owner of that house was Constantine, a Greek sculptor who was carving angels at the National Cathedral. One time he took us up on the scaffolding to watch him carving a marble wing and explaining in detail about the construction of the Cathedral. Another big influence in my life was Millie Huffman. She lived with her doctor husband and four children in one of the old houses on a very large double lot on Waverly, near the post office. Millie mentored and coached me as I was getting ready to leave for college and I've never forgotten her. It was at her house that I first met civil rights workers coming out of the south. This was in the early sixties and civil rights workers would drive all night from Mississippi to safe places to stay. The Huffman's was one of those houses and people would gather to hear stories of the struggles in the south and to sing together. Then later, when the Huffmans hosted civil rights workers, I became very close to one of them, with whom I traveled to NYC. I don't know why my parents let me go to New York at sixteen with a 22 year old man. And I remember his friends whose apartment we stayed in were pretty shocked. In those days, my parents were seen as pretty cool. They were only twenty-one when I was, born and my father's rampant alcoholism wasn't acknowledged then.

Later during high school I was close friends with Jessica Meyers' family across town. I was introduced to Jewish culture through them. I'd never been to a Seder and remember taking a huge bite of horse radish not knowing what it was. Jessica, along with Laura Finkler, a transfer student, was my best friend through high school and the college years.

My favorite seasonal event was the annual Fourth of July parade in which all the kids decorated their bikes for prizes, and fireworks were set off at the elementary school. One year, my mother had seen a picture of a room painted purple with pink curtains and bedcovers. So she redid our room. Sputnik had also just gone up, so my sister, Sam, wanted her bike to be a space ship for Fourth of July that year; without telling our parents we painted Sam purple to be a Martian on the space ship, using oil-based paint left over from the room paint-

ing. She won the prize that year but my parents spent weeks getting paint out of her hair and skin.

Halloween was also a huge event, and my mother made our costumes every year. One year, she made me an elaborate witch's costume, making everything from the shoes to the hat. Every year we'd plot together about the next costume. In those days families could hand out anything, and I remember houses where you dunked for apples and got homemade donuts or cookies.

I was in fourth grade when we moved to Garrett Park and I started at Garrett Park Elementary. Later I attended Kensington Junior High and Walter Johnson High School. During my junior high school years, my father was president of the Montgomery County School Board. The teachers I remember most were from high school. I particularly remember Mrs. Whitman, who ran the Year Book class and taught me to edit and to write in ways that still stay with me. I also remember an English teach-

Sherry in Pope's yard around 1959

er and an art teacher (whose names I've forgotten, but I do remember that they were having an affair) did a project where they gave prints from the National Gallery to English students and asked us to write a poem or prose poem about the art. Then they gave the art students our writing and asked them to paint from that description. I've never forgotten that project and used it when I was a camp counselor in high school at a camp for underprivileged children in DC.

I was in junior high and high school during the early sixties, and the civil rights movement had a big impact on me. I remember the big fight when the first black family (a dentist) tried to buy into a neighboring community. Garrett Park organized to welcome them with a coffee event at one of the homes and a clear message that there was no color bar in Garrett Park. Jessica, Laura and I all became student activists in college and early civil rights activities in Garrett Park helped make that happen.

I loved growing up in a true small town adjacent to a big city. One could bicycle or drive (after turning 16) anywhere in town and know almost everyone you met. On the other hand, with friends in high school, we'd skip school to go downtown to the Library of Congress for folk and blues concerts. Also there was a strong streak of early political activism there, with founding members of Women's Strike for Peace and safe houses for civil rights workers. It was small town life with an active social justice conscience.

I have had a very eclectic and changeable life. After college, I moved to California and started a sheep ranch on the Mendocino coast (on 100 acres my parents helped me buy). I also earned money as a State Park Ranger in the summers. While on the farm, I started a magazine called *Country Women* which later became a book published by Doubleday: *Country Women: a Handbook for the New Farmer*. Two years later, I wrote another book for Doubleday about old women in rural communities - *We Didn't Have Much, But We Sure Had Plenty*.

After that I moved to San Francisco and became a partner in a women's bookstore and then went on to found a feminist publishing company, Spinsters Ink. We produced over sixty books of fiction and non-fiction sold all over the world.

I was hired to help create the Gay and Lesbian Center at a new Main Library that was about to be built. From there I rose to the Executive Director of the Library Foundation, raising $30 million for the library. My spouse and I also wrote another book during this time for Warner Books - *Out In All Directions: the Almanac of Gay and Lesbian America*.

I held a series of non-profit jobs, and in 1999 I moved to New York to take a position as the National Director of Development for Lambda Legal Defense. While in living New York, I studied landscape design at Cornell's Master Gardener Program. I have now built a successful landscape business in Orient, at the tip of Long Island, where we have a second home.

I married my longtime partner in 2011. At the time of this writing, we've been together thirty-one years. I haven't been back to Garrett Park since the early 70s. My parents only returned for short stays between overseas postings. When my mother had her last child (my brother) while her oldest two were in college, they moved overseas where they would have full time help. My father served as a country director for USAID in Thailand, Malaysia, Pakistan, Syria, Egypt and Greece. Sam and I got to travel the world for visits and the two younger kids grew up in all those countries

Orient NY where I now live is a similar town, with 4th of July bicycle parades and poetry slams. We still have a real post office and no delivery. And there's just one through street in town; but the railroad stops ten miles away. Being in Orient has made me think a lot about Garrett Park over the years and how rare such communities are.

My childhood in Garrett Park has influenced me all my life. As I mentioned above, I had a lot of encouragement around writing early on that has stood me in very good stead. Though I never formally studied writing, I've published three books, edited a magazine, and owned a bookstore and ran a feminist publishing company. I've also never forgotten my mother taking us each year to pick out our dahlia bulbs to plant. Those seeds eventually led to my thriving landscape design business on Long Island. And Garrett Park left me with a template for what community can be and a strong moral compass for social justice. That's a lot for one little town to do, but Garrett Park was unique in all the Washington suburbs. You belonged there, you didn't just live there.

(Written by Sherry Thomas)

JESSICA MYERS ALBERTSEN

You can't travel in time, but when I used to visit Garrett Park I could almost see us as children - bicycling to the pool, trying to play tennis on the tennis court; we were just around the corner - shadows, so close. And the magic moments are so vivid that I can almost reach out and touch them.

My father's name was Henry Joseph Myers. His father was a doctor, and his older brother was the rebel who became an artist. As the good boy in the family, my father went to medical school to become what his father was hoping he would – a doctor. He had just finished his internship at St. Elizabeth Mental Hospital in Washington, D.C., when he was drafted during the Second World War, and because of this, he was used as a psychiatrist during the war. Psychiatry became a way out for him. He had found something that really interested him and became a psychiatrist and psychoanalyst.

My mother, Viola Aronson, came from Chicago. She had studied economy at University of Chicago, and she got a job at the Treasury Department during the war. After the war, my father came back to Washington D.C., and since he didn't know any girls, a friend loaned him his address book. My mother's name was the first one in the book, so she was the first one he called, and he didn't get any further. They were married, and I was born in 1948. At first they lived on Valley Avenue in Washington DC, and there they met the Franzes. Jay Franz found Garrett Park, so my parents discovered it through Jay. Al Richter had bought up an estate on the edge of the town, and at first he lived in the original farmhouse there. It became the Hartmann's house eventually, and Al parceled out the land, first developing Keswick Street, then Oxford Street, and then Weymouth. Our house was the first one on Weymouth Street with the Lehman house next door shortly afterwards. Then he built the house next door which he lived in, and then the McLaughlin's house across the street. Of course, Donal McLaughlin designed his own house which was radically different from the houses Al designed.

I was only two years old when we first moved to Garrett Park. The McLaughlins moved in a half a year later, so I met Karen when I was only two and also Ellen Bortman and Anne Lehman. I already knew Terry Franz. Mary Winegarden moved in a year or two later at the corner of Oxford and Weymouth.

My sister, Rhoda, was born when I was four, and that was our family. My mother was originally a housewife. But when I was ten years old my father had a heart attack, and my mother got really scared and started thinking about "What am I going to do if I lose my husband?" So she went back to school, deciding to become a school librarian, because she wanted to have the same vacations that we had. After that, she got work in the Montgomery County Schools and worked as a school librarian until she retired. The school librarians were really teachers. I think she was very creative in her work - for instance, she used to make these puppet theaters with the children. My father had his own practice, and his office was downtown in Washington. He would drive early and come home late to avoid the rush hour, which meant that he was gone around twelve hours a day.

Henry, Jessica, Viola, and Rhoda Myers

My father was a high energy person, and my family was very active. We would go bowling several times a week and played mini-golf. I could bring my friends, and Mary Winegarden came along quite a bit. My father liked to play golf and my mother learned how to play. We had a lot of picnics. I think that was the best thing we did together. We often went with the Franzes to Sugarloaf Mountain. My mother would make fried chicken and potato salad, and we had a great time. We also took long summer vacations together. My parents would rent a beach house, sometimes with another family, the Franzes or the McLaughlins. There was one year in Kitty Hawk when the Franzes, the McLaughlins, and the Richters all came along, and all four families had cabins next to each other.

As children we had our own world of play, separate from the adults. Sometimes I would get really bored and say, "What should we do?" and my mother would say, "Make a list". She never offered to do anything with us. I think today we are much more inclined to engage with our children, to play with them, but it was very different then.

Garrett Park was just the best place to have a children's world. We had this enormous area that we could use, and parents weren't worried about us wandering around by ourselves. We had the woods and the creek, we had our bicycles, and after a few years there was the swimming pool in the summer. We could bicycle to the town library, to the store and the post office where we could buy candy, we could pretend we were playing tennis on the tennis courts, and we really used the area. It was our own mini-world.

We played a lot in the woods and the creek. Behind the houses on the one side of the street, was a slope with a strip of woods bordering Rock Creek, and there was a vast expanse of woods where the street ended. Before the apartments were built, the woods seemed endless. The path into the woods started where the street dead-ended. I think it was Karen McLaughlin who decided that we should name the landmarks along the path. Walking the path, we would stop to look at The Vine - there were vines growing on all the tall trees but this one hung down, making a swing - then there were the Upside Down Tree Stumps, then Little Rock and finally Big Rock. Big Rock was on the top of a slope overlooking the creek and woods below. Here we would stop and sit and enjoy the warmth and safety and isolation of this rock. Big Rock was so big, and I was so disappointed when I returned as an adult and found a not so big rock. Watching how stones in my garden can disappear after very few years, I have since wondered if Big Rock too, has sunk deeper into the earth or had we really been so little? At any rate Big Rock was big then, and a good spot to hang out and philosophize over how the boys could be so cruel as to shoot birds with bb guns, or why all the girls in the class wanted to do the same as Kathy Z - or just to stop and choose a direction before venturing into the woods.

The creek was shallow, and we could wade through it or balance on trees that had fallen across it. The woods were dense - there were swampy areas, areas with small trees covered in honeysuckle and other vines, and areas of larger trees. Once in a while we would see a large black harmless snake in a tree, and nearer the houses we often found box turtles. We never saw the raccoons that later became a problem for the house owners, because they were so good at opening garbage cans of any kind. Of course they are nocturnal, but I don't think they were around then.

The woods were big and once in a while there would come rumors of kidnappers hiding out there. This put an edge on walking around there, and gave me nightmares of a kidnapper in a checked suit, like Pinkie Lee, sneaking down the street. One day I saw two police cars parked at the bottom of the street, and the policemen came out of the woods with Karen McLaughlin and Ellen Bortman and their barking dogs. After the police cars drove off, they told me how the policemen had asked them to show them around the woods, and how they had found something that could have been used as a shelter. They wanted to show it to me, and I followed them with my heart hammering in my throat, searching among all the trees for movement and trying to convince myself that the dogs would certainly see someone first. They found the shelter again, and

Rhoda and Jessica

then we discovered how fun it was to jump on the small trees wrapped in vines – "Funfulls" we called them. They were small trampolines- bouncy - we could jump, roll, bounce and for a time forget all about kidnappers. But I still looked over my shoulder the whole way back to Big Rock and was happy for the dogs. At Big Rock the safe world began - the street was not so far away.

I don't know who discovered the good swinging vine, but suddenly everyone wanted to swing on it all the time. We would stand in line and take turns and gradually we got bolder and bolder. Soon the thing to do was swinging upside down. Then Terry swung upside down and let go with one hand. I decided to outdo her, and just when the vine was at the highest point from the ground, I let go with both hands - and fell flat on my back. My back was not hurt, but I couldn't breathe- I had knocked all the air out of my lungs. I lay there thinking - if I can't breathe I must be dead- and I wondered when and how my mind would die. I thought about how I had quarreled with my mother and wouldn't be able to make up. Karen and Ellen thumped my chest, and I thought about how they didn't know what they were doing, and how it didn't seem very helpful, but never the less I soon was breathing again. My friends were the focus of my little world, and usually my mom or dad had a struggle to get me home. But this time, I walked home willingly and quickly and couldn't wait to see my mom again.

Two more stories about the woods. Once Mary and I decided to walk in the woods at night. She spent the night with me, and we slept in the rec room in the basement. The basement was on ground level at the back of the house with windows and a door towards the woods. These windows and doors towards the woods made me nervous, and I always kept the curtains shut when I slept there and double checked that the doors were locked. But this night we kept ourselves awake and snuck out at three am and wandered a short ways into the woods behind the house. There was a moon that evening, and we could see the creek below. We didn't stay long- it was too forbidden and scary, but we were proud that we had done it. My mom was furious when she heard about it.

She was also furious the day we decided to do a prank. Terry and I, and maybe a few others, were down at the creek behind the house. There was a bridge where the road ran over the creek, and we stood in the shallow water by the bridge and screamed Help! at the cars driving by. I don't think we believed they could really hear us, but one car stopped. The driver was very angry and chewed us out, and at home my mom did the same. I think she must have been in the backyard and heard us and was running down the slope terrified that something awful had happened.

In my adult life I have had many dreams about walking in the woods - in my dreams the path at the end of the street goes up one hill and then down and then up another hill and into the big world. It is an exciting and important journey. On waking, it has always confused me that the real path into the woods was so different- flat and twisting, and then down the hill at Big Rock. Revisiting Garrett Park, I realized that my dreams had melted two landscapes into one. When we were small, our path to school went up a hill, then through a different finger of woods where a dirt road went down a hill and up a hill. Later houses were built in this finger of woods and the road was paved, but my dreams had travelled back in time and moved this path through the woods to the end of the street and let it lead to the large area of woods down there.

I would guess that Richterville was something of a neighborhood within a neighborhood. On Weymouth Street, all the houses were built at the same time, there were many children of a similar age, and the neighbors were very close. Donal McLaughlin was a dynamo and a fun organizer, which contributed to this feeling. There was always a lot of contact, always good feelings between the neighbors, a willingness to help each other and have fun together, and it gave you a very safe, secure feeling as a child.

Weymouth Street ended where the woods began, which meant that it was a great place for kids to play, and in the wintertime we could sled down the street. When Parkwood Apartments were built in the woods, on the south side of town, Donal McLaughlin led a committee that fought successfully to stop the roads of the apartments from joining the roads in Garrett Park. Instead, they ended in dead ends. If this hadn't happened, the quiet streets on the south side of town would have become busy thoroughfares.

We knew everybody on Weymouth Street, Oxford Street, and Keswick Street. It was a special feeling - nobody locked their doors, and the adults also had a great relationship. They walked in and out of each other's houses all the time, and borrowed things or just sat and talked. Because of Donal McLauglin, the men played poker once in a while, as well as ping pong and golf. They had the handicap golf tournament, which was a really good idea, because even though my father was probably the worst golf player, he was able to win one year. Donal made a great plaque that he could hang on the wall. The women were active in the women's club and the book club. As a kid, it was just a wonderful feeling that everybody knew you, and the parents all knew each other.

When we couldn't play outdoors, we had our indoor games. For me and Karen, and I guess for Mary too, dolls were really important. We played mainly in Karen's attic, and I remember her dolls were always the best. Karen had wonderful dolls, classy dolls, like the Madam Alexander dolls, that were so expensive. She told me recently, that her mother had bought them at the thrift shops. Both of our mothers made beautiful doll clothes.

We each had our own little world of dolls and their doings. First we would choose which dolls we were going to play with, and then we would tell the story of our dolls, who they were, their personality, their lives, their families. I have a feeling it was more parallel play than interactive play with these dolls, that each person was more interested in talking for themselves than listening to the other. We were each living out our own fantasies and exploring our own ideas about the world and how people interacted. Because it was in the attic, we didn't have to clean up. We could just leave our doll game and come back to it another day, and just go on with the game.

Sometimes we played board games, and sometimes we would draw or write. In fourth grade my class had this amazing teacher, Mrs. Weymouth, who encouraged us to write creatively, and that became a big occupation among my friends. We sometimes wrote stories and sometimes books. We would sit and write and then share and read what the other people had written. Sometimes we would write collectively, but mostly we would just write on our own. Reading was always a big occupation, and we often went to the library to borrow books, and when we came home, we would sit together, each absorbed in reading one of these books. We loved fantasy books, especially the Narnia series, which was so real to me that I really thought I could find a fantasy world like Narnia.

We were not above money making projects. We used to make puppet shows, and then round up the younger kids on the street and charge them a penny each to come see it. I remember the puppet shows being rather poorly planned or practiced, with rambling plots, but the little kids kept coming. The most ambitious project was when Mary and I made a kindergarten for the little kids in our rec room one summer. It lasted a week, and we rounded up the kids every morning and had activities for them. I think maybe I was ten and Mary was twelve, and she was definitely the primus motor of the project.

The swimming pool was the focus in the summer. There were swimming lessons when we were little, and then the swimming team. I was only on it for one year, but Sherry Thomas and Terry Franz and Karen Modine went on to competitions and prizes. There was racing for fun and different water games, one where you held hands and then all went under at the same time, seeing who could swim underwater the longest ... I can't really remember all of the different games.

It got really hot in the summer. As a kid it didn't bother me, but when I hit puberty it did. Sometimes I'd sleep in the basement or on the porch at night. The hot weather could begin early, and it seemed unfair that the swimming pool first opened on Memorial Day. Why not May 1st? It seems to me, that one year when we were teenagers, Laura McLaughlin (Karen's mother), Karen and I would sneak into the closed swimming pool in the evening during all of May - so glorious to have the pool to ourselves and the safety of being with an adult. One evening, Karen and I swam without Laura and that was much scarier.

I was proud of running around barefoot all summer and getting thick leathery soles and wide feet that were unhappy when it was time to buy new shoes for school. The only danger was stepping on a bee, and this happened every year, and there were mosquitoes and mosquito bites - tons of them - and I would scratch them, and they would make ugly scabs, and I had a fantasy that there would be a contest - who had the most mosquito bites? - and of course, I would win, and the prize was that they would mysteriously be healed and disappear.

On summer evenings, we played "Capture the Flag" in Judy King's back yard that bordered into the woods. It would get dark, and the flag was hidden between the trees, at the edge of the woods. I would sneak through the trees, trying to be as silent and hidden as an Indian - feeling real suspense - but usually was discovered and then, rarely, had the thrill of getting the flag and running so fast, but oh, not fast enough. And my father's voice from the street calling and no I didn't want to go home and to bed – never - now it was pitch black and really fun. My stupid parents still thought I should go to bed at 8:30 and I thought that was crazy - we were having such a good time, and I wouldn't listen, I would just keep on playing. It was really special.

Fourth of July was the parade. Every year you would decorate your bicycle, and we would walk through the town, and there were prizes for the best decorated bicycle. Of course everyone knew that the parents had probably done most of the work, especially with the prize winning ones. But Rhoda's won second prize one year. And I remember that afterwards, at the school yard, there were races for all of the kids. I remember that one year Terry and I were the only ones competing in all these activities, and so we won the prizes. Of course Terry won the first prize and I won the second prize. Terry was such a social kid, I think she let me win first prize a few times too, because she really had a social conscience. And after the games, there were fireworks.

Fall was all the wonderful leaves falling down and the crackling sound they made when you walked in them. My dad would sweep all of the leaves into the beginning of the woods in the back of our lot, our property went to the edge of the woods, so there were huge piles of leaves to jump in and tumble in. It was so much fun. After a rainy day, the street would be covered in earth worms. It was impossible to walk without crushing an earthworm, and I didn't like them. One morning, before school started, Ellen and Terry threw earthworms at me, and I got very upset. Maybe I fainted. The teacher was involved and I think her conclusion was that I was mildly hysterical. I used to faint easily, and I fainted several times at school. Later in life, I have realized that this was because of anemia. I don't know why my dad, who was a doctor, didn't realize this.

Halloween was always dark and often wet. It was usually too cold for the costumes we had, and there was the choice of showing off your costume or putting on a jacket and being more comfortable. We had paper grocery bags for candy, and they would always break. We always went in a big flock. I think about that a lot because today, no kids are allowed to trick or treat without parents. Times have really changed.

Halloween was about candy. It was so disappointing when we got apples, cookies were also a downer. It was just a question of staying out long enough, in spite of the wet and cold and bags that broke, because we would end up with so much candy that it often lasted almost to Christmas.

The next day was the most exciting. We would gather in someone's living room and empty our bags, count the loot and sort it after what we liked and didn't like, and then it was time to trade. Our parents respected that it was our candy, and the bag of candy was something we dragged around the first few days, and then hid in our rooms and gradually consumed. There was a certain prestige in not eating your candy too quickly.

When I was younger, my mom would sew elaborate costumes. The most elaborate was after our visit to Williamsburg. She must have bought a pattern there for a real colonial fancy dress. Maybe my dad bought a wig too. Then there was Peter Pan and many others.

I remember the older I got, the less important the costume. It was always easy to be a gypsy or a ghost. And then there was the question how old could you be and still trick or treat? I think it was mostly an elementary school thing. Then it was possible to go with my sister and a group of her friends as an older chaperone. I remember one year Ellen and I went out when we were about thirteen and no one complained. I think we decided to dress as gypsies and go on the other side of the creek, in Kensington where no one knew us.

The next big holiday was Thanksgiving. As a child I somehow got the impression that Thanksgiving was about thanking the Indians for saving the Pilgrims' lives, and it was only recently that I realized that actually it was about giving thanks to God, and it was a big shock for me. I had always thought, wow, we have this great holiday, we're giving thanks to the Indians, and I was wrong.

We were Jewish, but my father saw Christmas as a fun holiday, so we had a Christmas tree, and we had Christmas dinner with some friends of theirs, and my father just loved to give presents. So Christmas was just made for him. And he would start two weeks before Christmas, he would say, "Can I give you your Christmas present now?" and it was the opposite of trying to keep the kids from finding the presents, it was me trying to keep my father from giving me my presents early. Otherwise Christmas just meant that Karen and her family would take so long to open their presents, and I just wanted to play, and they were still opening their presents.

Winters were unpredictable. I remember the pure joy of waking up and looking out the window and seeing snow!!! Quick, turn on the radio and listen and hope as they read up the schools that were closed. Luckily Montgomery County extended into some rural area which often caused the schools to close and kept them closed for days - the most, a whole week. One strange day, there was no snow and the schools were still closed. We went outside, to find a layer of ice everywhere. Out we came, with baking sheets and slid down the street, the grass, everywhere. This was before the flying saucer sleds- when sleds had real runners, so this was a novelty.

The best sledding was on the big hill running down from Holy Cross School at the other side of town, St. Angela's Hall. It was good walk, but then terrific sledding with the added thrill of a little creek at the bottom which you didn't want to run in to. We would sled and sled and sled until our fingers and toes were frozen and hurting- no good insulated winter boots or nylon water tight mittens back then. We never calculated with the long walk home, so by the time we arrived, we were in severe pain and afraid of frostbite. My mom would always remind us to run our hands and feet under the cold water, not the hot, and this seemed terribly illogical, but we did as she said. They would tingle and burn for hours and look beet red, but finally they were normal again, and all was forgotten the next good sledding day.

One year, when there was an unusual amount of snow, Brian McLaughlin and Tommy Richter made a snow tunnel the whole length of the McLaughlin's driveway. I think they charged money for the chance to sled through their long tunnel which was lit up with candles. That was the year we made a big snowman for some radio show's contest. Donal photographed it for us, and we sent it in and waited and waited and didn't win. Brian and Tommy had other engineering projects like a large cave made under the earth - also lit up with candles, and where they also charged entrance money and an elaborate tree house which you had to pay to get up in.

Spring came early in Garrett Park. I didn't experience spring as a child the way I experience spring today. I think it is first when you have been away and come back, that you can really feel the texture of spring and summer. I remember arriving a warm May night from Denmark, after a whole day's travel, and how the evening air was thick with perfume from the lilacs and the azaleas. Coming in July, and seeing the fireflies (how could I forget them?), hearing the crickets, feeling the hot humid air that embraces you sensually and overpoweringly.

Garrett Park Cooperative Nursery School might actually have been a subdivision of Kensington Cooperative Nursery School. At least my first year in Nursery School was in a big wooden house in Kensington not far from the intersection of Knowles Avenue and Connecticut Avenue. The next year it moved to the Community Center in Garrett Park. I think the first year we were also more kids, because we were divided into two groups by age with one group on the ground floor, and another on the first floor. There was a big garden to play in too. I remember that I would try to sneak into the four-year-old group when they were having a birthday party, to get some cake. Sometimes it worked. One day Ellen suggested we stay with the four year olds, and we did all day.

Being a cooperative nursery school seems to have meant that they hired one teacher, and then the mothers took turns helping her- one or two mothers at a time. There was also a carpool for driving us back and forth. Having the mothers as teachers, was not always such a good thing, depending on who the mother was. I remember once when we were in the Community Center and one mother thought I was talking too loudly. She told me I could only paint with red paint. Even at four, I knew that was absurd.

At that time, the library was in the Community Center. Once Ellen had been acting up and was banished to the library. Terry and I snuck in to see her, and we all three enjoyed being in the library with all the books. But a mother found us and told Terry and I to leave. Ellen was not supposed to be having fun.

Kindergarten and school were not frightening for me. The kindergarten was in the old school house which was built as a two room school house. It was a large room, and we were lots of kids it seems to me, but I have no idea how many. I think we mostly played, but some of the time, the teacher would gather us all together in the back corner and read a book and ask questions. I remember once she asked what animals, other than cows, give milk. A flock of hands went up, including mine, but it turned out that no one really knew the answer. I didn't really know the answer either. She called on me. I mumbled cows, and she said "That's right Jessica, goats. See, Jessica knows the answer." I realized that she expected me to have the right answer, and because of this, she heard the right answer. I basked in her praise of me to the class, but felt guilty over the deceit.

That year, Terry and I had matching winter hats. They were navy blue velvet with a fur trim, fake fur I imagine. One day we got them mixed up and I brought home her hat. The next morning, as soon as I saw Terry, I yelled "Terry, I've got your hat!" The teacher scolded me for yelling. Here, I thought it was the most natural way of giving Terry the message in a noisy crowd of kids arriving, but according to the teacher, yelling was really a terrible thing to do.

The first grade teacher punished the naughty kids by making them sit in the corner. I wasn't ever naughty, but I still ended up in the corner one day. I was sitting next to Ann and we started playing the hands game, where you stack your hands and try to keep your hand on top. The teacher thought we were slapping each other, so we ended up in the corner, even though we explained it was a game. She was impervious to this. I sat in the corner full of indignation over the unfairness of it all.

In first grade, we would bring lunch boxes with little thermos bottles. I remember the horrible feeling of opening the thermos and seeing glass splinters. It seemed to happen all the time. It was a relief when we could buy milk for two cents. One year, tetra packs were the big invention. Everyone was enthralled with the smart and practical design. For twenty-five cents we could buy a hot lunch in the school cafeteria. I would watch the menu and only buy one if they were serving spaghetti. We had an hour's lunch break and could walk home in good weather. Sometimes we would go home with each other. The biggest treat was when Ellen Bortman's mother, Esther, invited me home to eat hot noodle pudding with Ellen. It was fun to get away from school for an hour, but also rushed. The walk itself was at least fifteen or twenty minutes each way. It was best to bicycle home for lunch.

I remember the first time I bicycled to school. Learning to bicycle had not been easy for me. I remember Dad running around Weymouth Street trying to help me. Finally, I was stable enough to make the trip to school and had arranged to meet Terry Franz and her older brother, Don. Terry had learned to bicycle much earlier. Everything went okay until we approached the school. Suddenly, there was a long line of bicycles bicycling down the hill towards the school. The line was moving slower and slower. I only knew how to drive and brake and didn't know about the possibility of braking a little bit. I could see that I would soon either drive into the bicycle in front of me, or if I braked, be hit by the bicycle behind. I chose to drive onto the sidewalk and fell off my bicycle. Terry lectured me the whole way home about coasting.

Once a year, the lower grades would get spring fever. For about a week, the most important free time activity was boys chase the girls and girls chase the boys. The chase would begin before school started in the morning, and continue during all the recesses. In first or second grade I did actually catch a boy and pin him to the ground. I didn't know what more to do with him and let him go. I then realized the point of the game was chasing, not capturing.

Otherwise, during recess, girls played with girls and boys with boys. However, the boys would ask Terry and Ellen to join their softball game. They were that good at it. One year, suddenly, Hula Hoop rings were the big craze. Then everyone, boys and girls, stood outside Hula Hooping during all the recesses.

Once we visited the Wonder Bread Bakery. It was quite an experience to see how the bread was blown up with air instead of yeast, or at least that is how I understood it. After the trip, the factory had a drawing contest. The winner, Kathy, got a tremendous basket full of hostess cupcakes, Twinkies and all the Wonder Bread goodies. I made sure to visit her a few days afterwards. As always, she was generous and I got to eat some of the goodies. She was already tired of them.

Terry had a greater social awareness than me. Already by second grade, she introduced the idea of giving all the kids in the class valentines. I was careful in choosing the valentines for the boys, nothing they could misunderstand. By third grade, she introduced me to the idea of going home at least once with every girl in the class each year. I faithfully did this, also going home with the immature and unpopular girls.

The third grade had the honor of raising the flag in front of the school every morning and taking it down at the end of the school day, or if it began to rain. Then they folded it in the proper way. Two children had this job for two weeks. I was very excited when it was my turn. We had been taught to respect the flag, and had been told that it must never touch the ground. If it did, it must be burned. I felt very grown up being trusted with this important job. However, one day the flag did touch the ground as we were taking it down. We were both terribly upset - now the flag would have to be burned. Maybe kissing it one hundred times was good enough. We tried to imagine if the school would burn the flag, or if they would send it to a special place for burning flags. With great reluctance, we told our teacher of the catastrophe. She told us nonchalantly, to fold the flag and put it away. First we were incredulous and had to ask again. Then the full impact sank in. Both the flag and my teachers lost much of their glory that day.

Our fourth grade teacher, Mrs. Weymouth, was unlike all the other teachers. She was very personally engaged in teaching, and she even invited the whole class to her home. She wanted to help us really think about things, and this was new. She tried very hard to teach us to think before we answered a question, and not just guess what answer the teacher expected. This is difficult to teach fourth graders. But the message made an impression, even if it was difficult to live up to. She also encouraged us to write creatively, and we spent a lot of time in school writing. As a result, there were many girls in the class who began writing stories outside of school too. Actually I would say, that I never stopped writing after that - stories, poems, diaries - more or less intensively in different periods of my life.

School outings were events for all of Montgomery County and carried off with a military precision. Half the fun was watching the logistics of the day - for example all the school busses descending on downtown Washington DC, so the school children could hear the symphony orchestra. This happened once a year. They always played lyrical, story-telling music and I tried to picture the stories in my head so I wouldn't fall asleep. The biggest school trip was a trip to Philadelphia. All the school busses had to let us off at Union Station and off we went by train, thousands of school kids to visit Philadelphia. There, we were divided into groups that saw the liberty bell and other sites after turn, and even got fed lunch at a cafeteria. Somehow, we all got to see all the sites and eat lunch and arrived safely back at school.

I think Sherry Thomas and I spent most of fifth grade out in the hall drawing murals. We drew on big sheets of brown paper, something related to what we were reading in class. We loved the freedom of standing in the hall drawing, so we kept volunteering and apparently, no one else was interested or dared or something. Sherry usually came up with an overall plan, and I would start drawing in one corner, and she would start in another. I cannot picture any of these murals today, but I know we were very involved in them and very proud of them.

In sixth grade, we were school patrols, an important job with a uniform and inspection, where our uniforms had to be clean and our shoes shined. Karen Modine and I were the kindergarten patrols. We were in charge of walking the kindergarteners in a line to the traffic cop on Strathmore. It was not easy to keep kindergarteners in line. I found the easiest way was to play a game with them. I would tell a story where we all had to run or crawl or climb or look up or point or something or just do follow the leader where they had to skip or dance or do what I did.

In elementary school most of my friends were on the street, Ellen Bortman, Karen McLaughlin, Terry Franz, and Mary Winegarden, who had moved to Keswick. In fourth grade, I met Sherry Thomas who had just moved to Garrett Park and lived on the other side of town. She became a close friend, and we were always in the same class throughout junior high and high school and kept in touch until I moved to Denmark.

I think all the girls in the class were in the Girl Scouts. It was different mothers who were the leaders, so it would change greatly from year to year depending on the energy of the mothers. My mother was the leader one year, and she was really good. In junior high, Sherry Thomas, Terry Franz, Karen Modine and I joined the Mariner Scouts, but I was only in it for the first year, whereas the others continued for many years and took many exciting trips kayaking whitewater rivers in Canada. Terry and Nancy Abrams even went on to become U.S. women's champions in whitewater kayaking.

Kensington Junior High was a horrible place with a very unpleasant atmosphere. It was so big, and the classes were very uninspiring. My home teacher was a very sweet old lady who had been teaching for hundreds of years, and she even said she had been teaching the exact same lesson for fifty years. She remembered every kid's name that she had ever taught. You had to give her credit for that. Our school bus was always the earliest in the morning and the latest coming home. We weren't allowed inside in the winter before school, so we joined the "morning chorus" just to get out of the cold. There were all these arbitrary stupid things. The disciplinarian would go around with his whistle and his leather strap, hitting boys with it.

Of course there were many cliques - we were all going through puberty. There was the cheap crowd, girls with teased bleach blonde hair who would steal cashmere sweaters and hide them in their lockers. In seventh grade I started wearing those horrible high heeled spiked shoes once in a while, and this peach lipstick that I had found in the restroom, but at some point I chose the beatnik look instead, maybe in eighth grade. When I started wearing black turtlenecks and black tights and tent dresses, people started making jeering comments about it. But that was just part of being a beatnik, and I chose that identity at that time.

It was a troubled time in history, where the threat of nuclear war was very real. We had a science teacher who would talk to us about "When the nuclear bomb falls, the first thing will be a big explosion and a very bright light. Whatever you do, don't look at the light or you will be blinded." And the drills all the time - crouching under your desk or in the hall, hands protecting your neck. We even had a drill where we had to all leave the school and go home with someone who lived nearby. It was the time when some people were building bomb shelters in their gardens.

When my mother left Garrett Park, she moved to a retirement community called "Manor Care". Kensington Junior High had been torn down, and it was on a part of those grounds. When I saw that Kensington Junior High was gone, it was such a wonderful feeling. There was a park there and there were wild flowers growing on the slope. And there were people there having fun – playing games and flying kites and it was just Wow! What a metamorphosis – that this terrible place could be transformed into this wonderful spot.

Garrett Park was an isolated enclave in this growing metropolis - curved streets, large trees, patches of woods, Rock Creek Park on the one border, lots of old Victorian style wooden houses. There wasn't much room for new houses, but they did get built where there was room. No one changed their houses back then as I hear is the case today. The residents of Garrett Park were very proud of their little town and decided to give up having their mail delivered to keep Garrett Park as their address. The daily stop at the Post Office was a time to greet neighbors, chat and gossip.

When my folks bought their house in 1950, it was considered moving to the countryside. But the city caught up, and this constant growth has been the back drop of growing up in the '50s. I remember when Wheaton Plaza was built and opened in 1960, and we were all very proud of having the biggest shopping plaza in the country, the first one in the DC area. Donal McLaughlin told us that this was the new trend and would be the future.

My Dad especially, welcomed the stores. He loved the quick food chains like McDonalds and Kentucky Fried Chicken. He loved going to drive in movies and sitting in the car at Howard Johnsons with trays clipped on to the windows, and girls in wide skirts running out with our orders. I think at one point they started using roller skates, so they could move faster.

Kensington was the next town up from Garrett Park. I remember when there was a large wooden white painted house on each corner at the crossroads where Connecticut Avenue met Knowles Ave. First came Knowles Pharmacy on the NW corner, then I think it was the gas station, a Shell, on the NE corner. Many years later it was a large office building on the SW corner and I don't even remember what ended up on the SE corner (some multi-story concrete building I think)- that was after I had moved away. The pharmacy corner expanded into more and more stores. This crossroads was in miniature, a picture of how the suburbs grew more and more metropolitan. Today I can barely find my way around the crisscross of highways and apartment buildings and shopping centers and new housing developments that keep blossoming up everywhere.

Our first ventures out into the big world were walking to Kensington. Knowles Avenue was heavily trafficked and not very interesting. But along the back road was a saw mill. There were giant piles of sawdust and we would slide and play in these piles on weekends, or when the mill was closed. Once we got woken up in the middle of the night. Everyone was out on the street. The whole sky was orange to the northeast, where the saw mill was. It was burning. I don't know if it ever got built again.

The next step was taking the bus to Silver Springs. There was a Woodies Department store, and we would play a game - dividing into two teams that chased each other. You had to stay on the stairs, the elevators or the escalators. Chasing involved running up the down escalators. It was a very exciting game, but unfortunately, always ended up with the Store Manager catching us and throwing us out.

Sometime later we started taking the bus to Bethesda, to a movie, or to Chevy Chase Circle (movie and Chinese Restaurant). Back then you went to the movies and bought a ticket and could sit there all day if you wanted to. Often, we came in after the movie had started and stayed until the same spot came around again. I remember I saw Peter Pan six times, on different occasions. The cartoons between shows were fun, and the big hit was Mr. Magoo and the Pink Panther.

When we were teenagers, we started going downtown, to Georgetown, to the galleries and to Dumbarton Oaks, sometimes to the zoo. Those afternoons, downtown - spending hours looking at Klee paintings, eating fresh bread and cheese in the baroque gardens at Dumbarton Oaks, looking at small boutiques in Georgetown, sitting in the sun at the zoo. If I was downtown alone, I enjoyed just sitting at drugstore counters or in small parks with fountains -watching people and sometimes sketching.

One beautiful April morning when Karen was driving us to high school, she said, "Let's go see the cherry blossoms." And off we drove. She must have been sixteen and just gotten her license. We were sitting in the car afterwards, writing excuse notes and forging our mother's signatures. The first time I was so scared. But no one ever suspected us, the top students. And skipping school became a needed escape valve - meeting Sherry and another friend, Laura, in the early morning when the school buses arrived and fleeing to the bus stop for downtown, school satchels over our shoulders - escaping to the real world.

We walked in and out of the small boutiques in Georgetown commenting on everything, buying nothing. I don't think we were popular with the store owners. Then we found Sam the Argentine baker (or Argentine/ Russian/Jewish baker). He was little old white-haired man who ran the bakery with his wife and baked every-thing in the big oven in the back of the store. He always gave us a warm welcome and chatted with us and invited us into the back where the oven was. He made the most delicious dark round whole grain bread in the world, with a firm crust and a moist delicious center. He tried to stop us from eating the bread hot from the ov-en with tales of how it was bad for the digestion, but we paid no heed. He also made fabulous knishes. My father soon became a faithful customer and so did many of our friends and families.

We had lots of advantages, being in a Metropolitan Area. Sherry, Laura, Ellen and I became volunteer ush-ers at the Arena Theater, and Ellen and I were volunteer ushers at a small experimental theater. We got to see all the plays for free that way. We went to many wonderful concerts in a concert room which wasn't too big and where you felt in contact with the performer. We saw Bob Dylan when he first began his career and sat in the second row. We saw Odetta, Aretha Franklin and Joan Baez. Maybe we also saw Sonny Terry and Brownie McGhee. I can't remember if that is where I saw them. There were some folk club we went to - maybe the Cel-lar Door, and one very informal place in something that looked like a canteen or cafeteria. Laura and Sherry and I went to International Folk Dancing somewhere downtown.

We were a group of girls from high school, including Laura and Sherry, who started tutoring once a week at a settlement house in northeast DC. I tutored a girl named Linda, who was very bright, but hadn't learned to read. I am afraid I did not make so much progress with her. Once I took her to the circus and picked her up in the apartments where she lived. I remember seeing giant rats as I drove up to her building.

A lot was happening in history when I was growing up. I remember the election with Stevenson and Eisenhower. At school, I volunteered to make a speech for Stevenson though I didn't really know much of anything, just what the adults said. I remember the Cuban Missile Crisis. Sherry was very upset about it, she seemed to understand the implications so much better than me. Ellen and Mary and I went with Peg Winegarden when Kennedy died, and stood for hours to see his casket. I remember picketing in front of the White House, something about segregation I think, and we went to rallies and meetings. I attended the March on Washington. My father drove us in, and he knew D.C. so well that he managed to park rather close. I remember some of the March, and Joan Baez singing.

Garrett Park was such an amazing place to grow up. There were lots of girls my age who I could play with, woods to explore, a swimming pool, a library, a little store, all these friendly, interested adults- a mini safe world to bicycle and run around, to learn to fly on our imaginations, to explore the worlds and worlds of books, to write stories, play doll games that lasted for days. Run, jump, hide....

Jessica and Rhoda

And still, sometime after puberty, it wasn't enough. I couldn't understand that my parents didn't want to move to New York City - that must be the real world- why would they choose the boring suburbs - the conformity of it? Garrett Park was a very little world. So when I became a teenager I felt it was limited, I hungered for the real world, and I wasn't sad to leave Garrett Park. I was ready to leave, and I didn't ever really look back with longing until much later in my life.

I graduated from Walter Johnson in 1966, when I was eighteen, and I attended college at the University of Chicago. Looking back it was a very poor choice for me, but I was following Mary Winegarden, who had gone off two years earlier and was very happy there. I don't think I really knew why I was going to college, and I didn't have any clear goal or vocation in mind. I was just doing what was expected of me. I dropped out after the first two years. It was the late '60s and it was a time when you thought about and questioned things, and so I had to leave the university to figure out what I had to do. After living in the Boston area for a year, I joined Sherry Thomas in California, helping her run this saltwater taffy shop in Bodega Bay. Her parents were in Thailand, and they would send us these great silver filigree earring, other jewelry, and woven bags, which we would sell. It was not a thriving business. At the end of the year I went home, and I decided I wanted to try living in another country. America seemed so messed up to me. I had been in Chicago during the riots, and I had a girlfriend who was raped.

In seventh grade I had had this girlfriend, Beatrice, from Denmark, and she had gone back to live there, so I went to Copenhagen and looked her up. In Denmark I met Carsten, my husband, who grew up in the Bronx, but had a Danish father and was living in Denmark. We lived on this little island for a couple of years, then in Norway for five years, and then we returned to Denmark where I attended librarian school for four years. We had our first child, and I took courses in writing, drawing, and Danish. I started writing, and I wrote a little children's book, I was active with a group of unemployed librarians, and eventually I got a job as a librarian.

I worked for some time as a librarian in a little town that also had a Camphill community for developmentally disabled adults. I fit in well there, and felt very at home because it was a strong community of active adults and reminded me of Garrett Park.

We have lived in Denmark since returning from Norway in 1978. Even though I am a Danish citizen and am certainly very formed by my adult years here, I'll never really feel Danish. We are on a river, the longest river in Denmark and surrounded by beautiful forest, which is something I really love about living here. As a child in Garrett Park, I spent so much time in the woods, and this contact with nature is a big part of who I am today.

"Walking Coffee" - painting by Jessica

Every morning I walk my dogs to this park close by that goes down to the river, and every day I walk in the forest with my dogs. (Yes I have become a dog person even though as a child I was afraid of dogs. In Garrett Park the dogs ran free. The front yards were open to each other and to the street. Sometimes several dogs would band together and run from backyard to backyard- there were no fences. It was probably wonderful to be a dog then, but less wonderful for a small child who was somewhat afraid of dogs. At least I didn't like it when a strange dog would come running and barking towards me as I walked by HIS front yard.)

I know there are other communities like Garrett Park, but I have never lived in a community like it. I can't pick out any favorite memories – there were so many. I sometimes wonder if it wasn't also a "Neverland" for me, and that it made growing up more difficult, because it was so wonderful to be a child there. I was lucky to be in Garrett Park, and I was lucky with my family. I had wonderful parents. When my father died, I was surprised about how many of my friends wrote "He was always there for me."

I know that Garrett Park has changed and is not the same today. I remember once after Dad had died, I was visiting Garrett Park and my mom and I were interviewed by a man about Garrett Park's history. Somehow, mom made some remark which revealed by father's left wing view on politics and the interviewer, a doctor, in his thirties maybe, who lived in Garrett Park, was shocked. Do you mean that Dr. Myers went in for socialized medicine? So the times have changed, and the once liberal Garrett Park is taken over by other interests. The library has moved down the road to Kensington. There is no general store, the houses are rebuilt to be bigger and bigger and to be hybrids of style. But I am sure the town still has its charm and a soul. I can see that from the Bugle that you can read online.

You can't travel in time, but when I used to visit Garrett Park (last time in 1998), I could almost see us as children - bicycling to the pool, trying to play tennis on the tennis court; we were just around the corner - shadows, so close. And the magic moments are so vivid that I can almost reach out and touch them.

I have lived in cities, in the countryside, in the U.S., in Norway and in Denmark. And Garrett Park just grows and grows - how lucky I have been to grow up right there and right at that time.

(Parts of this narrative written by Jessica Albertson, parts from an interview conducted by Lee Pope)

Jessica with her puppy, Luna

22

ANNE CRICHTON PTAK

We weren't so centered on the T.V. and everyone was so much more social back when we were growing up. I have always regretted that my own son did not have the great childhood neighborhood that I had. David and I often comment on the unique and wonderful childhood we had in that unique and wonderful community, Garrett Park. You really can't describe Garrett Park to someone who didn't live there. You can try to get it across, but they can't fully understand what it was like. I will always be grateful that I got to experience it as a child.

My parents, J.C. Crichton and Elizabeth Anne (Lizanne) Crichton, bought their house in Garrett Park at 11016 Rokeby Ave. in 1952. Dad worked for the State Department in the Foreign Service for a while and ended up in Cultural Exchange with communist countries. My mother initially had come to Washington during the war and worked for the Civil Service Commission for the War Department. Later, from 1960 to 1979, she worked in personnel at the National Institute of Health.

I was born in George Washington University Hospital in 1949. My older brother, David, is two years older than me, and my younger brother, Mark, is two years younger. In 1953, our sister, Laurie, was born. Because Laurie was born with a heart condition, the family was always watching out for her, which she hated. As a child she spent the summer after first grade in the hospital at NIH, and she finally had open heart surgery at eighteen after her first year of college, which enabled her to live an active life. Unfortunately, in 1979 at the age of twenty-five, Laurie died in a car accident. My parents were never the same after that. You do not recover from the loss of a child.

Mark, David, and Anne - 1954

Mark, David, Anne, and Laurie - 1955

Before moving to Garrett Park, my family lived in Prince George's County. My brother, David, was getting ready to go to kindergarten, but Prince George's County didn't have a kindergarten. This horrified my parents, so they moved to Montgomery County, which did have kindergarten.

I don't know how my father actually found the town, but the fact that Garrett Park was named after the president of the B. & O. Railroad, John Garrett, probably attracted his interest. Dad had a great love for trains. They found the house in Garrett Park, right across the street from the train track, which he just loved. They actually looked at a few other houses in Garrett Park, but the one they ended up buying was across from the train track.

The train was a big presence in our lives. We were not supposed to go anywhere near the tracks, but I'm sure my brothers probably did. What I do remember about the tracks was that there was a mail train that came by to pick up and deliver the mail via a mail bag, that had to be pulled in by a hook, and occasionally the bags that they would toss off would open up and the mail would go all over the place. I remember when I was little, my siblings and my mother and neighbors picking up the spilled mail from the ground.

Wells Park was right across the street, with swings, a slide, and a creek. Behind it was a hill where the train tracks ran. We played in the park but we weren't supposed to go up the hill. David had a friend who lived up on Montrose who wasn't supposed to play in the park, because his mother was afraid the train would fall off the tracks into the park one day. His family later moved to Kensington.

Anne, David, Mark, Lizanne, and Laurie - 1957

I have many early memories of that playground, which I loved. We made dams in the creek, played games like "Spud" there, swung on the swings. On the other side of the creek was a large field area, and we used to play games there, and as we got older, the boys would play football there – the older boys like David and Ron Horn were called The Garrett Park Bombers and the younger boys like Mark were the Rokeby Raiders. Bomber/ Raider games were contested for years. When we played in the park in the afternoon, I remember talking with the other kids, about how we all had to be home by the 5:15, which was a commuter train that went by every day about 5:15. After dinner we would go back and play in the park some more.

There were not a lot of girls my age in the neighborhood, so I played a lot with my brothers and the boys. There were basketball courts next to the tennis courts down by the post office, and we used to play basketball there. We used the tennis courts sometimes – we called it tennis baseball, we would take these tennis racquets and use them for bats. We had the run of the town and our parents never worried about us. They knew we were alright.

We lived a short distance from the general store and the post office. Garrett Park was very unique because everybody had these post office boxes instead of having the mail delivered to their houses. This made it a real gathering place for the town. I really enjoyed going to get the mail. When we were little and couldn't reach the mailbox, we would go to the back and ask Mrs. Parsons, who was the postmistress, for the mail, and she would bring our mail to the counter.

Mr. and Mrs. Karsh ran the store for a long time. We called them Mr. and Mrs. Louie, and they were just the nicest people. It was a regular general store, and they even had a butcher there at one time. For kids, the store was a place where we could buy candy, and we ate a lot of candy. My sister loved this one kind of candy, it was purple, and we called it "purple balls" only she couldn't pronounce the word, she called it "puhple". I can still hear her asking Louie, "Do you have any puhple balls?" And Louie would let us go behind the counter and get our candy. That was the thing – take a nickel and go to the P.O. and you could get five pieces of candy. I remember at Halloween, Louie would just throw the candy on the floor, and we would scramble to get it.

The whole town was a friendly place to grow up, and it seemed like everyone knew everybody. A neighbor I really remember was Mrs. Stevens. They lived in a Chevy House next door and Mr. Stevens actually built our house. Before he died in 1960, Mr. Stevens used to take movies of us at Christmas. Around the corner were the Boltons and the Horns. Ron Horn was a good friend of my brother David, and Mr. and Mrs. Horn were wonderful to me. Unplanned visits were common. Barbara and Roger Pope were such good friends with my parents. I remember the Normans and how they were so accepting to me and David. Mark and Laurie were good friends with their kids, Paul and Storry.

My parents were big on taking advantage of the cultural opportunities that came from living so close to Washington, D.C. We went to Arena Stage, which is where I learned to love Shakespeare, and we went to the Folger Library. We visited the Smithsonian a lot, and the National Gallery, and the zoo. Laurie was an art history major, so it was really a good experience going to the National Gallery with her.

There was a lot happening in the world of current events during the period when I was growing up and both of my parents were liberal and very political. I was never very political, a fact that was hard for my parents to accept, but some memories of significant events from that time do stand out.

I was in ninth grade when Kennedy was shot. I remember coming home from school that day, and my father coming home from work and saying to my mother, "I'm more upset and worried than when Roosevelt died." It was a memorable occasion for our whole family when my brother, David, joined the Marines in 1967, and went off to Viet Nam, and of course it was a really big deal when he came home as well. In 1969, I attended the Peace March on Washington to protest the Vietnam War. I was a junior in college at the time. Since David had been in Viet Nam, I thought I should do that for him. That was big for me, not the kind of thing I did very often.

In 1989, when the Berlin Wall came down, I remember my mother crying on the phone and saying to me, "Your father should be here to see this!" (My father had died before then.) In his work my father spent so much time dealing with the issue of Communism, so the end of the Berlin Wall would have been a really exciting moment for him.

As a community, Garrett Park encouraged active citizen participation. My mother was a councilwoman for a couple of years and she was in charge of the trees. I remember the big fight over the proposed town houses behind the P.O. – this was in the 70s after I had left. The whole community came together to fight it, to keep it from being developed. It would have been so out of character to have those there and the community effort to block the development was successful.

One memory from early childhood was when the whole town had a box supper on the school grounds. It was a big community event that took place before the first addition was put on the school. I remember Barbara Horn talking into a microphone on those steps. It made a big impression on me, the whole town being invited.

All of my school memories are very positive. When I was little I attended the nursery school in that gray building down by the school. It was really a co-op nursery school. Mrs. Gootenberg ran it for a long time. She wrote me a letter when my mother died to say how much of a big help my mother was when Laurie, Mark, and I were in nursery school.

From kindergarten on I attended Garrett Park Elementary. I had very good teachers at Garrett Park Elementary and I did well in school. I also remember going on many fantastic field trips in elementary school. I remember Mrs. Duey who was the principal, as well as my kindergarten teacher. My father just thought the world of her; he thought that she was a fantastic educator who really cared about the kids.

For first grade I had Mrs. Kingman. When Laurie had her first heart surgery when she was in first grade, Mrs. Kingman used to call and visit her after the surgery. I thought that was so nice of her.

Mrs. Shombert was my second grade teacher. David had Mrs. Bradley for second grade, and my dad thought she was fantastic, so he was very disappointed and upset when I got Mrs. Shombert. Mark saw Mrs. Shombert at a1993 reunion at the school and she remembered Mark and Laurie and me. All of us, including Dad, thought she was a great teacher as well.

Mrs. Weymouth was probably my favorite of all my teachers. I had her in fourth grade, and she was fantastic. She was such a good teacher and very kind. I remember that at the end of the year, she had a backyard picnic at her house for her whole class. I also remember that every day we would take a sheet of paper and do a multiplication test. As a result, I have known my multiplication tables really well ever since. Another thing I remember about Mrs. Weymouth was that we used to do these great hallway murals of what we were studying – the pyramids, or other scenes from history. She was really good and all the kids seemed to enjoy her class.

I had Mrs. Strayer in fifth grade. She always wanted us to come to her house when we went trick or treating. Then in sixth grade, I had Miss Eisenburger who was very creative.

I was a safety patrol in sixth grade. Most of the kids were patrols, and if you weren't a patrol, you were sort of shunned. On the days you wore your uniforms, it was really obvious who wasn't a patrol, and I always felt badly for those kids who weren't patrols. Looking back, I regret that I didn't make more of an effort with those kids, because I was aware that they felt like outsiders, but I didn't do anything.

Once I started school I became friends with Pam Barclay, who has since passed away from cancer, and Carolyn Nance. Karen Modine was a year older than me and we were very good friends in elementary school. Carolyn's basement had a ping pong table and we had lots of fun playing ping pong there. We rode bikes all over the place, played war games, or played in the park. We played long Monopoly games on the weekends. We didn't watch T.V. that much, preferring to spend most of our time outside. We had our bikes and we were really mobile.

We could go to the library on our own. I remember Mrs. Bunker, when she was the librarian. She was wonderful. I remember asking her, "Are you related to anyone from the Battle of Bunker Hill? And she would say "Probably. That's my name." I remember Mrs. Payne too, with her quiet voice.

In the summer, the swimming pool was the main focus. Of course we loved going to the pool. My mother would always try to get us to spend time up at the recreation center near the school, but we preferred to spend all our time at the pool. I took lessons at the Garrett Park pool, starting out there as a beginner. I remember my swim teacher, and I think it was Andy Sonner, inviting me to join the swim team, which I did. Once my friends and I were on the swimming team, when we weren't playing we would be practicing, and there were the swimming meets on Saturdays. It was different for Laurie, because she couldn't swim because of her heart.

The Fourth of July was an important community event, with a parade in the morning, and a community celebration with fireworks later in the day. Initially, we would decorate our bikes for the parade but after a few years, Dad started decorating our car as a float. When Hawaii and Alaska became states, Dad painted the states on the car doors and had "E Pluribus Crichton" painted on the hood. Laurie, Mark, and I rode on the top with the sunroof open – we were Miss Hawaii, Miss Alaska, and Uncle Sam. David and Ron Horn walked in front of the car carrying banners for all the other states. Quite elaborate – the Crichton car floats always won first prize.

What I remember most about fall was that there were always lots of leaves to rake and burn. When I was in high school I wanted to go to football games on Saturday, but the leaves had to be raked as well. And then there was Halloween. When we were younger my father was into dressing up for Halloween, doing his face up like a monster or a ghost for the kids who came trick or treating at our door. We went out in a group with our bags and we didn't need an adult with us. When we were older we could walk over to the Estates to trick or treat. My grandmother would sometimes make us costumes when she was still alive, but for the most part, we made our own. Mark and I were pretty much always bums with charcoal on our faces, in our dad's old shirts.

On Halloween the big thing was to ring the bell in the church tower, what is now the town hall. It was a prank that boys in junior high liked to do. When I was in sixth grade David and Ron Horn did go and ring the bell, and it was a big deal.

It was very exciting when it snowed in the winter. I have wonderful memories of sledding on Donnelly's Hill, which was a great sledding hill for the whole town and right around the corner from our house. The snow plow was not allowed to plow that street, so the kids would need to pack down the snow for sledding. One time it snowed on Christmas Eve and it was when David was in Viet Nam and so my parents

Karen and David Crichton, Anne holding Karen and David's daughter, Lindsay, Lizanne, J.C. and Mark Crichton

made a movie of it snowing at Christmas, which it rarely did.

After sixth grade I attended Kensington Junior High. It was a big change – the school was so much bigger and you didn't know everybody. I was excited to go to someplace bigger and meet new people and I had a pretty good experience there. I made new friends and I liked going to different classes. I got involved with sports, but I have bad knees and they started to bother me in ninth grade. I developed constantly swollen knees and I couldn't play sports other than swimming any more.

After junior high I went to high school at Walter Johnson. The biggest thing in high school for me was joining the Mariners, a senior Girl Scout troop. That was the most fun I ever had and I still think about it. My friends Carolyn Nance and Karen Modine were Mariners, too. We just had the greatest times. Mrs. Abrams, who was the Mariners' leader, was like a second mother to me. I really loved her! I almost dropped out in ninth grade because I didn't think I had time for both Mariners and school. Mrs. Abrams called up my mother and said that she really thought I would enjoy the Mariners and that I should stay in. She was right! We were very involved in white water canoeing and kayaking. We went to white water races in Maryland, Virginia, Pennsylvania, Delaware., New York, and Canada. We spent my whole senior year raising money so we could go to Europe for a month, staying in hostels, and attending the White Water World Championships in Czecho-slovakia. We rented a VW bus, Mrs. Abrams bought a Volvo station wagon and we drove all over Europe. What an amazing experience that was for me.

In high school I had Mr. Harrison, for biology and he was such a fabulous teacher.   It was because of him that I ended up majoring in biology in college. Nobody else in my family liked science, but I was the odd one out. I hated writing papers; I was a science person and I did well in it.   I liked the classes in high school, but I didn't like the social environment and I couldn't participate in any sports activities because of my knees. I graduated from Walter Johnson in 1967.

After high school I went to the University of Rochester in Rochester, N.Y. I graduated from college in 1971 and got a teaching job in Buffalo, N.Y. I was a science teacher for ten years. In the early 80s I got laid off due to declining enrollment, so I went to pharmacy school from 1982 to 1985 and became a hospital phar-macist. I loved teaching, but being a pharmacist gave me a good life.   I married John Paul Ptak in 1986 and I had my son, John Cameron Ptak, in 1992.   I'm retired now, still living in Buffalo. I swim a lot, now that I am retired. I swam a lot through college, and a couple of years ago I took it up again. I can credit my childhood in Garrett Park for that.

I think what I liked best about growing up in Garrett Park was the fact that everybody knew everybody. The comradery of the whole neighborhood amazes me when I look back on it now. I don't think it's like that anymore. David and I have talked about it, the way things have changed. We weren't so centered on the T.V. and everyone was so much more social back when we were growing up. I have always regretted that my own son did not have the great childhood neighborhood that I had. David and I often comment on the unique and wonderful childhood we had in that unique and wonderful community, Garrett Park. You really can't describe Garrett Park to someone who didn't live there. You can try to get it across, but they can't fully understand what it was like. I will always be grateful that I got to experience it as a child.

Anne with her son, John Cameron Ptak, and her husband, John Ptak

23

CHIP FITZPATRICK

I was like a train spotter, and I was really into it...The trains had sort of a baseball card quality to them, because there were so many railroads before they were all consolidated. You'd see box cars from all over the United States. They had the Katy (the Missouri-Kansas-Texas Railroad) and there was the Frisco Line, the Sioux Line, the Nickle Plate Road, the New York Central, and the Wabash. I'd look at all those box cars and think, "I've seen that one before." It was like collecting baseball cards, and I got to know the ones I saw all the time.

My parents, George ("Fitz") and Molly Fitzpatrick, both grew up in Philadelphia, my dad in the East Falls neighborhood of Philadelphia, and my mom in Narberth, a suburb of Philadelphia. They met as summer camp counsellors at Camp Hilltop, courted for five years, and were married in 1945. They had a one-weekend honeymoon in Atlantic City, since my dad was in the Navy, and he had to go back to work the next day in the Philadelphia Navy yards. The Navy sent my father to Panama at the end of the war, and my parents lived in Panama for two years. When my father was discharged from the Navy, he got a job with the Office of War.

My parents moved back to D.C. when my dad got a job with the Operations Research Office, an early think tank like the Rand Corporation, which was what he was doing in 1950, when I was born. At that time they were living on 29th street in D.C., and soon after they moved to some apartments on East-west Highway in Silver Spring for about five years. In 1955, when I was five, they bought their house on Rokeby Avenue and moved in. My sister Meg was born in 1955, and my little sister, Marla was born in 1961, so I didn't have any siblings until I was five. My dad went to Korea in '52 or '53, and my first memories were that it was just my mom and I. She was lonely, because my dad was gone almost two years, so I was like her puppy.

When we moved to Garrett Park, the first thing I noticed was the woods at the end of the street. I remember how excited I was to think about the fun I was going to have exploring those woods. Also, I was totally into trains, so I thought it was really exciting that the town was on the B. and O. main line.

I had a good time playing on that street, though the wooded area started to be developed within a year of when we moved there. I was friendly with Mr.(Pop) and Mrs. Wells, who lived at the bottom of the street before it got developed. Mrs. Wells was really sweet, while Pop Wells could be a little gruff. Because they were so old, we kids were intimidated by them, but I think they were really just very nice. Even though it was private property, they let us wander all around and explore there. It was kind of an enchanted place, like a little pixie land, with a little bridge that went over a tiny little creek. The creek ran into a culvert that went under an embankment for the B. and O. The culvert seemed really scary to me when I was a little kid.

Then they started to build houses down where the Wellses lived, and over time they cut down the woods and put up that G.E.M. store. I remember that Wisconsin Avenue used to be a two-lane hardtop, and then shortly after the G.E.M. store went up, they built Congressional Plaza, which was the first shopping center there. At pretty much the same time they widened Wisconsin Avenue to a four-lane hardtop all the way from Bethesda to Rockville, which really changed the landscape. Before then there was just Georgetown Prep and it was kind of isolated with no other structures around.

I was very shy at first, and I didn't have any friends. I think Lee Pope was the first kid I played with in the neighborhood, which was probably set up by my mother, who wanted me to have friends. Lee took pity on me and befriended me, even though she was three years older than I was, and for a while she was kind of like my tomboy big sister.

A little later Paul Norman became a good friend. Paul lived just down the street on the corner of Rokeby and Clyde. It was good that we made friends because there was no other eligible boy in the neighborhood. My mother and Paul's mother, Peg, spent a long time trying to get me and Paul together since we were both so shy. But their efforts paid off, and after six months we finally became buddies. As soon as we could play baseball, we used to play whiffle ball in Paul's back yard. When we graduated to playing with an actual baseball we broke the neighbor's (Mr. Benson's) window. Paul and I were best friends and we are still good friends today, both living in Portland, Oregon.

My mother was terrified about me playing on the tracks. At first, when I was really little, she let me go across the street to the neighbors, who had a chain link fence, and I was allowed to stand behind the fence and watch the trains. But I couldn't get any closer than that. When I got to be ten or eleven, my mom, with great reluctance, said it was ok to walk on the tracks, because she figured by then I had enough sense to get out of the way if a train came. I used to walk to the store a lot from there, as it was a shorter and more interesting route. I could walk on that path all the way to my friend Frank Punga's house. Later, we kids spent a lot of time walking up and down the tracks, and I remember how we liked to put pennies on the tracks and watch them get smushed by the trains. I don't know why it was so fascinating. Maybe it was because the trains were so big and threatening.

I used to spend a lot of time watching the trains, and I would always report back what was on them. I was like a train spotter, and I was really into it. At 6:00 there were two passenger trains, express trains, the Capital Limited and I can't remember the name of the other one. They left out of Union Station within fifteen minutes of each other. One ran from Washington to New York, and ten minutes later there would be one that went to Chicago. So I would always watch for them. Or sometimes I would watch to see if there were any new cars. They had sort of a baseball card quality to them, because there were so many railroads before they were all consolidated. You'd see box cars from all over the United States. They had the Katy (the Missouri-Kansas-Texas Railroad) and there was the Frisco Line, the Sioux Line, the Nickle Plate Road, the New York Central, and the Wabash. I'd look at all those box cars and think, "I've seen that one before." It was like collecting baseball cards, and I got to know the ones I saw all the time.

I remember that when they still had passenger train service, they used to put the mail up on a semaphore right above Wells Park. A guy would walk down and hang the mail bag up on that thing, and an inbound passenger train from New York or wherever would put a hook out there and grab the mail bag and take it to either Silver Spring or downtown Washington. I used to like watching that.

Of course I played in Wells Park. I liked to pal around with Mark Crichton, who lived across the street from the park. Frank Punga, whose family was from Latvia, also lived near the park. I got to be friends with him because, like me, he was a total motor head. I was really into cars and anything mechanical, especially lawnmowers, but anything to do with machines, and we shared that interest.

We had a family dog, a collie named Puck. One summer when we were camping, we put her in a kennel and she escaped, and she was missing for six months. My mother was diligent in looking for her. She placed ads in the local newspapers, and sure enough someone finally found her. She had wandered a hundred miles from where she was lost. Sadly, after that she was never the same. Maybe she had been abused. Every time you picked up a broom she would disappear. She was really weird from that time on.

When my family first moved to Garrett Park I was in kindergarten. In Silver Spring I had had this really cool kindergarten teacher who let me draw train cars on the newsprint and put my train cars all around the classroom, the coal car and the caboose and the tank car, about thirteen different cars, and when I came to Garrett Park Elementary, the teacher was more like an overgrown babysitter. She didn't bring much to the party, and my mom thought she was a huge step down from my Silver Spring teacher. I think she went and complained to Mrs. Duey that the teacher wasn't bringing any intellectual stimulation, and that it was more like day care.

In second or third grade I had Mrs. Buckman. My mom liked her, but I was terrified of her. She was really thin with dark hair and wore these pencil tight skirts; she seemed to me like an evil villain or something. I think she was actually a good teacher but to me she was so scary.

One person that I remember from Garrett Park Elementary is Mrs. Murray. She was a really cool mom, and she was also the school librarian. Everyone in the Murray family was a voracious reader. What I remember about Mrs. Murray was when there was snow, and the teachers hadn't made it in, they would send us into the library and they'd call Mrs. Murray (who lived on Keswick Street not far from the school) and she'd come in and read to us. She read us all kinds of stuff, and she had this incredible voice that was really hypnotic. When they would come in and say "Ok, you have to go to class now, or you have to go home, it's a snow day" I remember almost crying in pain because I just wanted to hear that voice. It wasn't until much later when I was eighteen or so that I became friends with Alan Murray. When I started talking to Alan's mother, I remembered that she was the person with that voice.

Mrs. Strayer, my fifth grade teacher, always began the day by reciting the Lord's Prayer. I think we might have had to recite it out loud right after the Pledge. After that, there was always a five minute reading of a Bible passage. I had no religious education and found the readings quite soothing. We all knew it was slightly taboo, but evidently no one complained. I can't imagine what the Jewish kids must've thought, but maybe she was careful to stick to the Old Testament. Then in sixth grade, the Jewish kids were encouraged to bring in articles, like the dreidel, and explain Hanukkah to the rest of the class. This was a complete revelation to me. I remember going home to explain breathlessly to my Mom that there were people who didn't celebrate Christmas!!

Speaking of Christmas, I can remember going around with Peg Norman and Storry doing caroling at Christmas time. One time Roy Gootenberg landed in the Garrett Park School in a helicopter, and did his "Ho ho ho" thing as Santa Claus. I wonder how they pulled the strings to do that. They must have had a military connection or something. I was beyond believing in Santa by then.

We had our own Christmas ritual in our family. My dad had a Kodak windup camera that he brought back from Panama. On Christmas morning, he would position himself at the bottom of the stairs with his camera, and there was a sheet he had put up across the stairs. My mother would pull back the sheet so we could see all the toys, and he would start filming. It was a Hollywood entrance, and we had years and years of those.

After Christmas I would count down the days to the Fourth of July, which was a holiday that I really loved. I remember putting crepe paper in the spokes of my bicycle for the parade, and putting playing cards there so it would sound like a motor, and I loved the fireworks most of all.

One good thing about growing up in Garrett Park was that there were so many interesting and eccentric people around – so many different kinds of people, like Sam Powell, George Norman, Clyde Hall, the Browns, and the Thomases. Most people were transplants, and it made such a hodge-podge of people from all over - Ohio, Michigan, Pennsylvania, all these liberals. There was also a pretty big political range, all the way from very left-wing people to probably some John Birchers in there too.

My friend, Frank Punga, provided me with a tiny little window on a different "reality". His dad had a lumber yard down in the district in S.E. and most of the guys that worked there were black. Frank would bring back all these exotic swear words to us. We didn't even know what they meant, but we thought they sounded great. I remember going home one time for dinner and calling Meg a "stupid cork-sucker" (that was what I thought the phrase was) and my mother just went white. I was eleven or twelve, and my mother wanted my dad to take me out to the kitchen and give me a severe tongue-lashing, which he did. He said "You would never ever call your sister that!" and I said, "I don't even know what it means!" Then he understood that I was really naïve and I was just repeating l what Frank Punga said.

Everyone who lived in Garrett Park at that time was white. The Jim Crow thing was the order of the day when I was growing up. Over time I think this gradually changed, so my sisters have had a different experience than I did. I had gone to school with African American children in Silver Spring when I was really small, but after moving to Garrett Park, I never saw any black people except when the trash men came around.

That whole trash collection thing seemed so primitive by today's standards. They had an open bed stake truck that said "Wooten Refuse" on its sides and these guys laid this great big piece of burlap on the ground, 6' by 6' or 8' by 8', and they would dump all the rubbish in one big pile on it: coffee grounds, cigarette butts, and beer cans (there was no recycling back then), and they took it all off to Rockville, where I think there was a landfill. And this guy would have to stand up in the bed of the truck up to his knees in garbage, and stomp it all down. There were four or five guys going to each house while the truck went slowly down the street. There was a step ladder on the back of the truck, and they would climb up with their bundle, and the guy in the back would grab the bundle, dump it, and hand back the empty burlap. Those were pretty much the only black people we ever saw. We went to see my dad at his office in Bethesda and I would see a black shoe-shine place or a janitor, always someone with a menial job, or a black porter at Union Station.

About half the families in Garrett were liberal, mostly northerners. The other half was southern and generally conservative. Some of the conservative ones interacted with the liberals in a 'don't ask-don't tell mode'. Others kept to themselves and were unknown in our parents' social circles. I became somewhat aware of this when I was a paper boy for the Evening Star, which was the Republican paper. I had to collect the monthly subscriptions from a roster of these folks, who would have otherwise remained a complete mystery to me, many of whom were covertly, if not overtly, bigoted.

This dichotomy was shockingly revealed to the liberals when Ann Brown started this program called "In the Swim" which involved bringing inner city kids who had no access to any kind of pool or any kind of summer activities out to these suburban pools so they could swim one afternoon a week. I think they came in a school bus. My dad was either mayor or in the town council when it was proposed. Most pool members thought it would just automatically pass - they thought it would be a no-brainer, but two or three people said it had to be put to a citywide referendum, which really surprised Ann Brown, my dad, George Payne and these others liberals. It passed narrowly, by less than fifty votes, something like 510/470. I can remember my mother just being horrified by the narrow margin. There may even have been a few pool resignations, but I'm not sure about that.

At that time, though there were a few Puerto Ricans in Kensington, I couldn't have told you if there were any U.S. citizens of Mexican ancestry. The only representations of Mexicans I remember was Bill Dana's *My name José Jiménez* humor, and Pat Boone singing "You better come home Speedy Gonzales and slap some mud on the wall". That song was a top ten hit in 1962. It came to me a few years ago that the first Mexican-American person I ever met was César Chávez. I used to mow the Brown's lawn, and Chávez stayed at their house for some days during the grape boycott. When I went in to get paid, Ann Brown introduced me to this short brown man, and I shook his hand. He wouldn't have seemed much stranger to me if he had been from Mars and had antennae on his forehead.

I had one friend in the neighborhood who had been brought up to be racist. He said the "n" word all the time, and when George Wallace was running for president, he was rooting for Wallace, and he never had anything good to say about Martin Luther King. He was otherwise a nice guy, and we were actually very good buddies. When I was about fourteen or fifteen, we spent a lot of time together, and I kind of acquiesced in all his politically incorrect behavior because I really liked him as a person and I wanted to be friends with him. And since he was a year older than I was, he got his driver's license before I did, and he would take me driving.

When I was sixteen, my family moved to Germany for a few years. After we returned, this friend was attending college in Virginia, and he had heard that I was back. He drove over from Virginia to see me, and I shunned him. What was really going on was that I was ashamed of myself because in the past I had aided and abetted him in his bigotry instead of opposing him. A lot of people thought that way back then, and that kind of bigotry was not all that rare. It wasn't his fault that he had been raised to think that way, but because he was the only friend I had who was overtly racist, I guess I felt the need to snub him. I still have it in mind that I'd like to apologize for treating him like that. I'd like to tell him "I did you a big injustice forty years ago and I'd like to apologize for it."

When I think about the effect on me of growing up in Garrett Park, I guess the bad thing about it was that it was such an insular world that it stunted me in a way. When my dad was fourteen, he had way more street smarts that I did. I was completely wet behind the ears about anything having to do with sex or homosexuality. I don't think I understood about half of what any of that stuff was. My dad, growing up in East Philadelphia with a gang like "Our Gang", running around the sidewalk, hanging out with all kinds of different people, was way more versed in the ways of the world as a kid. I didn't realize this until I was about forty.

I think that being so sheltered as a child was somewhat crippling to my development, and I kind of resent that even when I was twenty years old I was so naïve. In 1970, I took part in the May Day demonstrations, and I was one of the few people stupid enough to get actually legitimately arrested. I had to go court, they gave me ten days in jail for disorderly conduct, and I ended up spending six days there. They let me out early for "good behavior". They sent me to Lorton, and when I was admitted there they took me through this holding area where there were all these black kids who were claiming to be heroin addicts. I was just terrified, and I thought they were going to slice me open. They walked me through the juvenile area, and I would have just gotten the crap beaten out of me there, but then they put me in with these old lifers on the top floor - drunks, pimps, winos, and petty criminals. That was a real immersion in African-American culture, and they were really nice to me.

Summer of 1972 - Front, L to R: Chip, Roger Barclay, a girl named Nancy, Sandi Miles, Paul Norman behind Sandi

When I came back from Germany, my friends and I were all nineteen or twenty. We didn't want to live with our parents, we wanted to be hippies and smoke dope, so we rented a house right over the district line in Friendship Heights, Maryland for $200.00/month. Two of my roommates there were Kevin Linton and Alan Murray. That's when we really got to know each other, and we are still friends. In fact, we went on a three day camping trip together this past summer.

Now I live in Portland, Oregon, as does Paul Norman, his sister Storry, and Cilla Murray.

Paul moved out there first, and I kind of followed him. I like it here, but there are some things I miss about living back east.

A gathering of GP alumni in Portland, Oregon: Chip, Lee Pope, Storry Norman, Paul Norman, and Cilla Murray - October 2019

I think having friends that go all the way back to childhood cultivates tolerance. Growing up in these small towns with all these weird eccentric people around them, kids can learn to live together with others. If they met each other in a different way maybe they wouldn't be able to stand each other, but in small town life it's just "Oh, that's just Joe White or so and so's weird father" - all these cranky, cantankerous, eccentric people and you just came to accept them. You took it for granted that they were in your neighborhood, this really broad assortment of personalities, and you'd just absorb it all.

24

PAUL NORMAN

Even from a young age, I thought living in Garrett Park was special, and I was proud of it. I was aware of town history, and I knew about residents fighting off "through streets" to preserve the town character. This was one of the special things about Garrett Park - that it was a defined, contained community.

In 1948, my parents, Peg and George Norman, bought our house at 4701 Clyde Avenue, where they lived until they moved to Portland, Oregon in the late 1980s. I grew up in Garrett Park from birth in 1951 until I moved away permanently in 1972. My younger sister, Storry, was born in 1953.

Even from a young age, I thought living in Garrett Park was special, and I was proud of it. I was aware of town history, and I knew about residents fighting off "through streets" to preserve the town character. This was one of the special things about Garrett Park – the fact that it was a defined, contained community. Because it had boundaries that were actually defended from encroachment by through roads, it felt like a contained community even though it was actually in the sea of suburbs. When I was a kid, my parents had no problem with me just roaming around without necessarily telling them where I was going. They thought it was safe for me to just jump on my bike and go wherever I liked, to explore the town, to go wherever I wanted. This was a function of the town being a protected community - it was harder for me to get out to where it was a more traffic-y and dangerous place.

Physically, I always thought that for a suburb the town was quite pretty. There were so many big trees, and I thought that it was especially pretty in the fall when the leaves turned colors. I liked the spacing of the neighborhood I grew up in, the fact that it was close enough that you could be neighborly, but not so close that you were on top of each other. And in my experience it was really neighborly. People were constantly dropping by to visit each other. I remember that when I first invited my wife, Sandi, over to my parents' house, when we were friends, she remarked upon the fact that people just stopped by all the time.

Another thing I thought was really neat about the town was that it had its own government. My awareness of this might have been fed by the fact that we were family friends with four Garrett Park mayors – Sam Powell, who lived across from us on Clyde Avenue, "Fitz" Fitzpatrick, Paul Edlund, and with longtime Bugle editor Clyde Hall, who also lived on Clyde.

The family friends that we interacted with most were families of my friends and close neighbors. The Powells, across the street, and the Fitzpatricks, who lived around the corner and down the street a bit on Rokeby Avenue were neighbors who were friends with my parents. I had my own neighborhood friends, and often their parents were also friends with my parents. Another good friend of mine was Mark Crichton, who lived down at the bottom of Rokeby. My mom and his got along well with each other.

Paul with Tim Powell

I was in the inaugural "class" at the Nursery School, and after that attended kindergarten and all six years at Garrett Park Elementary. I have this memory of all the kids in the neighborhood heading off to school at the same time. We walked to school when it was snowing, but otherwise we rode our bikes. Garrett Park was very bike-friendly for kids back then. We biked to Garrett Park Elementary, to the pool, to the store. We kind of lived on our bikes, riding back and forth to each other's houses all the time. We had a lot of freedom to do that.

The first opening of the Garrett Park Swimming Pool was memorable. The pool was built with a lot of community support, volunteers helping to make it happen, and I was proud that my father had helped build the wooden walls of the dressing rooms. I spent much of the summers at the pool, and swam on the team.

Fall leaf-raking was a major event. I can still smell those piles of leaves. It's hard to believe now that we burned the leaf piles on the curb, actually making a project of seeing how much smoke we could produce! Yikes.

Snowy winter days were exciting, and the snow itself was beautiful. I remember thinking that it was really pretty to have all that snow and it was so quiet. When it snowed, you didn't have to go to school, which was a big icing on the cake, and you would go sledding, which was a really big deal, and it just transformed the town.

Donnelly's Hill as viewed from the bottom

Storry and Paul

Paul and Chip Fitzpatrick

Everyone went sledding on Donnelly's Hill. There would be a fire at the top of the hill, and I remember the nights when we would be standing around the fire and occasionally jump on a sled and go down the hill – it was really great. If you wanted a more exciting hill there was St. Angela's Hall. I've got this picture of me and Chip Fitzpatrick standing out in our yard in about a foot of snow when we were kids.

I remember Christmas caroling as a big highlight. First the carolers would gather and have a few drinks at someone's house – often it would be our house. It was very festive, and then we'd all bundle up and go out and carol at pre-arranged houses. It was pretty great to roam around town in a big festive group and to see the enjoyment of the people we caroled-to. At some point liability fears moved the caroling indoors. There was a liability concern about all these people roaming around in the dark, a concern that someone might break their leg or something, resulting in someone getting sued. That's what I heard at the time. It was kind of a come down when the whole event got moved inside.

Another Christmas memory is of the treasured tradition of Roy Gootenburg dressing up as Santa. This was his thing at Christmas - he roamed around and visited a lot of houses, showing up to surprise the kids and acting just like the department store Santa. There was this good natured joke about the fact that he was Jewish.

The transition to Kensington Junior High was a big change, though most of my friends were still there. Now we had to ride a bus to school, though strangely, even though we spent over an hour a day on the bus, I have zero recollection of actually being on the bus. You'd think you'd remember it but I don't. Compared to Garrett Park Elementary, Kensington Junior High was definitely much more impersonal, and the student body was also different, more diverse.

During my time at KJH I got into trouble with some friends for getting these little papers typed up that purported to be a conspiracy that students were to take over the school in an insurrection and imprison the teachers. We quickly got busted for that. I'm pretty sure it was Mr. Cross, the school disciplinarian, who lectured us and called our parents. You can imagine that in this day and age something like that would be taken very seriously, it would be a huge deal. But I remember that Mr. Cross told me that he knew it wasn't serious because the note was too well written.

The town has changed a lot since I was a kid. Houses have been replaced, new houses built, lots of remodeling. Our house has been remodeled, but I think they did a good job. My father would always hang a nautical lantern on his garage, and they completely rebuilt the garage, but they, too, hung a nautical lantern there when it was done.

In the 1970s, my sister Storry, Chip Fitzpatrick, Alan Murray, and Pricilla Murray, all moved to Portland, Oregon. We somewhat presumptuously called ourselves "Garrett Park West" – which I think was symbolic of our attachment to the town. When we were house-hunting in Portland in the early 80s, I was finding myself frustrated by the search, and only later realized that I had been looking for a Garrett Park neighborhood in Portland, which didn't exist. I was looking for specific features that I remembered and valued from my own childhood. When my son was born in Portland, we lived in a house with a big lot and no close neighbors. We had very little interaction with neighbors, and you definitely couldn't jump on a bike and go anywhere, and I remember missing that neighborhood connection for him.

I actually kind of wonder about other people, how much they had an experience like mine. For others, was it just a place to live, a place where they happened to have grown up? I've wondered if some people were not aware that they lived in such a unique suburban community, and if some people didn't think they grew up in a place that was really special.

Paul and his wife, Sandi

CILLA MURRAY

Garrett Park was always a special, mystical place for me. Because Garrett Park was filled with children, there was always someone to play with. It was a small village amidst suburban Washington, a place buried and hidden from the outside world; I was both amused and bemused, to learn this from my fellow students at Kensington Junior High and Walter Johnson, who had never heard of it...

My parents, Jim and Marguerite Murray, moved to Garrett Park in 1948. Prior to moving there, they had been living in an apartment downtown. My father had been in the army, so they probably had an FHA loan, and they were looking for a house close to D.C. that they could afford. They ended up buying a lot in Garrett Park and finding someone to build the house for them. My parents had seen some plans in a magazine that they liked, but they had to adapt the house to the shape of the lot, which was very narrow and deep. They actually designed the house themselves, which suited my father, who had a great interest in architecture and really would have liked to be an architect. To fit the lot, our house was narrow from side to side and extended quite far back into the yard. Later, my parents had an addition built on to it.

There were three children in our family. My sister, Jennifer, was born in 1946, my brother, Alan, was born in 1950, and I was born in 1952. Garrett Park is where I grew up, living there from birth to age seventeen, when I went away to college and graduate school. I returned home for summers and holidays, and I once again lived with my parents in Garrett Park for about eight months after I finished graduate school and was working downtown. Once I had saved enough money to get my own apartment, I moved into D.C., from whence I moved to Portland Oregon where I have lived since 1979.

The Murray house

Our house was on Keswick Street, which was on the south side of Strathmore where the school was, the smaller side of town. Keswick was a dead-end street, and Oxford, the next street down from Strathmore, was only used by people in the neighborhood, so there wasn't much traffic on the street, making it very safe for children to play on. I have many wonderful memories of playing on the street - hide and seek, kick the can, tag, Frisbee, kickball, foursquare, hopscotch, jumping rope, roller skating, and racing each other – all up and down Keswick street. We played half-court basketball in the street, using the hoop attached to our butternut tree. That tree later was uprooted in a storm, and by the time I returned from work that evening, it was all gone.

My main neighborhood friends were Joan Hartmann and Martha Abrams. I played some with Elaine French, who lived across the street, and sometimes with Briane Pinkson, who lived next to Joan, and with Rhoda Myers, who lived on Weymouth Street. But Joan and Martha and I were together pretty much all the time.

Marguerite with Cilla and Alan - 1955

My brother, Alan, had three boys that he played with. There was Robert Eddy, who lived up the street on the corner of Keswick and Strathmore, John Hartmann who lived at the end of Keswick, and Roger Barclay who lived on the next street over, Clermont. The four of them were always together and stayed friends for years. Alan and Roger are still friends. So as John and Alan were always together and Joan and I were always together, the four of us sometimes did things together too.

Compared to children today, we had a great deal of freedom to do things on our own. I remember walking to elementary school with my friends, and that there were no parents needed to walk with us. Even at a very young age we could walk to the swimming pool without parental accompaniment. I loved going to the pool, and I remember enthusiastically pinning the copper tag onto my suit which indicated I had passed my swimming test. (My mother used to describe how I wiggled my way through the course.) Though I was a good swimmer and spent

Cilla and Martha Abrams at Pricilla Maury's Easter egg hunt - 1957

a lot of time at the pool, I was never interested in joining the swimming team, as I wasn't into competing.

There are some special memories from our neighborhood that stand out for me. I have wonderful memories of the Easter egg hunt at Pricilla Maury's, which she hosted every year, and also wonderful memories of Halloween. These days you always have packaged candy, as anything homemade cannot be trusted. Back then, we had Mrs. Weaver, and she always made either caramel apples or Rice Crispy treats in addition to the packaged candy. Though my mother did make excellent desserts, we normally never got to eat that kind of stuff, so we would make a bee-line to Mrs. Weaver's house to make sure we got some before they ran out. We never went trick or treating in Garrett Park Estates, and we hardly ever went across Strathmore. When we were real little my older sister would go around with us, but I don't remember our parents ever having to be there. But that's just how it was back then in Garrett Park. Even at night on Halloween we weren't highly supervised as kids are today. I would be curious to know how they do Halloween in Garrett Park today.

My parents liked to have a large group of people over for Thanksgiving. I remember one Thanksgiving in particular when we had the Popes, the Ritvos, and the Franzes. The night before Thanksgiving, the parents had prepared a treasure hunt for us, with written clues. We were in two teams - Donnie Franz was the head of one, and Carl Pope was the head of the other. It wasn't real cold that year, but it was dark, because the treasure hunt was after dinner. And we were allowed out, all over town, by ourselves. One of the clues was the tennis courts down by the post office, way on the other side of town. We were all over the place. I was on Donnie's team, and he knew all of the back ways, and our team won. Each team was rewarded with one of two little metal treasure chests - I think they had candy or something in them. They were these cool little metal trunks, with strapping on them. I remember Liz Ritvo asking me whether she could have our team's treasure chest, which was silver, and I said yes, though it was mine to keep, because I was the youngest. Jennifer got to keep the other one, which was blue. She had that little treasure chest for years, and I was really envious, sorry that I had given the silver chest to Lizzie when I could have had it.

On weekends, my parents' friends often came over for a few drinks and snacks a couple of hours before dinner. I remember the Reynoldses, the Popes, the Paynes, and the Chrislers coming over a lot. There was conversation, it was all very informal, and I really enjoyed those occasions, the friendly feeling that accompanied them.

Life in Garrett Park wasn't all bliss. Our street was near the curve on Strathmore Avenue at the top of the hill from Kensington. People would come roaring up that hill and not be able to make that turn, and they would crash into the trees. We would hear the ambulance sirens, which put our dog into a frenzy, and we would know that someone had crashed. I walked home from Kensington Junior High a few times, and it was very scary to cross the bridge over Rock Creek; I too-well remembered my parents talking about the car crash that crushed one or two little girls who were on the bridge when the car came over it. I would wait for a lull in the traffic, and then run across the bridge and up to Weymouth, where I could get off Strathmore.

I remember two instances when crime came to Garrett Park. The first was when Mrs. Ostrander was murdered, which happened when I was around eleven. I remember the "It can't happen here" feeling that I had when I heard about it. I didn't know her, but it was really shocking. And then later, when I was living with my parents after graduate school in the mid-1970s, a man started breaking into houses and raping women. One night, when I was housesitting for the Chrislers, who lived across the street, I was sleeping in the bedroom, when I woke up with a very strong feeling that there was danger outside. I knew these break-ins had been happening in the town, and I just froze, listening hard, trying to figure out what was going on outside, wondering what to do. The doors were all locked, but I knew it was possible for someone to break a window if they wanted to get in. I wanted to call my father, who was just across the street, but I hadn't closed the curtains on the windows, and it didn't feel safe to try to get to the phone. Finally, after a long time, I heard the cat eating the food off of the table outside; from that I knew that there wasn't anyone out there, and I was able to calm myself down. The next morning when I was riding to work with my father on the train, I told him about this experience. He told me later that somebody on the other side of town had been raped that night, so the fear I had felt was based on something that was really happening at the time. They finally caught the guy who was doing this, and I remember how relieved everyone was.

I have another memory of being afraid in a strange house at night. As a children's librarian, my mother was very knowledgeable about children's literature, and she read *The Hobbit* to us when it first came out. I was very little at the time, too young to follow the story, but there was one passage where Bilbo was in a dark, narrow passage, underground in the mountains, and something evil whooshed past him in the dark. This passage really made an impression on me, it really frightened me. As a result, I avoided reading Tolkien as a child, and I didn't read the Ring Trilogy until I was in college (though I have read it many times since). I remember this one night: I was in college at the time, when I was babysitting for some people at the bottom of Weymouth Street. I never really liked babysitting very much, didn't like being alone in an unfamiliar house at night, and I always thought Weymouth Street was a little spooky with the park right there so close to the houses. I was reading *The Fellowship of the Ring*, and had come to the part where the Ringwraiths rode into Hobbiton and sacked one of the houses there. It was a cold, dark and very windy night, and the shrubbery that grew up close to the house was scraping against the sides and the windows, and then a door banged in the wind. I was in an unfamiliar house in a part of town I didn't like, the part of the book I was reading was very scary, and I was really terrified! I had never been so glad to see anyone as I was to see those parents when they finally came home.

In addition to being a librarian, my mother taught at Garrett Park Elementary for a year or two. Sometimes she would bring home stories about her experiences with her class. She talked about one boy who had a really hard time staying in his seat. He was a very big boy of Swedish extraction, and she described him as a "Swedish farm boy" who really belonged striding over the fields, not shut up in some little classroom behind a desk. She liked him and was very sympathetic towards him. When he started to act restless, she would ask him if he wanted to go outside and walk around, and he was always happy to do that. She could still keep an eye on him from the window, so it was safe. I think my mother must have been a teacher with a good understanding of the needs of her students.

My school experience at Garrett Park Elementary was good. I had Miss Gooken for fourth and sixth grade and I adored her. I think she was my best teacher. For second and third grade, and also for fifth and sixth I was in split classes. They kept putting me in those classes, I guess because I could learn independently. When I was in the second/third grade class, we learned cursive. The second graders weren't supposed to learn how to do script yet, and they were still printing. Then I went into a different third grade class for a while when they were having a dictation, and I was writing script, and one of the other students noticed and said, "We aren't supposed to know that yet!" and I erased everything I had written and did it over in print.

The older classes at Garrett Park Elementary changed teachers for different subjects, with one teacher teaching math, another science, and another, language arts. Miss Gooken was the language arts teacher. When she was teaching poetry, she allowed me and another girl named Barbara to write in our own journals, to write our own poetry without following a form.

I was a safety patrol. I remember washing my belt so many times that it became pretty ragged. At the end of the year the patrols got to attend a special Baltimore Orioles' baseball game for free as a reward for their year of service – it was called "Safety Patrol Day". I don't remember anything about the game, but when I got home, Roger Barclay came over and said, "Are you safe? Did you see it?" See what? I didn't know what he was talking about. At the stadium there had been a terrible accident with the escalator, severely injuring many of the kids who were guests at the game. They had closed the gates and kids kept piling on to the escalator and then falling back down on each other. Somebody might even have been killed. My parents were trying to hush Roger up because they knew I would be upset to hear about this. Since then I have always associated baseball games with escalators.

Kensington Junior High was a big change, but because we had changed teachers in elementary school, it wasn't such a shock going from class to class. Still, it was very different from elementary school. A lot of the students at KJH had grown up in these neighborhoods where everyone had a lot of money, and these kids already knew each other and were quite cliquish. There was a girl in my class who was the daughter of the owner of The Villager, a shop that sold Villager clothes. I wanted a Villager outfit but I had to settle for Pandora. Families living in Garrett Park didn't have a lot of money, though for the most part they were well-educated; many of the town's residents were government workers, which meant they weren't all that well paid. It was in junior high that I first began to be aware of class differences based on money.

I attended Walter Johnson, and I hated it. I was ready to move on, to go to college, and I just wanted to grow up and get out of there. After graduating from high school in 1970, I attended Grinnell College in Iowa, majoring in anthropology. After Grinnell, I got my graduate degree in urban affairs at Washington University in Saint Louis, Missouri. At that time, the real focus in urban planning was on architecture. What I wanted was social planning, and I wasn't particularly interested in the physical structures. I was interested in the social dynamics of communities and neighborhoods. After graduate school, I worked for a small non-profit research firm that did housing for the elderly in Washington, D.C., and I stayed there until I met my future husband, Tom.

In September of 1979, Tom got a job in Portland, Oregon, and I moved to Portland with him. Paul Norman was already living there, as was my brother, Alan. After that, I only went back to Garrett Park for short visits to my parents, at occasions like Christmas. The town looked much the same, but it felt different somehow. What really surprised me was how small the house I had grown up in felt, and how low the ceilings were. Also, I noticed that the quality of the water was really bad, and it was very over-chlorinated, especially in the summer. Our house in Portland has very high ceilings, and the Portland water is excellent.

Today, Paul Norman and his wife Sandi, Paul's sister, Storry, and Chip Fitzpatrick are all living in Portland, and we all have our childhood memories of Garrett Park in common. I am retired from working for the county in various positions. The last one was as a senior business analyst, supporting enterprise systems. Before that I had been planning and managing contracts, supervising people, doing social services for the elderly.

My parents were still living in the Keswick Street house when my father died in the 1990s. My mother con-

Marguerite and Cilla in the garden of the Garrett Park Town Hall - Christmas 2003

tinued to live there alone for many years after that. Around 2005 or 2006 she began to not be able to drive any more, and my sister, Jennifer moved her into an apartment she had added on to her house in Virginia. Right before she moved, we had our last Christmas in the house, and then said goodbye to Garrett Park. Since then, I have never been back.

I think that what I liked best about living in Garrett Park was having friends who all lived within a short walking distance from my house. This close physical proximity of friends made it easy to connect, and I loved just being able to drop in on people who lived nearby. As kids we were able to move in packs freely around the neighborhood, with a wonderful sense of freedom. It was great not having to get in a car to go anywhere.

When my sons were growing up in Portland, I used to think about how differently I approached childrearing from the way I grew up. I wasn't exactly a helicopter parent, but I didn't allow my small children out in my unfenced yard without supervision, nor did they walk to school alone. I wondered whether it was a difference in time and/or place; I live in a very urban environment with sidewalks, cars, and lots of foot traffic, not all of which is benign. That's definitely a change in place, but is Garrett Park still the enclave of security and comfort I experienced as a child?

Garrett Park was always a special, mystical place for me. Because Garrett Park was filled with children, there was always someone to play with. We could walk all over the town and play in at least three playgrounds that I can remember - the school yard, Wells Park (on Rokeby near the post office), and a small park by the swimming pool. We could walk to the post office and market to pick up bread and milk, in addition to buying penny candy and six-ounce cokes, which were chilled in an ice-filled, self-standing soda cooler. It was a place where we could bike and walk safely, even without sidewalks, to our own swimming pool, just a short walk away, a place to safely trick-or-treat on Halloween. When it snowed, we could sled down a steep road into the park at the bottom (once the County stopped plowing the hill). It was a small village amidst suburban Washington, a place buried and hidden from the outside world; I was both amused and bemused, to learn this from my fellow students at Kensington Junior High and Walter Johnson, who had never heard of it.

(Parts written by Cilla Dieterich)

Christmas 2018 - Robin Richards (Martin's wife), Martin Dieterich, Joel Dieterich, Cilla Murray, Thomas Dieterich, Jennifer Lapp

STORRY NORMAN

I have wonderful memories of caroling at Christmas. We had practices at our home and on the night of the caroling, my mother would make cider and Swedish Rosettes, delicate butterfly and star shaped confections dusted with powdered sugar. The carolers would first come to our house to practice with Newton Blakesley as our conductor. Then we would walk around the neighborhood with lanterns, flashlights, and little 4" X 6" caroling books. I still have many of these little books, printed by the banks and insurance companies.

My parents, George and Peg Norman, met through mutual friends, John and Mary Krasny, who took them hiking on the Appalachian Trail. John invited George because he had a car to transport them to trails and cabins, and Mary and Peg were roommates in DC. A love of the outdoors, hiking, canoeing and camping were passed on to me from my parents. In fact, the Norman and Krasny kids are the same age and shared many activities in our youth. George used to say, "Ain't Nature Grand" and I wholeheartedly embrace that feeling to this day.

My mother, who was born in 1911 in Brecksville, Ohio, moved to Washington D.C. to work as a microbiologist at Walter Reed Army Medical Center. My father, who was born in Philadelphia in 1912, moved to D.C. from Virginia Beach where he worked as a mechanical engineer for the Navy. As an instrument design specialist at the David Taylor Model Basin/Naval Ship Research and Development Center in Carder Rock, he designed dynamometers, motors, engines and rotors and obtained three patents.

My parents were married a week before their life-long friends, the Krasnys, on Sept. 11, 1948. That's a sad date to remember but a happy one as well. Before they married, they purchased a Chevy House on the corner of Rokeby and Clyde, 4701 Clyde Avenue. The previous occupant was a woman whose dogs had worn pathways through the high, un-mowed grass of the yard. With help from their friends, my parents brought the house I grew up in, and which they occupied for fifty years, to a cozy, comfortable condition. My mother was thirty-nine when my brother, Paul, was born in 1951, and I was born two years later in 1953. This was a very advanced child-bearing age at that time.

My father was quite a builder. He built the white picket fence around our house, which involved fashioning the pickets and designing and making metal forms for the cement pillars he cast to support the pickets. He also built our garage and a three-story back yard fort for Paul and me. Earlier, when we were very young, he had built us a jungle gym. The fort was a magnet for neighborhood kids, so once we outgrew it, George took it down to avoid liability from possible injuries.

While George was building, my mother was cooking well-rounded meals for the family as a stay-at-home mom. She was an excellent seamstress - she had sewn her own golden wedding dress - and made Halloween and Fourth of July costumes for us. She was also an accomplished candle maker. For years, she and I made candles with metal molds in the basement, decorated them with glitter and chains, and gave them as Christmas gifts. She played the piano for the children's service of the Episcopal Church we attended, and I sang in the children's choir. (George didn't go to church because he claimed he was a Druid.) In the mid - 1960's Peg was recruited to continue working as microbiologist at Walter Reed, and later for the American Type Culture Collection with a focus on mycoplasma.

Supposedly, our parents bought our first black and white TV to entertain Paul when he was recovering from a tonsillectomy. Initially, we were each allowed an hour of TV, only on Sundays, with Walt Disney as our preferred show. My favorite childhood memories are simple things: playing with nearby friends including Kathy Brown, Abby Franklin, Meg Fitzpatrick, Martha Abrams, Amy Gootenburg, and Laurie Crichton; getting candy from the candy counter and soft drinks from the water cooler at the Garrett Park store (near the railroad station); riding my bike to school and to the swimming pool in summer; jumping in leaf piles in the autumn; hiding behind towering oak trees in our yard at night when cars came by; collecting acorns; catching fireflies in summer; looking out the windows while perched on our home's warm radiators; hearing my mother's special descending eight -note whistle to call us inside; and sitting on the screen porch on summer evenings. We usually had dinner there and could wave and call to neighbors as they walked by.

One of my favorite places to play was Wells Park, at the bottom of Rokeby Avenue, partially because it was right across the street from the Crichtons, where I spent a lot of time with Laurie Crichton, who was a very dear friend. I also remember catching crawdads in the stream at the other (Franklins' and Lintons') end of Rokeby, where Rokeby came to a dead-end and there were no more houses. Instead there was a scrawny pine forest that we used as our own U-cut Christmas tree lot for a few years... Another favorite memory was swimming on the Garrett Park swim team. Ron Horn and Tom Powell were my coaches, as was Tim Powell later on. When I was in high school, and Paul was away in private school, Tim, who had long since graduated from high school, acted as an older brother. He very kindly showed me the ropes for dining out and making conversation. Tom and Tim's parents, Iris and Sam Powell, were my very special godparents and lived across Clyde Avenue from us.

There was a period when kids were encouraged to hold carnivals in their yards as charity fundraisers. Paul and I had one or two at our house where the primary activity was "spin art" that created colorful cool designs. Neighborhood kids would drip different colored paints onto spinning paper squares attached to a rotating platform our father had made with a spare motor and parts... On Halloween I remember walking all around Garrett Park to get candy. Once, very scary eerie music was projected from what may have been Mr. Hill's house, a big white house with columns on Kenilworth. That's how I remember experiencing it as a young child.

In the winter when it snowed, we all went sledding on Donnelly's Hill. There was often a big fire at the top of the hill, and neighbors, Manny Flanders in particular, who lived in a big house at the top of the hill, would have us in for hot chocolate. I remember having snow storms every winter and building snow men and snow forts. Kids would grab on to the back of snowplows for a free but dangerous ride. I was too frightened (and wise) to do this though.

I have wonderful memories of caroling at Christmas. We had practices at our home and on the night of the caroling, my mother would make cider and Swedish Rosettes, delicate butterfly and star shaped confections dusted with powdered sugar. The carolers would first come to our house to practice with Newton Blakesley as our conductor. Then we would walk around the neighborhood with lanterns, flashlights, and little 4" X 6" caroling books. I still have many of these little books, printed by the banks and insurance companies. My contemporary, Scott Mader, still lives in Garrett Park, and I heard he is heading up the caroling now. I've wanted to get those caroling books to him for tradition's sake but haven't succeeded in contacting him.

Another Christmas memory is family friend Roy Gootenberg , who was Jewish, dressing up as Santa Claus and bringing good cheer to our home. Maybe I am hallucinating this, but it also seems like a helicopter would arrive at the Garrett Park elementary school and Santa Claus would jump out!

Abby Franklin was a good neighborhood friend from when I was very young. I have an early childhood memory of playing in Abby 's "rock garden". It seemed like a huge area at the time, but when I went back as an adult and saw it, it looked tiny. I remember playing with Abby and Mark Antosz, also with Kathy Brown, who was two years younger than I and lived across the street. Kathy went to Holy Redeemer while I went to Garrett Park Elementary. We would meet up at the end of the day and ride our bikes home together. Walking through the Browns' back yard and along the path above the railroad tracks to the post office was an adventure for me. Another friend, Susan Modine who was a tomboy, declared it was not cool to play with Barbie dolls. My dad had built a bear house for me, so bears, not Barbies, entertained me.

When I was in fifth and sixth grade, some Garrett Park girls and I had a Beatles Club at Debby Harris' house. We each had our favorite Beatle, with mine being Paul, and we all sported black leather hats like they wore. We had so much fun in Debby's basement listening and dancing to Beatles music.

In high school I was close friends with Laurie Crichton, and spent a lot of time at her house. Laurie died in a car accident when I was in Gabon, Africa in the Peace Corps. I didn't hear the news until a month later because the mail didn't get to me right away. After three successful heart surgeries, Laurie had actually run a marathon. She was beautiful, creative, bright, and fun, and I still miss her today.

As an older teen, I joined the Mariners, conceived of and promoted by the incredible Annavieve Abrams. The GP Mariners were an offshoot of the Girl Scouts. We did a lot of canoeing and kayaking, and it was formative and wonderful. Marianne Krasny, whose family lived nearby in Kensington, and I paddled canoes together along with other Mariner scouts in a number of regional slalom races.

After graduating from Walter Johnson High in 1971, I went to college at Saint Lawrence University in upstate New York but came home for the summers. After college, I returned to D.C. and lived next to Rock Creek Park in a beautiful old house with a group of friends. During this time I worked in downtown D.C. with Garrett Parkers Ann Smith and Molly Fitzpatrick. Two years after graduating, from 1977 to 1980, I was a Peace Corps volunteer in Gabon, Africa, where I taught English as a foreign language to French-speaking students in two different towns.

Upon my return to the States, the congestion of the DC area and reverse culture shock prompted me to drive across the country to join my brother, Paul, and his wife, Sandi, in Portland, Oregon where we all still live. Because there were so many of us who moved here from Garrett Park, we called ourselves 'Garrett Park West'. Paul and Sandi came out first, then Alan Murray, then Chip Fitzpatrick, then Cilla Murray. I was the last to come out. Now we and our families get together for Thanksgiving and birthdays, and we have dinner together from time to time. I'm still in touch with Abby Franklin, and I recently visited her in New York City.

Storry on Mt. Rainier

I met my husband, Jack Hollis, at weekly contra dances in Portland. We shared a love of cross country and telemark skiing, backpacking, and white water canoeing. I worked as an English as a Second Language teacher with immigrants and Southeast Asian refugees for ten years, and then I switched to a State of Oregon volunteer program management position for another twelve years. Our son, Nolan, who was born in 1993, now lives in Denver, Colorado. Both of my parents came out in 1996 to live in Portland when they got older. My mother died in 1999, three years after moving out here, and my father died in 2002. It was a difficult but important part of our lives. We had great solidarity with Paul and Sandi in coordinating care for our parents.

Taking care of a young child and two elderly parents in the mid-'90s, feeling the "sandwich generation" crunch, I stopped working for pay and instead did volunteer management in Nolan's schools.

I still volunteer with public school students in and out of the classroom. Currently, hiking with a woman's hiking group is my primary exercise along with leading group excursions. I am a wild flower enthusiast, and have been since even before the Peace Corps. Hiking, gardening, volunteering, book groups, singing in a choral group, and adventuring with Jack are gratifying activities that fill up my time.

The house I grew up in is still there. It's been remodeled and so has the garage. When I was in DC for the Women's March on Washington in January 2017, Martha Abrams Meehan and I drove through Garrett Park and it was really quite sad. The town has changed a lot, with in-fill and remodeling. In the vicinity of the Franklins' house at the end of Rokeby, the newly built houses initially prevented me from locating their house. Betsy White's nearby house on Kenilworth was replaced long ago. There is a totally different feel to the Park now. Instead of seeing kids riding bikes and gathering with friends outside, one sees nannies pushing strollers.

I like to think Garrett Park was unique, and I've been thinking about what made it so special. It was a small town with a mayor, a town council, and a cohesive community spirit as experienced in the building of the swimming pool. It was in many ways a self-contained community; we had our own kindergarten and elementary school, as well as our own swimming pool, community center, town hall, post office, store, library and railroad station before it was torn down. But I think other small towns may be like that.

However, the fact that we were close to D.C. and not entirely insulated, that we were aware of what was going on in the rest of the world while at the same time feeling safe, made it different. People were politically active and aware since the federal government and international affairs were omnipresent. Ann Smith (Ann Brown) got me involved with the Kennedy campaign, helping out at the Garrett Park Elementary polling place, which was a fabulous experience, really consciousness-raising. Ann was also instrumental in helping me connect to my first full-time job in D.C. And then there were the anti-Vietnam war marches in D.C. and Garrett Park's nuclear free zone.

Another thing that distinguishes our town from other incorporated towns was not only the political piece but the cultural piece. I went down to the Washington Mall frequently for cultural events with Marianne Krasny. It may have taken twenty-five minutes by car to get to there - imagine that! For instance, I remember seeing Kenneth Clark 'Civilization' movies at the Smithsonian regularly and attending music concerts in the Rotunda of the National Gallery. There were so many wonderful recreational activities close by too: hiking the Appalachian trail; walking on the tow path near Great Falls; canoeing on the Potomac; swimming in the ocean at Rehoboth and Bethany beaches; and sailing on the bays, to name a few.

Garrett Park was such a very warm, supportive community, such a tight knit community. My name for Molly Fitzpatrick was Aunt Molly, Jane Franklin was Aunt Jane, and Ann Brown was Aunt Ann. Growing up there felt very idyllic. Those were the halcyon days.

27

BETSY FRANKLIN

I can see the changes from the time when I grew up in Garrett Park to how it is now. When I was a child I could wander all over the place, and my mother had no fear. I feel like Garrett Park was the last gasp of small town culture. We just don't have that anymore, where people stay in one community for a long time, really come to know each other, and help each other out. I think that is how it used to be in small towns.

My parents, Ben and Jane Franklin were both born in New York City. My mom grew up in Mount Vernon, N.Y., and my dad grew up on Morningside Drive in Manhattan. When he was a teenager my dad's mother, who was by then a widow, moved her family to Washington. My dad's mother was the first female press attache for what would later become the Social Security Administration.

My mom and dad met when my mom was in college and my dad was still in high school (actually away-prep school). Prior to having her first child, Mom worked for retail stores, but after my older sister, Abby, was born she became an at-home mom. My dad was a news writer for Edward P. Morgan, before subsequently going to work first for the Evening Star, and later for the New York Times. He was working out of the D.C. bureau, and after doing some time as a librarian, he became the middle Atlantic correspondent for the Times. During his years as a newsman, he covered a lot of really fascinating stuff: the Spiro Agnew scandal, George Wallace's rise to power, assassination attempts, the Yablonski murders, Wounded Knee, the race riots in Cambridge, Md., and the nuclear power plant disaster at Three Mile Island. He worked for the Times for thirty years. As I was growing up, I attended a lot of political rallies because of my dad. I was at the March on Washington, and saw Martin Luther King there.

I was born June 24, 1954 at George Washington University Hospital, the second of three daughters. My older sister Abigail is fifteen months older than I am, and my younger sister, Clare was born on June 23, 1967 – the day before my thirteenth birthday! I had told my parents I wanted a brother and I wanted him born on MY birthday, but this is how it worked out! She was a good crash course in the responsibilities of baby duties, so great birth control for this budding teen.

Abby was born in 1953, while my parents were still living in an apartment in Bethesda. Shortly after that they found and bought a modest house in a really nice suburb. That house, on 11310 Rokeby Avenue in Garrett Park, was the house I would come home to about a year later. I'm sure my arrival really cramped Abby's style.

In 1959, our family relocated just down the street to a new house that my parents had built. It was at the end of Rokeby, and we moved into just in time for Christmas. Just before we moved in, the neighbors had a big housewarming party for us. I remember there were almost no furnishings at that gathering – just a big decorated tree and some tables.

My parents had bought the land from Mom and Pop Wells, who lived in a beautiful little log cabin right across the street from us. I used to go over there all the time and drink cambric tea, which was just water with cream and sugar, with Mom Wells, who loved having me visit. I loved visiting her too, and I especially fell in love with all of her beautiful Tiffany lamps. They had a big vegetable garden and they kept goats, because Pop Wells had an allergy to cow's milk. My family had a very friendly connection to Mom and Pop Wells. When Mom and Pop Wells moved from Garrett Park to Berkeley Springs, West Virginia in the early sixties, we would sometimes go and visit them. The family who bought the Wells' house later sold it to Pam Payne and her husband, who rebuilt it and doubled the size of it. Just the other day I came across an old picture of Pop Wells on this big agricultural tractor.

Next door and also across the road from us lived the two Williams twins, Don and Deward, who were both semi-professional baseball players. They were country people, very different from my family. Don and Deward both chewed tobacco, which I had never seen before. And I remember this time when the Williamses were driving in their Cadillac, and they hit a squirrel. I was amazed when they brought it in and cooked it for dinner. They also ran a summer camp with a pony and a small horse. Don and his wife Ann Williams had three daughters - Donna, Janice, and Karen. I played with Donna Williams, the oldest, and I did visit the summer camp in the off season and rode the ponies.

Next door to Don Williams were the Belters, who had two sons, Steve and Terry, and a daughter named Nancy, who was a little older than us, and very precocious. I remember her as always wearing patent shoes and white socks. One time Abby and I went over to her house and she spilled the beans about everything - Santa Claus, the Easter Bunny, and how babies were made! However, I was so disgusted by what she told us that I just rejected the whole thing. I went on believing in Santa Claus and the Easter Bunny for a long time afterwards, because it was too gross to believe what she said about what people did to make babies.

The Fitzpatricks, Molly and George, or "Fitz", had lived next door until we moved down Rokeby in 1959. They were very close friends with my parents, and like another set of parents to me. They were lovely neighbors. There is this story about them from when I was about four, during a time when I was very smitten with Mighty Mouse. Abby had a nurse costume with a blue cape. One day I snatched the cape because I wanted to play Mighty Mouse, and wearing the cape I tried to ride my tricycle over the garden wall, which dropped down to a lower level. But the cape didn't make me fly. Fitz found me and picked me up, and apparently I was a mess.

Betsy and Joe White, who lived around the corner at the very end of Kenilworth didn't have any kids or dogs, but they had a kazillion cats. I liked to visit them, and I think Betsy really liked it when I visited. The Whites were pretty eccentric. Joe was a brilliant guy who spoke fifteen languages, and he spent all his time in his little attic room, translating for the CIA. He was a man of few words, but a very nice one. He was such an introvert. After Betsy died, Joe was ostracized a bit, so my parents kind of took him in. We had him over for Thanksgiving and things like that. Otherwise he would have been totally alone.

In terms of age, I was always kind of odd-man-out in the neighborhood, and I played a lot by myself. There were also neighborhood kids that I sometimes played with. I played with Meggie Fitzpatrick and Kathy Brown, but because they were both a year younger than me, I felt sometimes like a fifth wheel. With Donna Williams and Johnny Mosler, I remember cutting bamboo poles and riding them around, pretending they were horses. I also have memories of putting pennies on the railroad tracks, and playing in the woods, and having lots of fun playing in and around a creek in our back yard, which was always good for tadpoles and other critters. I remember collecting bottle caps and bottles in Wells Park, and taking them to the general store, where Louie the butcher would let us exchange them for penny candy. And of course we loved to ride our bikes all over the place.

I have wonderful memories of the Fourth of July parade, decorating tricycles and bicycles. One particularly fun Fourth of July I remember was the year we decorated our Radio Flyer wagon, dressed up as printer's devils, and distributed copies of the Declaration of Independence along the parade route. And I remember there was always a ceremony down by the tennis courts after the parade, with prizes and popsicles and small town speechifying.

I was crazy about animals, the pet whore of the neighborhood who loved visiting people who had animals. I remember people largely by their dogs. The Fitzpatricks had a beautiful, sweet collie named Puck. They had had another dog before Puck, but that dog bit me, and so they replaced it with Puck. Harry and Betty Rothenbach, who lived next door to the Belters, had a dachshund named Fritz, and Elaine and Weber Luttenberger, who lived up the street from us, had a Kerry Blue Terrier, Duncan.

If there was something stray or injured I brought it home, and my poor parents were very good about it. I brought home turtles, toads, birds, cats, dogs, anything. One of my favorite teachers was my fifth grade teacher, Mrs. Hall. That year we had science fair, and for me, any science project where I could acquire an animal was good. My mom took me out to the Hines Hatchery in Olney, Maryland, where we got two dozen eggs and rented an incubator. My science experiment was the study the eggs in incubation, handling them to see if they were fertile, candling and culling the eggs (only keeping the fertile ones), turning them twice a day. I had to open the egg at various stages of gestation – four days, seven days, fourteen days, and twenty-one days. It actually got a little traumatic, and yet it was all for science. In the early stages, it didn't look at all like a chicken, but every time it was closer and closer to a baby bird – the last one was beginning to get feathers and it squirmed, and that was beastly. Out of that whole experiment I had a rooster and five hens. Ultimately I had to take them back to the hatchery, where I imagined that they would have a happy life and raise children, but of course they probably ended in somebody's soup pot.

While I have always loved animals, my most consuming passion was horses. I nattered at my mother until she found a place where she could take me for riding lessons once a week. I rode with a woman named Joe Duckett for years. I would hang out there all day, grooming the horses and helping out in any way I could. I also took ballet, but the riding was expensive, and I had to choose between riding and ballet so I chose riding, and Abby was into the ballet. Abby got fancy private piano lessons, and I mostly focused on the riding. I credit my mother hugely, for making that happen. She wasn't really an animal person, but she allowed me to follow this passion.

I was musical but I wasn't a diligent music student. I had to take group piano lessons at Garrett Park Elementary, which I hated. Mom and Dad were quite involved with the church, and we were brought up in the Episcopal Church, St. Luke's over on Grosvenor Lane. And although I really disliked church, I did get involved with the church choir, because I loved singing.

I went to Garrett Park Elementary through sixth grade, and I remember all of my teachers. For some reason I was always in combination classes after first grade. For kindergarten I had Miss Chloe, and I had Mrs. Boyd in first grade. She was a very loving, matronly woman. I remember making a project at Christmas time and we made flower vases out of orange juice cans. I made mine red and pink, and Mrs. Boyd said, "You can't do that, you can't combine red and pink." I couldn't understand that at all. In second grade I had Mrs. Fitzwater, and then Mrs. Cobb, and then Mrs. Brill, and then Miss Gooken and Mrs. Hall in fifth grade, and then for sixth grade I had Mrs. Strayer.

Mrs. Strayer was my nemesis; she and I just didn't click. I was much better at writing than I was at math, and I was lazy, and I think she had a problem with that. To this day I am better at verbal things than I am at math. Maybe if I had had a better relationship with Mrs. Strayer I would have a better relationship with math.

Of all these formidable teachers, I think my favorite teacher was Miss Gooken. She was funny and light, and she made learning fun. She was really into literature and language arts, and she had this great Long Island accent. I also loved Mrs. Hall, a young black woman, which, sad to say, was a novelty at Garrett Park Elementary in 1965. She was great.

Jane, Betsy, Clare (in front), and Abby

Abby and Clare

After Garrett Park Elementary, I went on to Kensington Junior High. It was at Kensington that I was introduced to Jewish culture for the first time, though there were only a few Jews there at that time. One thing about Garrett Park was that there was no ethnic diversity, and actually I got my first real taste of ethnicity when I attended college, at Wellesley.

I remember these two southern teachers that I had. One was Miss Stickley, my English teacher, who was very old school. I learned a lot from her, especially about writing. The other southern teacher was my math teacher, who gave me my first Ds in math. I was basically doing the minimum, so those Ds were a big wakeup call for me.

Mr. Henlein, the school disciplinarian, was really scary, and I even got in trouble with him once. Because Abby was always the chief of everything, chief of the Safety Patrols, Class President, and so on, I strove to be different from her, and sometimes that meant being naughty. At Garrett Park Elementary, as a Safety Patrol, I never even got the gold badge. It seemed like people were always expecting me to be like Abby, but I wanted to be me. So at Kensington, I experimented with being naughty in order to be me.

When I was in seventh grade at Kensington, the dress code was revised so girls could wear pants. However, my mother didn't agree with this. Because she didn't think girls should wear pants to school, I was not allowed to, even though the dress code had changed. So I used to take jeans to school and leave them in my locker. Go figure: my mom would buy me fishnet stockings, which she preferred because they didn't run, and I would wear them to school with these really short mini-skirts. This was when I was only fourteen! My mom was a little out of touch that way. We would throw parties when I was in high school, and sometimes we would burn incense, and my mother would come to the top of the stairs and say, "Now you shouldn't be smoking that weed, you need to stop that!" and we would say, "Mom, it's incense!" Then a week later we would be smoking weed, and she would say, "Now that incense smells really nice." We used to call her Mrs. McGoo.

At that time everybody from Garrett Park was to be redistricted to attend Charles Woodward for high school, but because Abby was attending Walter Johnson, I could have been grandfathered in there. However, I was tired of being Abby Franklin's little sister, so I didn't go to Walter Johnson. Woodward was a much smaller school, and I found myself a big fish in a little pond, and I also learned that I didn't have to do all that much to do well. I was supposed to take AP courses and I didn't, but I sang a lot and I went to county and state courses for a few years, which was really fun.

I also took art classes at Charles Woodward from this wonderful hippy art teacher named Mr. Moran who was busy keeping the kids busy, and so he didn't care what I did as long as it was interesting and independent. One of my favorite art stories is when I taught myself how to silk screen. With my new found skills, I made a number of "YIPPIE" flags with the red star and the marijuana. But really my favorite thing was when I got into crepe paper plants. You could make these incredible flowers and you could press veins into them, and one day I was making a marijuana plant in a ceramic pot that I had painted with stars and stripes. I had just finished painting the pot, and had put the plaster of Paris into the pot to make my plant stand up. I was holding it to make it stand up when the fire alarm went off, and the plaster of Paris had not yet finished hardening. So Mr. Moran cradled my art piece in his arms and we all trooped out to the blacktop with this huge marijuana plant. And nobody cared. Even the principal noticed it and grinned.

After high school, I attended Wellesley College in Boston, as did my two sisters, my mother and my youngest daughter, Gabrielle, who just graduated from there in 2016. My mom was really thrilled that Gabby

Betsy (in middle) with daughters, Gabby and Amanda

Gabby, Jane, and Betsy at Gabby's graduation

attended Wellesley. At Wellesley, I learned I could kind of reinvent myself, and I thank Wellesley for the ability it gave me to survive all the hard things that I have gone through as an adult. After graduating from college in '76, I went to London for a year and studied design at the College of Printing.

When I returned from England, I got back into riding. I kind of had to learn to ride over again, because by that time Dressage had hit. One thing led to another, and so I was back into horses again. Today I have a small farm in Frederick, Maryland. My childhood dream was to have a little farm with horses and other animals – just what I have today. Both of my girls got into horses, and I think that saved them from the mean girl thing and the mall and all that.

I have never wanted to go back to live in Garrett Park, but not because I didn't like it. My childhood there was really good, and my memories from that time are very happy. I just never thought I would come back to the Maryland suburbs. Garrett Park was really a great place to grow up, but by the time I grew up and left home, I had sort of an aversion to suburbia.

My parents still lived in Garrett Park when I came back to live in Maryland, and I used to bring my kids there to visit. We went there for the great small-town things like the Fourth of July and Halloween. And Halloween had totally changed. When I was growing up there, the kids used to go trick or treating by themselves, and it was totally safe. But when I took my kids there, about fifteen years ago, Halloween ended when the sun went down, and parents were hovering, helicoptering, as their kids went up to the door. It was sad, not at all like I remember Halloween.

Of course the town has changed along with the rest of the world. One thing that has really changed in the world is a loss of community and security. I can see the changes from the time when I grew up in Garrett Park to how it is now. When I was a child I could wander all over the place, and my mother had no fear. I feel like Garrett Park was the last gasp of small town culture. We just don't have that anymore, where people stay in one community for a long time, really come to know each other, and help each other out. I think that is how it used to be in small towns.

I have a neighbor out here in Frederick County who has motion-detecting cameras all around his house. What is he trying to protect himself from? The wildlife?

Betsy with her grandson, Spencer

28

JOAN KENNEDY

When there were big demonstrations, my parents would open the house to college students who were in town for them, and after one march where hundreds of people were arrested, held in RFK stadium, and my parents and some other people from the town went down and bailed the kids out and brought them to our house to stay and gave them a meal. I remember before one of the big moratorium marches, Rennie Davis, one of the Chicago Seven, came up to the community center and talked to us for a while one night. I was raised on activism, and I still go to demonstrations, try to speak up about injustices and find ways to live according to the social and political values I grew up with.

My parents, Tom and Elaine Kennedy, moved to Garrett Park in 1951 or early 1952. I was born in 1955, the third of five children, all of us born between 1951 and 1960, so I grew up in Garrett Park from the beginning. My older brother, Thomas, was born in 1951, and my older sister, Ann, was born three years later in 1954. I have two younger brothers - Paul, who is two and a half years younger than me, and Chris, who is five years younger. My family lived in the town, in the same house, until 2011.

My father worked at the National Institute of Health. NIH was his universe. He started out as a research doctor in the clinical center, later becoming an administrator. Over the years, he was a head of several different institutes there. My mother had been a nurse when my parents met, and she returned to nursing when I was in high school. Around that time, she got very involved with the women's movement and started to rebel against the traditional role of homemaker and mother. She was tired of having to manage all the kids and take care of everything at the house, of being in a submissive role all the time.

My parents had contracted with Al Richter to build our house at the bottom of Weymouth Street. The Weymouth Street houses, almost all designed by Al Richter, are Frank Lloyd Wright inspired, which makes Weymouth Street and parts of Oxford and Keswick Streets unique among Garrett Park neighborhoods.

Our house was built into the hillside so that the entry level was the upstairs, and the downstairs was open to the back yard which ran down to Rock Creek. It's funny – I thought we had this enormous house when I was growing up, and then when it came time to sell it five years ago, it seemed very small.

As with all the Garrett Park houses, there were lots of big trees around. We also had Rock Creek Park right in our back yard, and until they built Parkside Apartments, we had the woods at the end of the street. We didn't go into those woods very often because of stories of kidnappers there. I think that was one of those stories that parents made up to keep the kids out of the woods. I don't know who started the story – we were kids, and we just knew there were kidnappers there.

Anyway, we had the park right in our back yard and we had Rock Creek. When I was young, kids my age weren't supposed to play down by the creek, but I did anyhow. My brother Thomas would threaten to tell my parents unless I shined his shoes and ironed his shirts for him, so I did a lot of that. The creek was maybe twenty feet wide, and in most places it was three feet deep at the deepest, though in plenty of places it was much shallower, maybe only a foot deep. Still, it was big enough not to be considered safe for little kids. The creek was also rumored to be so polluted that you would get really sick if you played in it. Another problem was that the big kids were always playing down there, and that was a little bit scary. You didn't want to mess with them, because sometimes they could be mischievous in a bullying sort of way. But we did play at the creek.

We had clubs and forts everywhere. A number of them were in my backyard or someone else's back yard, the yards that backed up to the creek. Our neighbors, the Snyder's, were in the Foreign Service, and after one of their postings they brought back a sports car in a shipping crate. That shipping crate ended up being a really great fort for us. And then I remember that we built an underground fort in my back yard, burrowing into the ground, probably only about two or three feet deep, with sheets of plywood over it.

Weymouth was a dead end, so we could safely play in the street. We played kickball, and the parents put up a basketball hoop at the bottom of the street. The kids who lived over in Parkwood thought all the Garrett Parkers were so snobby, because when they built Parkside Apartments, the town put barriers up at the ends of the streets so there wouldn't be any through traffic, even though their streets ran right up to ours. Most of the streets in Garrett Park except Strathmore were dead ended, and it kept a physical boundary around the town. We had the creek on one end, the railroad tracks on one side, and all of the dead end streets. I think that did a

Weymouth Street girls: L to R: Sidonie Xavier (Amy's daughter), Lizzie Friedman, Amy Lichtenstein, Joan Kennedy, Sally Baldwin

lot to create and maintain the real community feeling of the town. And it's still like that. It wasn't until I was much older that I realized that all the dead end streets in Garrett Park were part of what gave it its character, and it was designed that way on purpose.

The neighborhood kids who were close to my age were all girls. There were some younger boys, boys my brother's age, but they were bratty and annoying. There were many girls on my street who were my age or a little older. I think there were five or six who were my age, so I always had someone to play with. The three that were my closest friends through high school and beyond, were Sally Baldwin, Amy Lichtenstein, and Lizzy Friedman. When I was younger there was Patty Cunnare, Pat Deasy, who lived across the street from the Cunnares, Betsy Lehman, and Gigi Voris.

The Cunnares lived on the corner of Oxford and Weymouth in a house that was almost exactly like our house, with the same floor plan. I remember when I was quite young, before I was in elementary school, feeling so proud because I could get my cowboy boots and jean jacket on by myself and walk all the way up to Patty Cunnare's house at the other end of the street.

One of the beauties of growing up in Garrett Park, or growing up in that age, was that we just played outside all the time, and nobody organized us. We just figured it out. If you're playing games together, and you have to figure out the rules and stick to the rules, you have to learn to negotiate. We played four square a lot, and we played hide and go seek, using four different yards. We played it at night, flashlight hide and go seek. We hardly used the streets because we knew how to get everywhere by cutting through everybody's yard.

We rode our bikes all over town, and I rode my bike to school. We didn't roller skate much on Weymouth Street because it was so steep. The only place I remember roller skating was down on Parkside Apartments, because the sidewalks were smooth. I remember wiping out once or twice, and trying out the early skateboards. The skateboards back then were just an old board with a roller skate attached to it.

On Halloween we did major trick or treating. The Hartmanns lived at the very end of Keswick in one of the original Garrett Park houses, a big nice old farmhouse, abutting the back of the Friedmans' house and the Kings' house. They always had the most elaborate scary

Kennedy Family Christmas, 1972 - Paul (in back), Elaine, Ann, Thomas, Chris, and Joan

stuff, like people hanging from the trees. It was scary and also exciting. We could go as far as we wanted on our side of Strathmore, and there was never any concern about our safety. But we didn't go across Strathmore. It really was a boundary that divided the two sides of town. It wasn't until I was in junior high that I started hanging out with people from the other side of the "highway". The exception to this was that we did have to cross Strathmore to go to the swimming pool, which was the center of our life in the summer, and also to go to the post office. I was eight or nine when I first began to do that.

I particularly remember the turtle races on the Fourth of July. There were so many box turtles in the woods back then. They were everywhere, and every kid in my family had at least one. Now there are almost none. We would identify our turtles with nail polish on the shell, and enter the turtle race. We had these window wells, so there would be daylight in the downstairs of the house. That's where we kept our box turtles, and my mother would save peels from tomatoes to feed them. Every time I smell tomato peels it takes me back to the turtles. After a while we would let the turtles go, but I think one or two may have died in the window well. I remember

a really bad smell from the dead turtle. We didn't have any other pets. Mom's plate was full enough with five kids to manage and a house to maintain.

Another childhood memory that seems unique to Garrett Park is the Easter egg hunt that Priscilla Maury held in her yard every year for the kids in the neighborhood. She lived at the corner of Keswick and Oxford and had a beautiful garden. Participating families decorated eggs and delivered them to the Maury's house the day before Easter. The "big kids" would hide them around the yard and on Easter morning dozens of kids would descend to hunt for the eggs. The adults would drink coffee, eat donuts and chat while we were hunting.

Priscilla Maury's Easter egg hunt

My father was a pretty serious Catholic until about the mid '60s. He had gone to seminary and had entertained the idea of becoming a priest for a long time. He became pretty radicalized over time, and his involvement with civil rights and the anti-war movement did not put him in a good light with the church.

Mom just went along with it. She had converted to Catholicism when they got married, so that the kids had to be raised Catholic. As I figured out much later, she was not Catholic, though I think she craved some kind of religion or spirituality, which really came out when she was in her eighties and nineties, when it seemed as if she was reverting back to the Protestant church of her youth. At one point I started learning about Buddhism and some of the other spiritual schools that were out there, and when I told her about it, she was fascinated, and wanted to learn as much as she could. I think she always had a craving for some kind of spirituality.

I attended Holy Cross Elementary School. It was just beyond the old library, right next door to Garrett Park Elementary, so we walked to school with kids who went to Garrett Park Elementary. Lizzie Friedman went to Holy Cross, as did Kathy Brown, who lived on the other side of town, on Rokeby. Kathy was one of my best friends from kindergarten through high school.

Holy Cross was much stricter than Garrett Park Elementary, and we had to wear uniforms. We also had to go to church and sing a high Mass every Friday. Women had to cover their heads in church. If you didn't have a hat to wear, there were these little lacy things called mantillas. The little ones looked like yarmulkes, but they were lace. If you didn't have a hat or a mantilla, the nuns would bobby pin a Kleenex to your head. At one point my father forbade my sister and me from covering our heads in church, and then he left it to us to say to our nun teachers, "No, I'm sorry I can't do that, my father has forbidden me to cover my head." So we were caught between my father and the nuns, who didn't respond very well. Dad loved to instigate controversy, but he was also very authoritarian.

Here is another thing my father did at one point: when the progressive nuns from different parts of the country started wearing shorter habits, he cut out an article from the newspaper with a picture of the new habits, and sent me to school with it, telling me to give it to my teacher and ask when the Holy Cross nuns were going to start dressing like this? I didn't know what I was getting into, but the teacher/nun did not react well. By giving me that article to show the nun, it was like he gave me the Molotov cocktail to take to school. I didn't even know what it was all about.

I remember another time when we had been down to a civil rights demonstration in front of the White House. Somehow the parish priest heard about that, and he came in on Monday morning to do our usual religion class and said, "Miss Kennedy, I heard you did something this weekend. What was it?" I didn't know that he would think it was wrong, but when I told him about the demonstration, he tried to humiliate me in front of the class. I was only about ten. I must have told my parents about this. I wonder how could my father not have known that it wouldn't go down well with them, why would he make me challenge the nuns like that? I left Holy Cross after fifth grade, and got to attend Garrett Park Elementary instead.   I was very happy with the switch.

There was a real community feeling in Garrett Park. No matter where I was, people would look at me and say, "You're a Kennedy, right? " No matter which one you were, they knew you were a Kennedy, and you just knew so many people in town. I remember having this feeling once walking to the post office, and I thought to myself, "I know someone in pretty much every one of these houses, and if I was ever in trouble I could run to one of these houses and have a refuge." And you knew that if you did something misbehavior-wise, even on the other side of town, your parents would hear about it.

Some neighbors were particularly special to me. My parents and the Kings were very good friends, and we used to have Thanksgiving dinner at their house. Barbara King was probably the first adult who ever really talked to me about things like finding out what I wanted to do in life.

The Lichtenstein family was very important to me. It was Sylvia Lichtenstein who really brought me in, and kept an eye on me when I was a teenager, and the situation in my family was very bad. I was very rebellious, taking drugs and hanging out with men who were much older than me, and things at my house were really ugly. I practically lived at the Lichtenstein's house for a long time. There were periods when I would spend the night there a few nights a week. Silvia knew my father, and she knew how strict he could be, and while it was never discussed, she was always very welcoming. Irv Lichtenstein was the vice president of one of the local radio stations. I remember one time when he actually got to pick the Beatles up at the airport. We were all so ripped when he sold that car not too long after!

As with much of Garrett Park at that time, there was a lot of social activism. When we were young, whenever there were elections coming up, my mother had us going door to door leafleting for the Democrats. There was only one Republican family that I knew of in that neighborhood. When Goldwater was running for office, my brothers and I were walking down the street and these people had a Goldwater sticker on their car, and we made my youngest brother, who was really a young kid at the time, go over to the car and rip the sticker off. I wasn't aware of the McCarthy hearings until later, when I heard stories from families in my neighborhood, stories of what had happened to them.

My parents were very good friends with the Browns. Growing up in Garrett Park, I learned about boycotting, which I still do, regardless of the impact it is (or isn't) going to have. I do it out of principle. I remember a story Kathy Brown told me when we were all boycotting grapes. They were at the grocery store one day and Ann Brown put a bunch of grapes in the cart, and then put everything on top to squish them, and then left them in the store to show support for the farm workers. I loved grapes before that, and to this day I can't eat them.

I must have been present for MLK's "Dream" speech, but I don't remember it. When I was cleaning out our house I found a bunch of buttons that you wear to those kinds of events, and I found one from that march. My mother tells me a story about how at the end of one of those demonstrations we were walking back to our car, and a limo pulled up, and it was Coretta Scott King, and she stopped and said something to us. My mother's whole face lit up whenever she told that story.

When there were big demonstrations, my parents would open the house to college students who were in town for them, and after one march where hundreds of people were arrested, held in RFK stadium, and my parents and some other people from the town went down and bailed the kids out and brought them to our house to stay and gave them a meal. I remember before one of the big moratorium marches, Rennie Davis, one of the Chicago Seven, came up to the community center and talked to us for a while one night.

I was raised on activism, and I still go to demonstrations, try to speak up about injustices and find ways to live according to the social and political values I grew up with. I was at the Women's March in 2017, which was unbelievably fun, and there was a March for Science the same year, and that was great fun also. It was pouring down rain the whole day but we had a great time.

When I was in seventh grade, at Kensington Junior High, girls still had to wear skirts to school. Isn't that archaic? When you think about cold weather, I remember wearing those terrible knee socks and your legs would just get raw with the cold. So in seventh grade, I remember that Kathy Brown and I, also Lizzie Friedman and Amy Lichtenstein, all decided to stage a protest. We knew all about protests at this point, protests and boycotting and all that stuff, so we staged a protest where all the girls wore pants to school. Not all, but all of our persuasion. We wore pants to school on the same day and I don't think we got in trouble. And it was right around that time that they changed the rules and allowed girls to wear pants. We actually made a difference with our protest.

Growing up in Garrett Park, I had a lot of chance to interact with nature, and that became a huge part of my life, of who I am. I was in the Girl Scouts with Kathy Brown, and my mother was our leader. But the only thing I really liked about the Girl Scouts was the camping trips. Later, when I was older and I had taken up smoking, I used to go out into the woods to smoke, since I couldn't smoke around my parents. As result, I spent a lot of time alone in nature.

In college I fell in love with botany and ended up with a degree in Ornamental Horticulture. I took a course called Environmental Conservation that blew my mind. This was in the early 70s and the environmental movement was in its early stages. I feel like that class set me on a path for my life. I became a middle school science teacher with a strong focus on environmental issues. (It was so Garrett Park of me to view teaching as a subversive activity).

We started smoking pot in seventh or eighth grade, which now just kind of horrifies me to think about it, especially since I taught kids that age for so long, which made me realize how young I really was. And the music we were listening to, both the lyrics and the feel of it, now seems pretty rough for me to have been listening to at age fourteen.

I graduated from Charles W. Woodward High School in 1973. That was the high school that kids from Garrett Park were going to at the time. The story that was going around at the time was that the Garrett Park kids were so wild that Walter Johnson didn't want them anymore.

After high school I took a year off and completely screwed up my life. After that I went to University of Maryland and graduated from there in 1978. I lived all over the D.C. area for a while - in D.C. near Dupont Circle, near the Chevy Chase line, in Takoma Park, in Bethesda, and back in Garrett Park. After college I got a job with Bob Frost (another Garrett Parker) at his gardening business Green Gardens. Later I worked at a telephone answering service in near Dupont Circle that was started by a guy from Garrett Park, Mark Efross. I lived downtown for several years around that time. In 1983 I moved to Connecticut, attended graduate school at the University of Connecticut and got my teaching degree. I lived up in Connecticut for twenty-five years, working as a middle school science teacher.

I moved back down here in 2010, and moved back to my parent's house. My father had died and my mother was living in an apartment in Chevy Chase. I ended up living in Garrett Park for a while. After selling our house I rented a room in the house that John Lamb grew up in. Later it belonged to the Brock family for about forty years. I remember a party at that house when I was in high school. The cops came to break it up and I think it was me mouthing off to the cops led to my brother, Thomas, and two friends being arrested. (Oops!)

I think that one of the best things about growing up in Garrett Park was that feeling of community, and how it always felt safe, and the feeling of knowing everyone in the town at least a little. I don't get that experience much anymore, though I've discovered that wherever I've lived, the thing that has meant the most to me has been having neighbors that I connect with. In Garrett Park, you could just go to your friend's house and walk in the door. You had access to all the homes, and it was comfortable and friendly and safe.

Another thing that was important to me was having so much access to the out of doors, and having the freedom to explore and have adventures, having the freedom to go wherever we wanted to. We had explorations in nature all the time, and having the woods around us was a big part of that.

I loved that because there were so many kids my age, I just had a slew of friends there, and I loved the dead end streets that we could play ball in at any time. When I moved back to my parent's house as an adult, it just warmed my heart when there would be five or six kids down at the bottom of the street playing, a new generation of kids playing there. There are still kids but not nearly as many.

I can't think of anything I didn't like about growing up in Garrett Park. I just think it was an amazing place to grow up, especially at that time in history. We had so much freedom, and we had access to the city, which fostered in us both political awareness and involvement. I attribute so much of who I am now to my upbringing in Garrett Park. It's not surprising to find that many of my closest friends today, the people I see most often are people who are also from Garrett Park.

29

BEN GALLANT

It was really idyllic growing up there, and I was always kind of proud to be living in Garrett Park. I think I always had a sense of how special it was compared to the McMansions of Rockville. My clearest memories are of tramping around in the woods, of learning the plants and learning the trails. I have always loved connecting to the ecology of a place, and I definitely had that as a kid in Garrett Park. The connection to nature and exploring continues to be an ever-present and essential part of my life.

My parents are Frank Gallant and Karen McLaughlin Gallant, who herself grew up on Weymouth Street in Garrett Park. I was born in 1975, and I have a younger brother, Nick, who is three years younger than me. We were both born in Maine, on the coast. Before moving to Garrett Park, our family lived in this little fishing village called Cape Porpoise near Kennebunkport. My dad, Frank Gallant, was working as a journalist, writing for a small paper called the York County Coast Star. My parents had good friends and a cool house in Cape Porpoise, and they loved it there. But in the late 70s, during a time when the economy wasn't very good, my dad was laid off. My mom's dad, Donal McLaughlin, who lived in Garrett Park, knew someone in Washington who was looking for a writer for his magazine, my dad got the job, and my parents decided to move in with my mom's parents on Weymouth Street in Garrett Park. I was four at the time, and my brother, Nick, was one. I have memories of leaving Maine and coming to Garrett Park, and of the anxiety of leaving my friends in Maine.

My first impression was that it wasn't my real home. Cape Porpoise was my real home, and while Garrett Park eventually became home, I was skeptical in the beginning. As I remember it, we all thought it was a temporary arrangement, since we had a lot of friends in Maine and thought we would go back some day. We didn't sell the house in Cape Porpoise, and we stayed connected there. Since my mom was working as a teacher and had summers off, she, my brother and I would basically go up there from Memorial Day to Labor Day. My dad would fly up for short visits in the summer. We held on to that house until I was in sixth grade.

My mom's parents moved into an apartment in the attic, and we moved into the main floor of their house. It was great living in that house, a house that my grandfather had designed. I thought the idea of designing your own house was really cool, and that idea really stuck with me so that, all my life, I had this dream of designing my own house the way my grandfather had. We recently did a major remodel on our house here in Santa Cruz, and it felt to me like achieving that dream.

It was neat to have all three generations living together, and it was a great house. The fireplace in that house was unique, built into the brick wall, with a broad bench in front of it so you could sit by the fire on cold nights. The bench, which ran half the length of the wall, was topped with dark stone and faced with brick. I once lost a Lego piece down a crack at the back of the bench where it met the fireplace. It must have separated a bit. I remember being heartbroken because there was no way to get it back - it was a goner.

My mother's sister Coille's first husband, Peter Hooven, was an artist. He painted my mom and three of her friends sitting in front of that fireplace. Two of the figures in the painting are seated on the bench, and the dark opening behind the second figure is the fireplace itself.

Painting by Peter Hooven of Jessica Myers, Mary Winegarden, Susan Roberts, and Karen McLaughlin

There were these big windows in the living room, which looked out into the garden. My grandmother, Laura, was a fantastic gardener, and she had beautiful azaleas. I did a lot of work in that garden for my grandma, and later for the neighbors. I could earn spending money that way, as many of the neighbors had big gardens. I was really aware of the neighborhood history and the families who had played a part in it, even if I didn't directly know them. I knew they were friends of the family and heard stories about them.

From what I have heard from my mother, my experience as a kid on Weymouth Street was different from hers.   The main difference that stands out to me is that on Weymouth Street, when she was a girl, there were a lot of kids her age, which was not the case when we were there. A lot of the same families were living there that had been there for many years, the parents of the girls she was friends with, like the Myers family, who were now of retirement age. But there were a few kids for part of the time when we lived there. In the house next door to us there was a boy, I think his name was Neal, a little older than me, who lived there temporarily. While he lived there I considered him my best friend, but it only lasted a couple of years, and then he moved out. After that, Heidi and Steve Lipman moved in. Their daughter, Leah, was a few years older than me, but she was at least our generation, and we were friends, and have since kept in touch. In fact, I visited her in Austin a few years ago.

My grandmother, Laura, was into progressive early childhood education. She knew people at a private, progressive k-8 school in Rockville called The Green Acres School, and she connected my mom with this school. My mom got a job as an art teacher there; hence this was the school that Nick and I both attended. So not only weren't there many kids on our street, but because I didn't go to Garrett Park Elementary, I also didn't have a connection with kids who lived in other parts of the town. This probably contributed to that sense I had that there were more kids around when my mom was a girl.

At some point we met a family, the Rothwells, who became family friends. David and Jenny Rothwell were the parents and Jessie, the oldest daughter, was my age. They had a son named Andy who was Nick's age, and their daughter, Lizzie, was a couple of years younger. Nick and Andy were like best friends, and I hung out with Jessie. So the Rothwells became our one set of local friends.

The Rothwells lived on Kenilworth near the elementary school, and we could bike over there where they lived. We liked to go over to the elementary school and play in the playground there or in the fields, and as we got older, we weren't limited to our side of the highway anymore. Later, the Rothwells moved to a house on

Clermont Place on the other side of town, and we kids would cross Strathmore (always being very careful as we had been taught to be) to visit them. We would go down to the post office, or get candy at the general store, and sometimes we left pennies on the railroad tracks. After the train went by, we liked to find them again, now squished flat. We also spent tons of time over at the Garrett Park pool in the summer.

Another place we like to play was Cambria Park, over by the pool. That was our stomping ground. I don't know if it was an official city park or if it was just a vacant area that we called Cambria Park. It was a great place to do jumps and other tricks on our BMX bikes. It wasn't paved, it was packed clay with a couple of little gullies and the jumps were designed around the gullies. They had some pretty serious jumps that the big kids could do, and we were always trying to push our limits, doing bigger and bigger jumps. I don't remember any of us getting badly hurt, but we definitely had some spills.

Halloween was a fun time in the town. I remember loving it, going around with a group of kids, and it was fairly lively. We would get dressed up and mostly go around our neighborhood, although we probably at the end of the night crossed Strathmore to see the Rothwells and compare our haul, to see who had more. My parents came along when we were little, but maybe we were on our own as we got older.

In the winter, we could have a fair amount of snow. At the bottom of Weymouth Street the plows would leave these big mounds of snow because it was a dead end there, and we would carve out forts from these mounds. We had one we called "The Otters Playground" and we made chutes that you could slide down. And we went sledding, sometimes all the way over on Strathmore Hall over on Rockville Pike, where they had a really good sledding hill. Strathmore Hall was on the Garrett Park side of Rockville Pike from Georgetown Prep, and there was an old mansion there that was being used as an event center. We also went sledding on this hill out behind Garrett Park Elementary School – I think it was the Holy Cross property.

Near our neighborhood there were all these places where the streets would dead end, where there was either a woods or another neighborhood on the other side. I knew all the little back ways through those dead ends, and I would just keep going to the other side. I did a lot of exploring on my own, especially the part of Rock Creek Park that was near Weymouth Street, where I was allowed to go alone. At the end of our street there was a row of trees, and Parkside Apartments was on the other side. In the back of the apartment parking lot you could go down a little slope, down to a flood plain of Rock Creek Park. I called it "the swamp", this area that was full of skunk cabbage and interesting "spice plants". There was a band of woods near the creek, and while I would go down to the creek sometimes, the woods and the swamp area was where I mostly spent my time. I remember the smells and the ecology there, how it was very moist and woodsy. I saw an owl down there once, and in the winter when it froze, I liked looking at the cool patterns, at the way ice froze, and the different depths of water. There was a culvert that I could go into, big enough for me to stand in, and there was some quicksand that was very exciting. The quicksand had a bottom, it was about thigh deep, if that, but it was real quicksand, and you could lose your shoes in it. I just loved getting to know that terrain, exploring it and bringing my friends down there. It was wild and magical.

My grandparents were very social, and they had this rich social network, while my parents were sort of new in town, and not such born entertainers. So a lot of the socialness in our house that I remember was more around my grandparent's friends. My grandfather, Donal, especially, was a super gregarious fellow. He had what he called "The Redskins Club". They were fans of the Washington Redskins football team, and his friends would come over to watch the game while eating chips and dip. I always thought those gatherings and parties were great fun. My grandfather, who was older but was still working, had a graphic design and an exhibit design firm. So we got to know his older neighborhood friends, and also people who worked for him who were my parents' age or a little younger. They would come over and hang out.

Then there was my grandparents' famous spring garden party. For the garden party, one of my jobs was to go harvest bamboo shoots, which we would steam and eat, peeling away the leaves and dipping them in butter. It was always a central part of the party. People were surprised that you could eat them like that. There was this really extensive bamboo grove, which we called the bamboo forest, down at the end of Keswick Street, back down towards those apartments there. We would go over there and harvest the young bamboo shoots and bring back a big bag of them. I had my knife, and I would know when they were too big, too tough to eat. I loved that. I still love any kind of natural food foraging. This spring we did this thing called the acorn gathering down in Santa Barbara, where we learned these food gathering skills, how to prepare them and so on. It really started back in Garrett Park with the bamboo shoots. Also, we used to harvest onion grass, we'd pull up the onion grass, we'd pull up the onion bulbs and my mom would sauté them.

It may just be part of my disposition as a kid that I was comfortable around adults, maybe more comfortable than I was around kids, so I didn't mind that I was surrounded by adults a lot of the time. In fact, I actually liked being the kid among a bunch of adults. I was always kind of a cautious kid, and I wanted to learn how you are supposed to be in the world before I jumped into it. Watching the adults around me interact really gave me an opportunity to learn from them, and my grandfather hung out with a lot of really interesting characters.

Donal McLaughlin with Ben and Nick Gallant

When I was in sixth grade, we sold our house in Maine and bought a house in Takoma Park. The neighborhood we moved to was a really cool neighborhood in its own right, and we had a really great block there with more kids. Since my grandparents were still living in Garrett Park, we went back a lot. We visited my grandparents, and the Lipmans, who lived next door to them, and we were still close with the Rothwells. We stayed members of the swimming pool at least for a few years, and I continued with the school in Rockville through eighth grade. So I bonded with Takoma Park while still being an honorary Garrett Park member.

After moving to Takoma Park and graduating from Green Acres, I spent one year at Montgomery Blair, which was a total shock - a two thousand person high school where I pretty much didn't know anybody. My eighth grade graduation class at Green Acres had been about ten people, so it was a really big change. After a year of that I begged my parents to scrape together the money to send me to Georgetown Day School where a lot of my friends were going, and that's where I went for the next three years. When I attended high school at Georgetown Day School, we were at the other end of the red line. Garrett Park was one of the last stops on the west side of the red line which goes down into D.C. and back up into Takoma Park and Silver Spring, so I could take the subway into high school from Takoma Park, and sometimes would take it to Garrett Park in the evening if we were having dinner with my grandparents or something like that. After high school, I attended Stanford University in Palo Alto, California. I loved northern California, the Pacific and the redwoods, and here I stayed.

I graduated from Stanford with a mechanical engineering degree and became a product design engineer. I did consulting for a while, and for the last seven years I have worked for Google, living in Santa Cruz. I first saw Santa Cruz when I was in college, and I immediately knew I wanted to live here someday. I think it reminded me of Maine. We live a little outside of town, on an acre with a hillside full of redwoods facing us. What is different for my kids from my experience as a kid in Garrett Park is that they aren't so free to wander.

Since my parents moved out here I don't go back to D.C. that often, maybe twice in the last five years. When I have gone back, I haven't noticed nearly as many changes as I have noticed in a lot of other places. It seems about the same to me; all of the growth in suburban Maryland seemed really different from the way it is in Garrett Park.

Ben, Frank, and Nick Gallant

It was really idyllic growing up there, and I was always proud to be living in Garrett Park. I think I always had a sense of how special it was compared to the McMansions of Rockville. My clearest memories are of tramping around in the woods, of learning the plants and learning the trails. I have always loved connecting to the ecology of a place, and I definitely had that as a kid in Garrett Park. The connection to nature and exploring continues to be an ever-present and essential part of my life.

Ben and Julie Gallant with Milo, age 10, and Caspar, age 4

SASHA BURCHUK

I've been independent since an early age, but I do think that growing up in a small community has taught me the importance of community and knowing your neighbors. Even though we weren't involved in each other's lives, everyone was stuck in this remote little community together, and we did things together, like trick or treating. That influence has stayed with me, and even though I've lived in cities for the past twenty years, I still know my neighbors, and I try and help them. That really is more of a small town thing.

My mom moved to Garrett Park in the 1970s when she was in her mid to late twenties. She was single at the time. My grandmother lived in Silver Spring, and I think my mother was living there also before she moved to Garrett Park. My family had a business in Silver Spring called Dale Music, originally started in 1949. My dad came to Garrett Park in the mid-1980s, but didn't really stay very long. My parents were pretty unstable.

I was told that Garrett Park at that time was a place where people were playing volleyball together, and just socializing a lot, and I think that appealed to her, the fun, young party atmosphere of the place. She was also Jewish, and the fact that it was kind of a Jewish enclave also attracted her. Over time, I think that some aspect of the party scene had gotten druggier. I have this impression of Garrett Park being this hippie utopia in the 1970s, but by the 1980s some people were starting to devolve into addiction, using a lot of alcohol and using a lot of drugs.

I lived in Garrett Park from when I was born (at Washington Hospital Center) in 1984, to when I moved away in 2001. I grew up on Montrose Avenue, on the Town Hall side of Strathmore. It was very idyllic, a "perfect suburb" - the really quaint houses, the big yards, and everyone was very friendly, with people in the neighborhood walking their dogs. I remember that both the town hall and the post office were these community hubs, where everyone came together to see each other and talk.

I am an only child, and growing up I spent a lot of time alone. Fortunately, Garrett Park was an okay place to navigate on my own. I had a strong community there, and some people took an interest in my welfare, looking out for me. One of these was Mike Henley. I knew Mike because he was friends with my mother. He was a good friend and neighbor, and he is the reason why I got through middle school. I dropped out at the high school level, though I eventually got my GED and went to college and got back on track.

Another important adult in my life was Susan Alexander, who often babysat me. She lived in and out of Garrett Park, sometimes living in Kensington and sometimes in Garrett Park. Susan was kind of like a progressive Catholic and a really sweet person. She died of cancer about ten years ago. I remember the Guernseys because Ben Guernsey (Tom and Adrienne's son) used to babysit me when I was a kid. He is about ten or fifteen years older than me. Still, I felt pretty invisible as a kid, even though I know that there were always these people looking out for me as I was growing up.

I was really independent, and I did what I wanted. I roamed around on my own a lot, riding my bike and going wherever I wanted to go. I had a dog, a Finnish Spitz named Yogi, who was a great companion. I got him when he was a puppy. When I got older I would take Yogi for walks in Rock Creek, which in hindsight wasn't the safest thing, but I survived it and always felt very safe. I walked down through the neighborhoods towards Kensington, to where there was a bike path and a bridge that goes down to Beech Drive, and once you get on Beech there's a trail and a bike path. So I spent a lot of time in nature. I explored, walking the trails and the bike path. I just loved the woods, loved checking things out there. I think I learned early the healing benefits of nature, which probably had a lot to do with growing up in a very natural setting. I learned that you could go for a walk in the woods and escape whatever was bothering you. I still do that when I have time. I'm an avid hiker and mountain climber.

I remember once when I was only six, I decided I was going to walk to Silver Spring to go find my mom, about nine or ten miles. I was walking down Strathmore and I came to this place where the sidewalk ended and a man came out of his house and started screaming at me, "Are you crazy? Go back to your house! Get away from the road!" and I thought, "Why is this guy bothering me?" I did listen to him, though I didn't like him.

I was fascinated by the trains and liked to hang out by the train tracks, waiting for them to come. I was a tree climber, and I spent a lot of time in trees - there was this magnolia tree I liked to read in. I was not a real girly kid, but I had this doll house, and I was obsessed with it. When I was first given the doll house my reaction was "Oh this is so girly, this is stupid. I don't want this." But afterwards I really got into it. Because my home life was so chaotic, it was a way to project myself into a more organized, clean, idealized space. You could say that the doll house was my first design laboratory.

I remember the Fourth of July parade that they had every summer. Once I dressed up as a Pilgrim for the parade. Looking back on that I think about how inappropriate that was. The theme that year was "Pilgrims and Indians". Don't get me started about that.

Halloween in Garrett Park was memorable. The Almys lived in a beautiful Victorian house on Kenilworth pretty close to Mike Henley's house. Dave Almy was an architect and he drove a very old Chevy truck probably 1930s or 1940s. They were eccentric. Every Halloween they would spend a few grand making their house very Halloween-y. Dave would dress up as a vampire and he would lie in a coffin and when you would go up to get your candy he would open the coffin and hand you the candy.

In the winter when it snowed I would go sledding at Holy Cross, at least until they redeveloped that property. Or I would go to Donnelly's Hill and hang out, but I didn't sled there because it always seemed kind of crazy, it was so steep.

I went to Garrett Park Elementary. At that time Garrett Park Elementary had three classes at every grade. It used to be a K-6 school when I first started, but it changed to K-5 and the 6th grade got shipped off to middle school. There were students from all over - students from Rockville, there were students from Wheaton, and there were students from Kensington. There were also kids from Nicaragua, and Mexico, and Japan. Since I was reading way above my grade level, and they didn't have enough resources to teach ESL (English as a Second Language), I became the ESL program. Also, because of my family environment I didn't have many friends. So the teachers figured, "Okay, here's a way to socialize this kid" by having me teach other kids how to read English. I taught a lot of those kids how to read English when I was in third grade. It was really fun for me, and I did make some friends. I went on to study abroad as a foreign exchange student in college, and I think that was a factor in my wanting to study other cultures and study abroad. But also I think it was a really great experience overall, because I came in contact with people from different cultures and I got to learn about them. It was fun, and it gave me a lot of confidence in my reading skills at a time when I didn't have that much to be confident about. I didn't have any foreign language skills, but it worked out anyway. It seems like the kind of thing that couldn't happen nowadays, at least not at a big school. Maybe it could still happen at a small school.

Miss Driscoll was my first grade teacher and she was a lot of fun. Another teacher I remember is Mr. Milner. He was a very tall black man who taught science in third grade, and he was just exceptionally kind and wonderful. I also remember Mr. Vogel, who I think is still there. He was a new teacher at the time, new to teaching. He taught fifth grade, and was very kind and patient.

But actually, I didn't like anything about growing up in Garrett Park. I hated it, and thought it was boring. It was boring because I didn't really have any friends in town, and the school district was so big that the only friends I did have lived far away and you had to drive to get to them. There wasn't a whole lot of action in Garrett Park. There was the swimming pool, which I wasn't a member of, there was soccer, which I didn't play, and there were the town hall events, which were for old people. Even though I did like going for walks in the woods, I really wanted more stimulation.

One thing that I noticed from early on was that the whole town was very white. It felt strange to be growing up in the weird bubble where there were no people of color. It's extremely strange looking back on it – it makes me wonder what was going on there, especially because, Montgomery County, if you study urban planning at all, is radical in terms of creating the kinds of policies that bring people together so as to create diverse communities. But even at the time it felt weird to me, because both my elementary school and the middle school I later attended were both very diverse.

For middle school I went to Tilden. It was much bigger and more impersonal, not like elementary school, which had been much more insular. I think that because I didn't have the best parents, the teachers at Garrett Park Elementary had been looking out for me. I wasn't that aware that they were looking after me, but I think they were. They probably had been looking out for me since third grade, and in middle school there was just none of that. And I think the middle school kids were meaner and more cliquey.

I very briefly went to high school. The first high school I attended was an alternative school called Parkmont. It was in Washington, D.C., near the Congo Embassy and the Walter Reed Medical Center. It was very small, a kind of Montessori school. There were kids with all kinds of personality disorders and behavioral disorders. To be honest, it was a bit of a sham. I think the headmaster must have been benefitting from some kind of a federal program.

I was sent there because I had an attendance problem. My grandmother and my mother had decided that I needed to try a different kind of school. They were trying to figure out what I needed. My problem was I needed sleep. (I have Hashimoto's disease, an auto-immune disease that causes thyroid problems, and one of the side effects is really bad insomnia, and it was extremely bad when I was a teenager and going through puberty, and I didn't fall asleep until 7:00 in the morning.) Because of this, I had a major attendance problem, and that is why I got sent to a remedial school for bad kids. While I was there I still wasn't sleeping, so I would just go to school, and there was this sofa, and I would lie down on the sofa and sleep for three hours, which was pretty much the only sleep I got, and then I would get up and I would go to my afternoon class. I got kicked out because of that. So I decided that I would try Walter Johnson, but because I had been sent to a bad kids' school, I had picked up some bad habits, like smoking. I was smoking at Walter Johnson and trying to hide it, and the principal found me and suspended me. So I figured, "All right, I already have a job, I'm not interested in these subjects, I can teach them to myself, I'm just not going back."

I was just barely fifteen when I tried Walter Johnson, and when I dropped out in October or November of my sophomore year, I was still fifteen. But no one came after me. I had a job. I worked in a bar called The Black Cat. I was the cook, and I wasn't allowed to serve alcohol. I was living all over at that point. I lived at my mom's house, but I also stayed at my older friends' houses a lot. A lot of my friends were college graduates. I had a group of twenty-eight year olds who had adopted me, and they did a pretty good job of looking out for me.

I left Garrett Park for good after I turned seventeen, just a couple of days after 9-11 happened. My mom had remarried and her new husband just wasn't very nice. 9-11 had a big impact on me, as it did on everyone else. Everything international feels personal to me, because I'm aware of the effect globalization has on people and countries, and I read a lot of news. I grew up in the D.C. punk scene, and my thinking as I was growing up was more about systems of oppression - colonialism, classism etc. - than it was about current events. I was still forming opinions in a pretty general way, but I was questioning a lot about the world I lived in.

When I left D.C. I moved straight to Portland, Oregon, where I live now. I was on tour when I was sixteen and my car broke down in Portland, and I really liked it. I thought, "Oh wow, a place where people are actually nice to each other." In D.C. it was very snarky and competitive and weird. People are more patient, more kind and considerate out here. I think it has actually gotten a lot nicer in D.C. since then. I hate to say it but I think it's the "silver lining" of gentrification. There is less crime, people can walk more slowly, can unwind and relax. Of course this means a lot of people have been displaced. But D.C. is a lot more laid back than it was when I lived there, like really laid back – I'm amazed.

I've been in Portland for seventeen years now. Eventually I went to college at Portland State University, the largest urban state school in the country, and I studied political science, and because of going to school there I studied and lived abroad. I lived in Argentina and in Mexico, and then I moved back here and I worked in the legislature, met my husband and got married. I wanted to do design, which has always been my passion, and Portland finally had a large enough community of rich people to support that. So I started my own business.

This is the second business I've started. I work in fabrication and interior design, I do a lot of furniture, and I'm a concrete fabricator. I do a lot of pre-cast stuff, and I do build-outs. I'm self-taught. I never studied design in college. I didn't want to go get a second degree and be that much more in debt. The degree might move your forward but the debt might hold you back. It's a damned if you do and damned if you don't situation.

I've been independent since an early age, but I do think that growing up in a small community has taught me the importance of community and knowing your neighbors. Even though we weren't involved in each other's lives, everyone was stuck in this remote little community together, and we did things together, like trick or treating. That influence has stayed with me, and even though I've lived in cities for the past twenty years, I still know my neighbors, and I try and help them. That really is more of a small town thing.

My life can seem chaotic because I'm never focused on just one thing. I eventually find my way through situations by just trying everything. My whole life I've been finding these back doors to get in to places, and so I figured I'd just find a back door. I find these opportunities even when I don't know what is coming next.

I've been doing this my whole life. I'm all about the doors, I say "push on three doors and see if it's locked." It's all about curiosity and trying everything.

Photo of Sasha by Robbie Augspurger

Acknowledgements

This project never could have happened without help from many people, most especially and obviously those of you who took the time to share your stories, whether by interviewing with me on the phone or writing them down. Karen Milam was an invaluable help to me in getting started - generous with encouragement and advice, she loaned me her recording device as well as sharing with me the documents she had used for her own book, also a collection or oral histories. I want to especially thank Mike Henley for his help in getting the word out about the book via email, so that I was able to greatly expand my list of willing contributors. I also want to thank Charlie Snyder for his generous help in opening up the town archives so that I could access interviews conducted in the past. And last but not least, without the love and patient support of my husband, David Daum, I'm sure I never would have completed this book

ABOUT THE AUTHOR

Lee Pope is retired from twenty years of working as a Waldorf class teacher and mentor. Her experience as a child in Garrett Park left her with a deep appreciation for childhood – for the value of free, unstructured play, the importance of ample exposure to the natural world, as well as the sense of safety and connection that comes from growing up embedded in a strong, supportive community. She loves reading, spending time with her four grandchildren, writing, and reminiscing. Lee lives in the foothills of the Sierra Nevada Mountains in northern California with her husband, David, and her cat, Willow.